MY

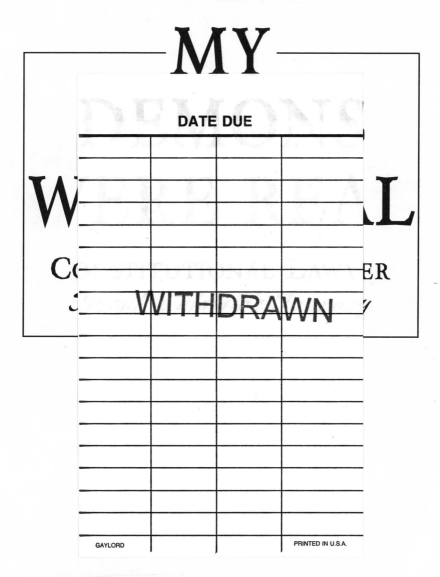

DEMONS

DATE DUE

W   AL

Co   ER

WITHDRAWN

GAYLORD   PRINTED IN U.S.A.

MY DEMONS WERE REAL

CONSTITUTIONAL LAWYER
Joseph Calamia's Journey

Bob Ybarra

Arte Público Press
Houston, Texas

My Demons Were Real: Constitutional Lawyer Joseph Calamia's Journey is made possible through grants from the City of Houston through the Houston Arts Alliance, the College of the State Bar, the El Paso Bar Association, the El Paso Bar Foundation, the El Paso Federal Bar Association, the El Paso Legal and Charitable Foundation, the El Paso Mexican American Bar Association, the El Paso Women's Bar Association, the Texas Bar Foundation and individual contributors.

Recovering the past, creating the future

Arte Público Press
University of Houston
452 Cullen Performance Hall
Houston, Texas 77204-2004

All photos courtesy of Mark A. Calamia, Ph.D.
Cover design by Pilar Espino

Ybarra, Bob
    My Demons Were Real: Constitutional Lawyer Joseph Calamia's Journey / by Bob Ybarra.
        p.   cm.
    Includes bibliographical references.
    ISBN 978-1-55885-608-0 (alk. paper)
    ISBN 978-1-55885-697-4 (cloth)
    1. Calamia, Joseph Albert. 2. Hispanic American lawyers—United States—Biography. I. Title.
    KF373.C325Y33 2009
    340.092—dc22
    [B]
                                                        2010033240
                                                        CIP

∞ The paper used in this publication meets the requirements of the American National Standard for Information Sciences—Permanence of Paper for Printed Library Materials, ANSI Z39.48-1984.

10 11 12 13 14 15 16   10 9 8 7 6 5 4 3 2 1

TABLE OF CONTENTS

The Quest Begins

A WHIRLWIND OF IDEALISM: YOUNG JOE

In the late 1940s, a strong wind swept through the judicial and political systems in the desert community of El Paso that occupies
the westernmost edge of Texas. Some forty years later, this dominant current was still packing strong gusty winds. As in many post-
World War II communities in the United States, the isolated
community of El Paso was fortunate to have many of its veterans
return. Many were warriors who experienced hardship in battle-
grounds thousands of miles away from home where they fought an
enemy that threatened America's way of life. These defenders confronted an enemy led by tyrants who suppressed personal freedom
through fear, force and even death. Armed with worldly knowledge,
the veterans returned home with the possibility of higher education in the form of the G.I. Bill of Rights. Those who realized this
opportunity soon found themselves positioned to test a judicial and
a political system that was subservient to the need to maintain economic and social stability in their hometown communities.

El Paso was the very epitome of this kind of community. As the
1940s drew to a close, political decision-making for El Paso's
190,000 inhabitants rested in the hands of about one hundred influential executives. The El Paso One Hundred defined the city's
priorities to provide a water supply and traffic control, attract new
industry, bridge the education gap and, importantly, control crime
and delinquency.[1] A culture of personal leadership prevailed, in
large part within the economic power of El Paso's two major
banks, the State National Bank and the El Paso National Bank,
and its two major department stores, the Popular and the White

House.[2] El Paso was ripe for changes that would reflect the pangs of political and social change that were beginning to grip the nation at large. A select group of young freedom-loving veterans, caught in a whirlwind of quixotic idealism, was poised to feed this upcoming storm of judicial and political change. This book is about one of those contributors and the methods, techniques, knowledge and hard work that he brought to the state and federal courts. This account is about a lawyer by profession. His demons were the institutionalized practices that favored expediency over rights of individuals. His quest became one of doing whatever it took under the law, even if faced with difficult odds, to see that lawmakers and law enforcers did not violate the Bill of Rights. The state and federal court system, that neutral ground of justice, served as his battleground.

Born in 1921, Joseph Albert Calamia grew up in a largely Mexican immigrant-populated neighborhood, near downtown El Paso. His house was only a few blocks from the Rio Grande, the international boundary with Mexico. For all the inhabitants of the area knew, the house might have been in Mexico, given that for several decades the United States and Mexico disputed the ownership of a square mile of land that encompassed El Paso's Second Ward. The Second Ward, or "El Segundo Barrio" as Hispanics called the area, was a neighborhood that attracted immigrants from Mexico. European immigrants also found their way to the United States through this southern route as an alternative to an overflowing Ellis Island. El Paso did not have to post words at the port of entry signaling the tired, poor and oppressed to come across the border. They came anyway.

Joseph's grandparents, Simone and Vicencia Abocato Calamia, immigrated to the United States from Sicily in 1896 at about ages thirty-seven and eighteen, respectively. They came not by choice but by fear. They came in search of freedom. Their Sicilian community was in the hands of the mafia. One did as one was told. "Simone," as Joe's grandfather was called in his native Italy, was a freedom fighter in that country's struggle for unification under King Humberto. Simone, who once aspired to be a Catholic priest, sought to confront the mafia with the help of his friend, the king. The king was helpless against that powerful organization. Unwilling to help, he justified his apparent weakness against tyranny by explaining, "Simone, even the great Napoleon was powerless against the mafia." For Simone, there was no option but to flee to some place where they could live in freedom.

The Calamias sailed to the New World, landing in Veracruz, Mexico, along the Gulf of Mexico, and then traveling overland to Ciudad Juárez, Mexico. Once they arrived, they opened a bakery. The couple brought with them José, their one-year-old son, and Nina Palmero, Vicencia's daughter from her first marriage. A second son, Leonardo, was born in Ciudad Juárez in 1898. "My grandfather got along well with the Mexicans," Joseph recalled. "They reminded him of Sicilians. He found it difficult to understand the demanding style of the Anglos." The Calamias needed to live at least two years in Juárez before immigrating to El Paso. The Mexican government sought to have these immigrants contribute to their new community with their professions and skills. At that time, temporary residency was necessary because U.S. immigration laws were becoming exclusionary, especially for Chinese immigrants, who had also established residence in Juárez. As those two years came to a close, the Calamias realized that running a business would be more prosperous on the other side of the Rio Grande. By 1899, "Simon" Calamia, as those in his adopted English-speaking country called him, opened a grocery store on the first floor of a two-story tenement that he constructed in El Paso's Second Ward.

In 1910, a new wave of immigrants came from Mexico. Fleeing the chaos of the Mexican Revolution, throngs of less wealthy Mexicans were attracted to the Second Ward.[3] These were individuals who had known hardship all of their lives. They had suffered injustices even before the overthrow of the dictatorship that lasted some thirty years. Most lost their lands, families and friends in the bloody ten-year struggle that claimed some one million lives. This new wave added another influence that transformed El Paso from a frontier town into a developing city with a significant copper smelting industry, irrigated agriculture and commercial and trans-

portation industries. At some 53,000 inhabitants, El Paso had dou-
bled its population since the turn of the century. However, even
with this wave of refugees from Mexico's civil strife, Hispanics remained a minority. This new wave simply added more Hispanics to
the crowded "Mexico Chico" between downtown El Paso and the
Rio Grande. In this little Mexico environment, the Calamia's two
sons, José and Leonardo, were educated first at a nearby elementary
school and then at a high school a short distance across the railroad
tracks in downtown El Paso. Soon the young men were at work as
meter readers with the local gas company. At age twenty-three, José
(1893–1969) married Laura Amity Miller (1898-1990).

Laura was the daughter of James Miller, Jr. and Beatriz Amity
Miller. Like the Calamias, the Amity Miller lineage followed the
lure of freedom and opportunity to America. Henry B. Amity,
born in Nice, France in about 1833, came to America via Mexico,
but on a very different mission than the Calamias. He was among
the French forces sent by Napoleon III to set up an aristocracy
headed by Emperor Maximilian, a French empire that was short-
lived. After a northward retreat, Mexican resistance fighters set up
their provisional government in Paso Del Norte, later Juárez, across
what would eventually be called El Paso, Texas. The United States
allowed the French occupation because it was involved in a war
between the states. With the Civil War's tide turning in favor of
union forces, President Lincoln later assisted Mexico's "legitimate"
president, Benito Juárez, with weapons and the blocking of
sealanes. Amity left the French cause and fled to America. By 1863,
he had enlisted as a clerk with the 1st New Mexico Calvary Vol-
unteers in Santa Fe in the Territory of New Mexico. This was the
third year of Apache Indian wars of resistance that would continue for the next twenty-two years. While in the military, Amity befriended William Brady, the Lincoln county sheriff killed by Billy
the Kid, and A. J. Fountain, another murdered Lincoln county
sheriff. While living in Lincoln county, Henry married Tomasa
Ronquillo in 1870. The couple had three children, Anna, Beatrice
and Henry, Jr. When Amity headed for Australia in an attempt to
return to his native France, Tomasa was left to raise the children.

Beatrice (1875–1909) married but that union ended in divorce in El Paso. She remarried James A. Miller (1876–1921). Miller was an adopted name. His biological parents, James Hosey and Sarah Ann Crowley Hosey, were born of Irish immigrants who moved west with the U.S. Army. The fourth child of the marriage between Beatrice and James A. Miller was Laura Amity Miller (1898–1996).[4]

In 1921, Joseph Albert was born of the José Calamia and Laura Amity Miller union.[5] Young Joseph's first few years were spent in the Calamia family tenement in El Paso's Second Ward. Spanish prevailed despite English-only rules in the public schools. El Segundo was a tough neighborhood in which to grow up. In a span of three weeks, young Joe saw his bicycle and two replacement bicycles disappear from his home.

His early schooling took place at a local elementary school named Alamo. It seemed as if all the public schools were named after heroes of Texas's war of independence from a tyrannical central Mexico City government. This was not a surprise. The city of El Paso was dominated by U.S. immigrants from east Texas and beyond. Wealthy individuals built southern-style mansions with lush green grass and live oaks, magnolia and other greenery north of the railroad tracks.

Young Joe waged his own war of independence in favor of basic school learning. Playing music and dressing up like a monkey for a school play was not for him. Young Joe's Italian background made little difference at school. To the predominately Mexican population, "Pepito" was a Mexican. Spanish was his first language. He looked and acted Mexican. But on the other hand, he stood out in his dress shirt and pants. Mama Laura was quite adroit at sewing. There was a rebellious streak in young Joe. On one occasion, an object hurled by a classmate interrupted Joe's concentration while at the blackboard. Nine-year-old Joe hurled himself at the other boy. The boys landed on the steam heater, bursting the pipes and sending the entire school into a sudden chill on that cold winter day. The other boy remained at Alamo, but young Joe was no longer welcome there.

José and Laura hoped that Catholic school would work out better. At St. Mary's Catholic School, the six-foot-tall principal was a nun of German ancestry and a strict disciplinarian. She demanded order in the classroom and was not interested in little Joe's argument about "mitigating circumstances" when he got in trouble. Once he rushed to the defense of an attractive little girl. The boy in the desk behind her was amused at how the girl's long braids rested on his desk so close to the inkwell. In those days, the wooden desks and chairs were attached in rows. The boy could not resist the temptation. A dip of the girl's braid in the inkwell set off a sudden passion in young Joe. The quixotic young man went to the rescue of his Dulcinea, indicative of a willingness to defend the weak.

These were also the years in which Joe began to explore what lay beyond his immediate neighborhood. He was very curious to find out just how south the river went. One time, Joe followed the river levee for a considerable distance, much to his grandfather's dislike. Grandpa was about to take a stick to the young lad when Grandma interrupted, "No, Simone. Don't strike the boy. *Il figlio indica corraggio!*" (The boy shows courage).

At the start of the Great Depression, a job opportunity in the prosperous natural gas distribution business in Mexico's industrial center of Monterrey lured the José Calamia family south of the border, more than eight hundred miles southeast of El Paso. For the next four years—until his mother's illness forced the family to return to El Paso—Joe mingled with the Spanish-speaking residents in and out of school. The school for Americans had a waiting list, so Joe enrolled at the Colegio Franco Mexicano. There was discipline in the classroom. Students had to wear traditional white shirts and dark trousers. Unlike the slang that was common in Calamia's Segundo Barrio, formal Spanish was spoken, and Joe quickly got used to being called the formal *señorito*. The curriculum was intense, but it consisted of more than reading, 'riting and 'rithmetic; there was an opportunity for debate. Young Joe was a perfect candidate to present the pro-American case in a debate over the American War of 1848, as the Mexicans called the war that ended with Mexico losing half of its territory to the United States.

Formally, Joe's academic experiences were supplemented with plenty of outside activities, particularly camping. Opportunities opened up when his father introduced him to the *YMCA de Monterrey*. Socially, young Joe learned valuable lessons from the school of hard knocks. The many poor, sick and weak who struggled in certain areas of Monterrey taught lessons of compassion. There was also a lesson to learn concerning the criminal element. Witnessing a shootout between police and two men quarreling over the attention of a woman, the young *Señorito* realized that there were bad people out there. On another occasion, *Señorito* Joe accompanied his father in his gas meter monitoring rounds at the local prison. He could hear the hoof beats of horses mounted by uniformed guards armed with pistols and shotguns. They struck fear among the populace that witnessed them escorting a long line of prisoners struggling with balls and chains. One prisoner dared to run out of formation as if to *fugar*, or escape. A shotgun thundered. The prisoner lay dead. "*Ley Fuga*," the startled young Calamia was told. "That is the law. No death penalty here. But if a prisoner flees, what can one do?" The boy thought about justice and law and order. "There must be a better way."

When the family returned from Mexico to an economically depressed El Paso, a certain quality of toughness came out in Joe. He had grown up as a batboy, watching his father play semipro baseball. He recalled how his forty-year-old father had rattled a much-touted ace pitcher with his solid hitting and had silenced the jeers of "*Viejo, Viejo.*" Through this shared activity with his father, Joe developed a love for physical fitness that led directly into the roadwork that is a must for any aspiring boxer. The police who patrolled the area soon got used to seeing Joe running in the wee hours of the morning, a far cry from other youth whose early morning jaunts had only one purpose—that of evading the law in a crime-ridden Second Ward. Joe occupied himself with workouts in one of several southside gymnasiums that offered an alternative to violence on the streets. To many poor youth, this was an opportunity to use their boxing skills to seek a better life. Calamia developed coordination as he rapidly hit the speed bag, alternating a left and a right. The bag flittered like the wings of a hummingbird. He hit harder and harder at that large stuffed punching bag, spotting the points of resistance with a careful punch and those of opportunity with a follow-through punch. He would venture to the real test of skills, the boxing ring.

Calamia, now in his teens, moved with his family to a house north of the tracks. There, the teenager lived in a predominantly Anglo neighborhood and attended a similarly structured Austin High School. Joe quickly sensed the prejudice and discrimination that many Anglos felt and displayed toward individuals of Mexican descent. However, it was a case of constant harassment by the class bully of a skinny Hispanic boy that motivated Calamia to confront the bully. Joe, however, prudently carried out this confrontation with his high school coach's permission. He made the challenge, and the coach, who would not let the boys fight in the locker room, arranged an after-school bout. By assuming an intervener's role, the coach instituted a procedure that followed the rules. The coach acted as an impartial mediator. Quite skilled at boxing, Calamia settled the score quickly behind the school field's bleachers. The bully went down after a couple of upper cuts. The question of justice was settled with knowledge, skills and techniques acquired through discipline and hard work. Moreover, the confrontation was settled "legally" within the jurisdiction of the school coach who served as a presiding official overseeing the fight.

His high school experience ended in 1938. The young Calamia turned his vision toward getting a college education at El Paso's Texas College of Mines (now the University of Texas at El Paso). Still, Calamia thought that boxing might be in his future: he had sparred with some pretty tough customers. He believed he was good enough to make it in the professional circuit. He had also been at close range with some fairly well-known boxers, including a much-heralded bout in El Paso. In Calamia's corner was former World Welterweight Champion, Fritzie Zivic, known as the Croat Comet. His opponent was Mexico's champion, Manuel Villa. Zivic was lean and did not seem to be much of a match for the stocky Villa. To the young aspiring boxer's surprise, Zivic could hit. So much so, that Villa suffered a fatal liver injury. Nonetheless, Papa Calamia would have none of that professional boxing stuff. He scolded the young adventurer, "What about college? What about law school? I thought that's what you wanted!" Calamia settled down, working at several jobs while attending college. In 1941, however, his education was put on hold.

The Japanese had attacked Pearl Harbor. In defense of its way of life, the United States declared war against the Axis Powers. Ten days later, Calamia enlisted in the U.S. Navy. After boot camp in San Diego, California, he served as an aviation technician on a small gunboat, which patrolled the icy cold waters off the Aleutian Islands. The base of operations was in Dutch Harbor, located on Unalaska Island about midway between the Alaskan mainland and the outermost part of the Aleutian Islands. Dutch Harbor was recovering from a Japanese attack in June 1942. There was fear that Seattle would be next. The island inlets were mined by the Americans to protect against intrusion of Japanese submarines. A soldier did his duty with the equipment that was available. The 84-x-18-foot diesel-powered boat was equipped with guns to protect against air attacks and with ash cans (i.e., explosives) to toss overboard on unsuspecting submarines below. The fixed position gun was no match against the better-equipped Japanese attackers. Calamia and a fellow sailor put caution aside and did the unthinkable. They tinkered with U.S. government property, turning the antiaircraft gun into a more effective sweep gun. Someone squealed on them, but to their pleasant surprise, their captain soon ordered, "Do that to all the other guns." On one occasion a Japanese aircraft scraped Dutch Harbor, seemingly uncontested. The arrival of a hot-shot Canadian pilot in a P-51 Mustang aircraft spelled hope. That hope was dashed when the Canadian's aircraft sprung an oil leak and the plane was grounded on Dutch Harbor. Calamia was put to work in the tool shop. After fourteen attempts to manufacture duplicate oil pressure fittings, Calamia succeeded. Once the Mustang was in the air, the pesky Japanese airplane was soon put out of commission. The war raged for the next several years until an Allied victory came in 1945.[6]

Discharged from the Navy, Calamia returned to the Texas College of Mines aided with tuition assistance, thanks to the G.I. Bill of Rights. The G.I. Bill provided veterans with a chance at education and training for up to four years and loan guarantees for homes, farms or businesses. The educational institution was paid up to $500 a year and the returning World War II veteran was paid $50 to $75 a month for subsistence. Nearly eight million American veterans were trained under the G.I. Bill until the program ended in 1956. While the war and the postwar years of college postponed the veterans' entry into the labor market, once they did enter the market, many were better prepared to support their families with a higher standard of living. Moreover, they were able to serve society with greater knowledge. At the program's peak, nearly one-half of the total U.S. college enrollment consisted of returning veterans eager for advancement. The veterans were more mature than the typically younger student population. More notably, the stereotype that higher education was a privilege of the well-born elite was disappearing.[7]

At Texas College of Mines, Calamia once challenged the grade given him by his professor and future state district judge Hans Brockmoller. After Calamia's strong argument in defense of his contention that he earned a perfect score, Brockmoller gave the young, aspiring lawyer that perfect score. While at the College of Mines, Calamia found a friend and mentor in his philosophy professor, Dr. Joseph Ross. Ross, a conservative Jewish rabbi, was ubiquitous in both his presentations and his appearance. He dressed in a long coat with tails and talked with ease and eloquence. In one instance, Ross lectured the class on his research and findings concerning the roots of poverty. Once Ross listed the various findings, Calamia interrupted, "You forgot one!" "Which is?" Ross inquired. "Apathy!" retorted Calamia. "So true," the philosopher mused. To Calamia's delight, Ross allowed Calamia to make use of his library. Even more to Calamia's delight, he found in his friend a mentor and a humanitarian who practiced what he preached. Calamia would often see Ross conversing with and helping out the lower-income Hispanics in the streets of El Paso. Even with the G.I. Bill, Calamia found that he still needed a job.

Taxi driving was a great test in the college of hard knocks and certainly in the down-to-earth school of life. This experience served to further open Calamia's eyes to the inequities between those running the political system and those marginalized by it. Moreover, it caused him to realize that the law could become a powerful tool against abuse and injustice. After all, this was a country that 170 years earlier declared equality and pronounced life, liberty and the pursuit of happiness as inalienable rights. It was a country based on a rule of law and freedom sealed in an inalterable Bill of Rights for all Americans.

In those days of ward-healer politics, there was always the tough, streetwise Hispanic policeman or influential person in the form of a strict public school principal, vice principal, or successful Hispanic businessman, all of whom yielded considerable power in maintaining law and order in the "barrios" near the Mexican border. Among these good guys was Police Sergeant Baiza, a sharp dresser and a good musician. As if through magic, Baiza managed to maintain a balanced liaison with both the Segundo Barrio "bad guys" and the guys that wore the white hats in downtown El Paso. One could argue that this modus operandi served to maintain law and order against the ever-present threat of street gang warfare, perceived immigrant-introduced lawlessness and an extension of the vices that had given a wartime Ciudad Juárez the title of Sin City.

On the other side were those voices of the returning World War II veterans who, like Calamia, saw some abuse of the practice.[8] As a cab driver, Calamia experienced these abuses firsthand. He recalled the familiar scene of Hispanic youngsters being slammed into the side of a police car followed by a quick confession and certain jail term. He also faced harassment by "cabbie checker" policemen who were assigned to keep an eye on taxi drivers. On one occasion an out-of-town woman, in distress after having obtained a quickie divorce in Juárez, left $3,200 in her purse in the back seat of Calamia's cab. Calamia quickly returned the purse and all the money to the cab company supervisor. Upon his return to the cabstand, a tough Anglo detective and an even tougher Hispanic detective met him. The Hispanic detective yanked Calamia out of his cab and rammed him against the side of the police car accusing him, "*Cabrón*! You stole the money!" Calamia might have received more severe treatment had not the Anglo detective intervened. Eventually, a call to the supervisor cleared up the issue. But after seeing this singular attempt to simultaneously act the part of policeman, judge and jury, Calamia made a major decision to attend law school.

During his years at the College of Mines, Calamia had installed a boxing ring in the basement of his parents' home at 214 West California Street. It was in the boxing arena that Calamia befriended Robert Galván. It turned out that Robert would be more than a boxing companion, as he also influenced Calamia to accompany him to law school at his brother's alma mater. Galván's older brother, Frank, had been practicing law in El Paso since the late 1930s.

While driving a taxi, Calamia took a liking to a fellow student, Geraldine Campbell. She too was working her way through college in hopes of a degree in English. Geraldine was assertive and tough. In her words, "Joe was the only one who liked me. All the other guys would shun away." Joe and Geraldine had a nice Catholic wedding in El Paso in 1946. A year later, Joseph Robert Calamia was born.[9]

Calamia graduated from the Texas College of Mines with a degree in history and government. After graduation, he attended law school at Southern Methodist University (SMU), while his bride remained in El Paso until the birth of their child. At SMU, Calamia lived in the rough-and-tumble Cement City, located a long streetcar ride from SMU. He stayed with Claude Pickens, who ran the construction operation in Cement City. Rumor had it that bank robber Clyde Barrow of Bonnie-and-Clyde fame once worked for Pickens in Cement City. Once reunited in Dallas, the Calamias braved the cold Dallas winters in a trailer park while both studied at SMU for the next two years.

Joe's law school studies included various aspects of the law. Corporate law caught his attention early on, particularly that involving the oil and gas industry. Dr. Masterson instilled in his mind the antiquity of natural resource laws in Texas. While Texas had abandoned the Spanish and Mexican Roman law principles when it obtained independence from Mexico, its adoption of British common law did not include the abandonment of Spanish land grants. The young lawyer-to-be quickly grasped these and other principles. Soon he was performing mineral rights research for an oil company in gas-rich Texas. A couple of things bothered him. Calamia could not see himself behind a desk at work on tedious routine matters all day long. He was used to excitement, and he had a penchant for independence and freedom. He was also concerned with the practices that oil and gas law condoned. Essentially, a person owned the land and had the right to extract whatever amount of natural resources he sought from the ground without any concern for his neighbors.

Corporate law also required a clear understanding of financial management. Dr. Raines opened his eyes to reality. Calamia and the other students had just spent their hard-earned dollars on expensive textbooks earmarked for this particular course. They were shocked at Dr. Raines's words, "Put the books away!" The professor passed out balance sheets, profit and loss statements and other accounting papers for a fictitious oil company firm. The task was to study and understand these numbers. Capital-to-assets ratios and sales income indicated excellent performance. Profits were astounding. The value of the stock was to be envied. However, an additional task was that of deciphering what was *not* revealed in these numbers. Inventories were over-valued, and, in some cases, the inventory did not exist. The price of shares was over-valued. Calamia shook his head at the thought that a company's finances could be built like a house of cards. Although corporate law offered a real opportunity for one to become wealthy, Calamia believed this would be at the expense of the underdog. The little guy needed his skills. Not the big guy.

Looking to his future, Calamia became more fascinated with constitutional law that established a social compact between the people and the government that was to be "of the people, by the people and for the people." The integrity of the compact was assured by a tripartite system of checks and balances. One branch of government enacted the laws. A second executed the laws. A third interpreted the laws. Each branch was to be completely independent of the others. Each branch was to keep an eye on the others to ensure that the social compact was not violated. The social compact included protection for the people under the Bill of Rights, which required all three branches of government to respect the rights of freedom of speech and religion, a free press and the right to bear arms. Americans were protected against the quartering of soldiers in their homes and against unreasonable searches and seizures. Persons accused of crimes were protected against an arbitrary criminal justice system through a number of guarantees. This social compact also protected the states against a central government asserting powers that were not delegated to it. It was one final protection that was ingrained in Calamia's mind: "The enumeration in the Constitution of certain rights shall not be construed to deny or disparage others retained by the people."

A federal district court was a lesson in the criminal justice system. Calamia and his fellow law students were greeted with the authoritative glare of a federal lawman as they entered the courtroom with a warning to be quiet, even though they had not uttered a word. The elderly federal judge, who spoke with a thick southern accent, frowned at two female African-American maintenance workers who admitted they had stolen typewriters from the federal building. They asked for clemency because they needed money to feed their children. But their plea went unheeded as the stone-faced judge declared loudly, "five years in prison." Next, an African-American man, who also admitted the theft of merchandise from the federal building, pled for clemency. He presented a long skit about how the "devil made me do it." The judge's pale face turned a rosy red and his stern look changed first to a smile and then to roaring laughter. Out of the judge's mouth came a sentence of clemency: "Probation!"

With a law degree in hand and a declining interest in following the big bucks in the oil and gas industry, Calamia followed his heart. He recalled the experience he had with a policeman acting the part of officer, judge and jury. There were the confessions extracted from South El Paso youth. There was the fatal shooting of a fleeing prisoner in Monterrey, Mexico. And so the Calamias returned to El Paso. In October 1949, Joe began a law practice with fellow SMU law school graduate, Wellington Y. Chew, in the downtown Caples Building. Geraldine handled the paperwork and other law office support.[10]

CALM BEFORE THE STORM
THE JUDICIARY IN THE 1950s

Downtown was the center for about one hundred legal professionals who served nearly 200,000 inhabitants of El Paso county. About 80 percent of them worked out of offices in the multistoried Bassett Tower, the El Paso National Bank Building, the First National Bank Building, the State National Bank Building and the Caples Building. The state and federal courthouses were a few blocks away.[1] This was a county whose legal community had evolved in some ninety years. The legal community was no longer made up of lawyers and judges dispensing frontier-style justice. Rather, it was one of trained judges and of attorneys specializing in certain areas of law. Increased opportunities in civil, business and corporate law gave less importance to criminal law practice.[2]

In the 1950s, El Paso—like many other communities—was positioned for social change. Of its Hispanic population, about 17 percent had completed high school compared to 64.7 percent of the English-speaking population. 60 percent had completed seven years of schooling or less. Regarding living conditions, less than 13 percent of Hispanics lived in homes valued at more than $13,000, compared to 41.8 percent for their Anglo counterparts. Few Hispanics held jobs that involved community decision-making and few held public office. The "100 influentials" that dominated El Paso were seen as "powerful men, older men who want to keep their monopoly on local affairs in El Paso. They control the council and the county judge." Still, in El Paso's Lower Valley and the south side, there was a strong and influential cadre of Hispanic leaders. These individuals were prominent, small businessmen who provided the "100 influentials" an assurance that all was politically quiet in the barrio front.[3]

Since 1947, U.S. District Judge R. E. Thomason had presided over the federal court system in El Paso and several other Texas counties bordering Mexico, all the way to Del Rio, Texas. Charles Boyton (1867–1954), his predecessor, was educated in Kentucky and Michigan and had served as El Paso's federal judge since 1924. Before Boyton, William Robert Smith Jr. (1863–1924), an East Texan and former U.S. congressman, served as El Paso's first federal district judge beginning in 1917 when Congress created the seat. Thomason was one of two federal judges that presided in the Western District of Texas. This district covered some 92,000 square miles west of San Antonio. Besides the El Paso Division, the Western District included divisions in Austin, San Antonio and Del Rio. San Antonio served as the headquarters where U.S. District Judge Ben Rice presided over the rest of the federal docket. Judge Thomason, seventy-one years old in 1950, had been moved to El Paso from East Texas because of his health. He and many other Easterners, some of them ailing from tuberculosis and other lung diseases, found in El Paso's dry climate and frontier environment a refuge from the crowded cities and polluted air. Judge Thomason began his career as an attorney for a prestigious El Paso law firm. He was elected to the Texas House of Representatives in 1917, and, in 1927 he was elected mayor of El Paso. He served as a U.S. Representative for the Sixteenth Congressional District from 1931 until his appointment as federal judge, a post he held until 1963.[4] It was Judge Thomason who, in the days of Operation Wetback in the 1950s, applied lenient sentencing to the overwhelming number of undocumented aliens appearing before him on criminal illegal entry charges. It was also Judge Thomason who vocally decried the practice of the U.S. Immigration and Naturalization Service and the Mexican government to repatriate deported Mexicans from Corpus Christi, Texas, to Veracruz, Mexico, in an overcrowded banana boat. A defendant, quizzed by Thomason, once described the plight of some five hundred deportees aboard *El Mercurio*: "poor food [. . .] and all slept on deck." It was not until after an incident in which some of the deportees jumped overboard and drowned that the Mexican government finally suspended the use of *El Mercurio*.[5] Judge Thomason was characterized as a politically astute, popular judge who maintained good relationships throughout the El Paso community.

Judge Thomason was succeeded in 1963 by U.S. District Judge William Homer Thornberry, a former congressman from Austin, Texas, who, in less than a year, moved to the Austin Division of the Western District. In 1965, Thornberry was appointed to the U.S. Court of Appeals for the Fifth Judicial Circuit.[6] U.S. District Judge Dorwin Wallace Suttle (1906–2001) succeeded Judge Rice of San Antonio in 1964 but presided over the El Paso docket. A self-styled country lawyer, who served both as city and county attorney in Uvalde, Texas, Suttle received his law degree from the University of Texas at Austin in 1928. For some thirty years, Suttle was the personal attorney for Uvalde, Texas, native John Nance Gardner (1868–1967), who served as vice president to President Franklin D. Roosevelt. Suttle handled Garner's interests in some nine financial institutions and roughly 50,000 acres of ranchlands.[7] Soon afterward, a second federal judgeship was created in El Paso. That seat went to El Paso attorney Ernest Allen Guinn (1905–1974). Judge Guinn was born in Palestine, Texas. He practiced law in Venezuela for about three years after graduating in 1927 from the University of Texas Law School with the highest scholastic standing in his law school class. A staunch FDR supporter, Guinn first served as city attorney in 1944 and then as an anti-crime, tough county attorney from 1939 until 1954 when he entered private practice with his wife.[8]

Joseph Calamia, described as "half Mexican and half Italian," began his practice in this legal community, characterized by not more than six Hispanic lawyers, two who had been in practice since the 1930s, another who was a real estate lawyer and a fourth who did not speak Spanish in spite of the fact that there existed a potentially large Spanish-speaking clientele, albeit many of low income.[9] At age thirty, the upstart attorney Calamia could not have envisioned that in the next twenty years he would be challenging decisions made by these jurists. Certainly he did not envision that he would gain their respect if not their friendship. Moreover, he could not have realized that the federal court of appeals would evolve into an institution that would set legal precedents favoring a marginalized segment of the society that resided in the segregated South.

Appeals from the Western District of Texas fell under the jurisdiction of the Fifth Circuit Court of Appeals seated in New Orleans, Louisiana since 1891. The Fifth Circuit extended through the states of Alabama, Florida, Georgia, Louisiana, Mississippi and Texas. This appellate court, like others in the United States, was created to relieve the caseload of the U.S. Supreme Court. However, unlike the Supreme Court, where the entire court sits on a case, the circuit court considered appeals in panels of three judges. On occasion, the entire court would sit *en banc*. Likewise, certain circumstances would result in a circuit judge presiding over a three-judge panel district court case. Up until 1954, the circuit court's record was typified by only a handful of civil rights cases. Among the most noted civil rights decisions was one that struck down Georgia's all-white primary elections (*Chapman v. King*, 154 F.2d 460 [5th Cir. 1946]). Another addressed the beating death of a black man by Georgia police officers (*Screws v. United States*, 140 F.2d 662 [5th Cir. 1944]), *rev'd.* 325 U.S. 91, 65 S.Ct. 1031, 89 L.Ed. 1495 (1945).

By the mid-1950s, the Fifth Circuit was positioned to become the busiest in the United States. This sudden surge in judicial reviews came after the landmark decision by the Supreme Court in *Brown v. Board of Education* (347 U.S. 483, 74 S.Ct. 686, 98 L.Ed. 873 [1954]). That decision reversed the long-held separate-but-equal principle of *Plessy v. Ferguson* (163 U.S. 537, 16 S.Ct. 1138, 41 L.Ed.256 [1896]), that in Calamia's mind was a cruel interpretation of the Fourteenth Amendment's guarantee of equal protection under the law. *Plessy* set the tone for the next twenty years when the court held:

The object of the (Fourteenth) Amendment was undoubtedly to enforce the absolute equality of the two races before the law, but in the nature of things it could not have been intended to abolish distinctions based upon color, or to enforce social, as distinguished from political equality, or a commingling of the two races upon terms unsatisfactory to either. (*Id.* at 544.)

Clearly, after 1954, the separate-but-equal principle was no longer the law of the land. However, there would be much resistance in the segregated southern states that fell within the Fifth Circuit's jurisdiction. This became more evident as the *Brown* ruling was extended to areas other than public school accommodations. While public notice focused on the Supreme Court in the post-*Brown* years, a great deal of credit belongs to the Fifth Circuit Court of Appeals. This was the court that extended the Warren Court's decisions in several rulings concerning application of the Fourteenth Amendment. Since the Supreme Court dealt with a small percentage of appeals, many rulings of the Fifth Circuit were to stand as the law of the land and as guidance to state and federal authorities. Credit for these rulings belongs, in large part, to the contributions of Judges Richard Taylor Rives (1895–1982), Elbert Parr Tuttle (1897–1996), John Minor Wisdom (1905–1999) and John Robert Brown (1909–1993). They were later to be known derisively as the Fifth Circuit Four after their courageous rulings in favor of a marginalized sector of society in the segregated southern United States.[10] In 1981, Congress divided the Fifth Circuit and assigned the Deep South states to a newly created Eleventh Circuit. However, the new circuit honored the case law articulated by the Fifth Circuit prior to its creation.

In 1950, the chief justice of the U.S. Supreme Court was Frederick Moore Vinson (1890–1953). Chief Justice Vinson was appointed by President Truman in 1946 and served as chief justice until his death in 1953. Among its rulings, the Vinson Court issued two significant decisions concerning the constitutionality of homeland security laws. It upheld application of the Smith Act concerning advocacy to overthrow the U.S. government against the American Communist Party (*Dennis v. United States*, 341 U.S. 494, 71

S.Ct. 857, 95 L.Ed. 1137 [1951]).[11] The Vinson Court also upheld the constitutionality of a requirement that a labor union officer swear to non-membership in the Communist Party (*American Communications Ass'n. C.I.O. v. Douds*, 339 U.S. 382, 70 S.Ct. 674, 94 L.Ed. 925 [1950]).[12] After Vinson's death, President Eisenhower appointed former California governor Earl Warren as chief justice with the intention that he would lead a conservative supreme court. Notably, under Warren's leadership, the court overturned numerous federal and state statutes and applied many provisions of the Bill of Rights to the states. These decisions provided opportunities to sectors of society that had been marginalized, if not excluded, from the political process.[13]

Already a tenacious barrister in the early 1950s, Joseph Calamia was on his way to becoming a leading criminal defense lawyer in El Paso. Perhaps ahead of other lawyers in El Paso, Calamia would come to understand the implications of the Warren Court's decisions involving the Bill of Rights. In light of these rulings and decisions from the Fifth Circuit, the courts begin to reject notions of legal expediency at the expense of individual rights in the South. Calamia would become well-known to these appellate court judges. But first, he had to start in a tough West Texas, pre-Fifth Circuit Court and a pre-Warren Court judicial system.

The Texas judicial system in El Paso was comprised of three judicial districts presided by elected judges, with jurisdiction over the more serious criminal offenses and civil disputes. The oldest district court was the Thirty-fourth District Court, created in 1884 to include El Paso, Presidio and Reeves counties. In 1950, Roy Dale Jackson presided over this court. At age sixty-nine, Judge Jackson was an East Texas native and a 1922 University of Texas graduate who began his legal practice in El Paso in 1923. Now in his third year as a district judge, Jackson had previously served several years as El Paso's district attorney.[14] The Forty-first District Court had been created in 1887, but El Paso county was not included in the district until 1899. In 1950 at age seventy, David E. Mulcahy presided over the Forty-first District Court. Judge Mulcahy had held this post since 1939. Prior to that, he served as assistant city attorney and in 1924 as county attorney.[15] The Sixty-fifth District Court had been in existence since 1915. In 1950, District Judge Morris Galatzan presided over the Sixty-fifth District Court. A native West Texan, Galatzan at age thirty-nine had just been appointed to fill the vacancy left by District Judge Ballard Coldwell. At the time of his appointment, Galatzan was one of the youngest judges in Texas. He had returned to El Paso a few years earlier, his El Paso law practice having been interrupted by the draft in 1942.[16]

The next lower court of record was the El Paso county court at law, which was created in 1915. This court was established to relieve the county judge of having to administer civil and criminal cases whose sanctions and penalties were less than those handled by the district courts.[17] Judge Milton Vaughn (Buddy) Ward (1880–1961) was the judge of the county court at law in 1950. He had presided over this court since 1936. Ward, known for his sharp and kindly wit, was well respected in El Paso. Like so many in his generation, the Kentucky-born Ward also claimed to have come to El Paso in 1913 for health reasons. To some extent, this was said tongue-in-cheek. After obtaining a law degree from the University of Michigan in 1906, Ward went to work as a railroad agent in Mexico until the Mexican Revolution got too hot for him. One night, while locked in a revolutionary jail cell and fearing that his life would be cut short, he fled to El Paso—for the sake of his health. Ward served as assistant district attorney from 1920–1928. After an unsuccessful run for sheriff, he served as a justice of the peace until his election to the county court at law in 1936.[18]

The El Paso county courts of lowest jurisdiction were the justice courts, presided by a justice of the peace with venues represented by precincts. In 1950, El Paso had two justices of the peace in the downtown precinct. Place One was held by Charles Windberg, Jr. and Place Two was held by Texas S. Ward, who was not related to Buddy Ward. Windberg received a law degree from Cumberland University in 1926 and maintained a private practice in El Paso through 1935, when he was appointed as El Paso corporation court judge. He was reelected to the position through 1935. In 1945, he was elected justice of the peace.

At the municipal level, the City of El Paso's court system consisted of a corporation court presided in 1950 by Judge Charles M. Lanier. He had succeeded Windberg in 1947. Corporation court Judge Windberg exercised jurisdiction over ordinances approved by the El Paso city council. The corporation court was not considered a court of record. Lanier had been a police chief in Monroe, Louisiana before coming to El Paso as a railroad company agent; he served in the El Paso police department from 1928–1945.[19]

The state appellate process in Texas was—and still is—bifurcated. Civil cases from the district courts were appealed to the intermediate court of civil appeals, and then to the Texas Supreme Court. The Eighth District Court of Civil Appeals, which originally served El Paso and nineteen other west-Texas counties, was created in 1911. Cases from the court of civil appeals then moved to the Texas Commission of Civil Appeals before reaching the Texas Supreme Court. Criminal appeals took a shorter route from district court directly to the Texas Court of Criminal Appeals. In 1981, the Texas legislature added a first tier of criminal appeals to the intermediate court of civil appeals and renamed them as Courts of Appeals.[20]

This was the judicial system in El Paso in 1950. The law office of Joseph A. Calamia and Wellington Y. Chew was open for business. For El Paso, and perhaps Texas, this was a first. Chew, an Asian-American, was in private law practice. This was a bold move for Calamia. El Paso had a history of discrimination against the Chinese. The office space was divided into a reception area and the consulting office. Calamia and Chew shared that office. Calamia's wife, Geraldine, was the secretary. "If one attorney needed privacy with a client, the other would step outside," recalled Calamia. "Our families knew one another. Wellington and I were good friends." He recalls inviting Chew to join him for exercises at the YMCA. "No, thank you," was Chew's reply. "I did my exercise walking from France to Austria during the war."

Competition was stiff. The large law firms had a lock on the lucrative insurance/tort business, and there were several other law offices in the Caples Building. Advertising was prohibited. With only a name on the building directory and the sign on the door, Calamia's law office was a long elevator ride to the seventh floor. Once on the seventh floor, prospective clients were prey for unscrupulous lawyers. Disturbed by the client-stealing tactics of one such lawyer in the building, Calamia and Chew decided to teach him a lesson. The pair arranged for a telephone call to the lawyer from a Mr. I. B. Free who requested legal services but needed the lawyer to come down to the first floor to escort him to the lawyer's upstairs office. The lawyer was quick to get to the first floor and asked several persons if their name was I. B. Free. It took a while, but in time the rogue lawyer realized that he had been set up with a fake client.[21]

At the same time, Calamia's mother and father had some international business connections that brought young Calamia some clients. It was in defending one of those acquaintances that the young attorney seized an opportunity to challenge an abuse of the criminal justice system by none other than the sheriff of El Paso county.

A QUICK START: CORRUPTION
AND CAVALIER ATTITUDES

While Calamia observed and at times experienced inequities, he was unaware of the organized or individual interests behind the actions that triggered them. Now as a member of the legal community with a self-imposed mandate derived from championing the rights of individuals, Calamia began to encounter the harbingers and protectors of the status quo. At the start of his practice, Calamia faced off against the sheriff and the county commissioner's court in what he perceived to be a corrupt practice. In his crusade for justice, he chose to defend Mexican truckers against a perceived abuse by the local sheriff. Not long afterward, he took on City Hall over what appeared to be a simple case of reckless driving. He also challenged the constitutionality of the city's use of jail inmates in chain gangs. To individuals who benefited from these and other practices, these altruistic challenges endowed Calamia with the "nom de guerre" of "Calamity Joe." Yet after a Calamia court victory, they must have wondered whether this idealistic young man was simply attacking windmills, believing them to be demons.

The status quo did not necessarily benefit the wealthy and the politically powerful. Calamia learned this in a test of honesty, with what at first appeared to be a routine real estate transaction. In law, as in business, there is often a middleman, sometimes honest and sometimes not so honest. Three men walked into Calamia's office requesting title verification and the necessary legal paperwork to close a land sale. The recently widowed owner of the five hundred acres was prepared to sell the land to the second person. The third person, a real estate broker, had made the arrangements. The proceeds would be distributed in a community property arrangement between the widower and his two adult daughters who lived in California. As Calamia prepared the paperwork, he overheard the conversation of the three men. Speaking Spanish, the potential seller asked why the sales amount reported to Calamia was considerably less than the actual sales price. He was told, also in Spanish, that this arrangement would provide cover for a $30,000 discrepancy that need not be shared with the two women. To their surprise, Calamia responded in Spanish that he would not take the case. The broker told Calamia he would find someone else. Calamia warned that the action amounted to stealing and potential mail fraud. Once outside his office, the three men argued. They soon returned and asked Calamia to prepare the paperwork in the full amount. Nevertheless, Calamia contacted the two women and advised them to hire an attorney. Calamia recalled, "Once the daughters received their share of the money, they returned it to their father." Without reservation, Calamia interpreted these proceedings as a good way to start practicing law in a tough and competitive West Texas environment. The California lawyer was impressed with Calamia's honesty, and he was rewarded by several referrals from the California attorney and others who heard of the story. It was a case of a cat smelling a rat, and the cat caught the rat.[1]

In June 1950, less than nine months into Calamia's law practice, Ignacio Tinoco, an acquaintance of Calamia's mother and the head of an El Paso lumber sales company, entered Calamia's office. He sought relief for his firm and other independent lumbermen from harassment by El Paso county sheriff Joe Campbell[2] over transportation of lumber from Mexico. Campbell, like his predecessors, was a tough law-and-order man following a course of conduct that he considered to be in the community's best interest.

At the time, El Paso—and indeed the entire United States— was going through a difficult spring and summer. This era was characterized by a peak in the ups and downs of the Cold War, which included Soviet expansionism in Europe, an atomic bomb threat and a battle between East and West for control of China. There was the Communist invasion of South Korea. At about this time, a congressional subcommittee[3] was investigating allegations by Wisconsin Senator Joseph R. McCarthy that some two hundred U.S. Communist Party members had infiltrated the Department of State. Subcommittee hearings started in February. In May, the resurrection of a 1945 case involving stolen, sensitive U.S-China policy documents dominated the front pages of El Paso's newspapers. In El Paso, the campaign by Sheriff Campbell against gambling came a close second to the Communist infiltration news coming out of Washington.[4]

Sheriff Campbell was responding to a Texas-wide antigambling sentiment that had resulted in a federal court injunction sought by the attorney general and future Texas governor Price Daniel. Daniel, prompted by religious groups and other moralists, obtained a federal court order enjoining Western Union from allowing its wires to be used to transmit horseracing forms and information to bookies in Texas. In El Paso, various private clubs and bars had telegraph-wire ticker machines on their premises. Campbell was concerned that the telegraph company continued to operate a telegraph line from a New Mexico shack located a stone's throw from the Texas state line. Lacking positive action from Western Union and with a message of support by County Attorney Ernest Guinn, Campbell had his deputy cut the telegraph wire at the state line. Before long, Campbell was enjoined by El Paso's federal district judge from cutting the telegraph wire. Western Union successfully sued for $75,000 in damages suffered to the regional wire traffic resulting from the cut wire. Nevertheless, Campbell, with renewed support from County Attorney Guinn, intensified his antigambling campaign with a series of raids on El Paso clubs and bars, seizing telegraph company wire tickers and racing forms.

It was in the midst of this campaign that Sheriff Campbell opened a hard-hitting crusade against Mexican truckers who were importing cheaper Mexican lumber into El Paso, much to the dismay of organized El Paso lumbermen who depended on American suppliers. In mid-June, Campbell posted a deputy as a truck checker at the international bridge at a cost of $250 per month that was covered by the organized El Paso lumbermen. The legal battle began with a blunder by Deputy Sheriff C.O. Colley, who detained a driver with a truckload of lumber entering El Paso from Mexico. Colley charged that the trucking firm had imported more than two truckloads of lumber from Mexico in a month, believing this was in violation of Texas law. He unsuccessfully tried to file a complaint with the county attorney against the Pearson Lumber Sales Company. Colley could not establish the dates of the shipments and mistakenly assumed that a Mr. Pearson was the local representative. Ignacio Tinoco, the real sales representative, observed that his company's trucks were in good mechanical condition, were not overloaded and thus not a problem on city streets. "We called this one off," Colley blared at Tinoco. "But if you bring over any more loads—over two a month—we are going to file on you. This load today will count as one."

Tinoco, other independent firms and customs brokers, hired Calamia. Calamia let out a passionate protest over the sheriff's actions. "We will take all the remedies in law we can, including any action which can be taken through the federal courts." It was no secret that Colley was on the payroll of organized El Paso lumbermen who feared the competition of Mexican lumber trucked into El Paso. Calamia threatened to appear before the El Paso county commissioners court to protest "the hiring of this lumberman deputy sheriff."[5]

Calamia's excitement was one of obvious concern over what he perceived to be blatant discrimination. Yet he expressed this passion in a tone that reflected an abiding respect for the law. This demeanor would characterize Calamia in the many court battles he would face in the halls of justice. Calamia's passionate reaction was vented at the behavior of the sheriff's office. But even so, he had chosen his words carefully. He was going against what was a common practice in a community run by powerful interests where peace officers were often used as a tool to preserve the status quo. Peace officers enjoyed certain immunity when enforcing laws. There was much legal research to perform. In Calamia's eyes, some occurrences had led to a blurring of independence between the legislative, executive and judicial branches of government. The sheriff and the county attorney, in Calamia's vernacular, were the enforcers. In his mind, the enforcers had a duty not only to arrest and convict, but also to see that justice was served. And it followed, in Calamia's mind, that this required respect for a defendant's rights that are guaranteed in the U.S. Constitution and in particular the Fourteenth Amendment:

> No State shall make or enforce any law which shall abridge the privileges or immunities of citizens of the United States; nor shall any State deprive any person of life, liberty, or property, without due process of law; nor deny to any person within its jurisdiction the equal protection of the laws.

This provision surely applied in federal cases under the U.S. Constitution's Bill of Rights, but in 1950, case law applying the Bill of Rights to the states was not all that convincing. Calamia looked for relief through the state courts. What was the applicable law that was being enforced? What authority did the sheriff have to limit imports to two trucks a month? Was not importation of goods a matter of federal jurisdiction and not a state responsibility? U.S. customs officials believed that the importation paperwork was in order. What authority did the sheriff have to require registration of Mexican trucks, when there was an apparent reciprocity between Texas and Mexico in drivers' license validity? Yet, law enforcement officers enjoyed certain immunity in their actions. In Calamia's mind, the sheriff's action was induced by corruption, and it amounted to harassment and an overextension of his authority. "No immunity in such cases," Calamity Joe thought. "Under such circumstance, there was justification to seek and obtain injunctive relief."[6]

As in many court cases, the environment outside the courtroom mirrored the larger and more complex social, political and economic picture in El Paso. To start with, Deputy Sheriff Colley's role as a "lumberman's deputy" had the full support of Sheriff Joe Campbell, County Judge Victor Gilbert and the commissioner's court. Each month, the organized El Paso lumbermen provided funds to the county and, in turn, the county passed the money on to the deputy. There was a housing construction boom in El Paso, as in other communities in the United States. World War II veterans, many of them returning from technical and professional training under the G.I. Bill, were buying houses for their growing families in this postwar baby boom era. There was also the lure of lower prices just across the border in Juárez that this included the lumber used to meet the housing demand. A house, like those many veterans were buying, would sell at less than $3,000. According to some accounts, construction of a house with Mexican imported lumber would reduce the cost by about $125.00.[7] That would be like taking $3,200 off an $80,000 starter home in 2004. At the same time, the organized El Paso lumbermen cried foul. They charged that the Juárez lumber carriers, in defiance of their import permits, were going directly to job sites instead of to consignees. U.S. customs officials thought everything was on the up-and-up. There were no violations of the permits. The El Paso lumbermen also charged that the Mexican trucks were so unsafe and so overloaded that they were damaging the streets in El Paso. During his protest before the county commissioner's court, Calamia got into a heated exchange with Sheriff Campbell. The sixty-year-old Campbell at one point erupted: "I'm not going to let any lint-faced young lawyer who isn't dry behind the ears try to tell me how to run the sheriff's department."[8]

Calamia filed the lawsuit before Forty-first District Judge Mulcahy and requested a temporary restraining order. The petition alleged that an unlawful arrest of the independent importer's truck drivers would cause irreparable harm. Calamia argued that there was no basis for requiring Texas registration and Texas licensing of Mexican trucks and drivers. After all, Mexico allowed Texas trucks and drivers to do business without harassment, arrest or the imposition of a similar requirement. He referred to practices and agreements between Texas and Mexico encompassing fifty years of reciprocal acceptance of the other's motor vehicle registration and motorist licenses. Reciprocal arrangements were honored in the Texas penal code. This was an unusual point as in the 1940s the

practice of "quickie" divorces in Juárez was a matter of some re-
pugnance in the El Paso area: Texas had questioned their applica-
bility. It was Judge Mulcahy who, in 1943, considered their validity
in the United States to be an infringement of Texas's sovereignty.[9]
Calamia further argued for municipal exclusivity concerning load
limits on city streets. He observed that no such ordinance had been
enacted by the City of El Paso. In short, Calamia argued that the
laws cited by the county attorney in defense of the sheriff's actions
did not apply, and therefore the El Paso county sheriff was ex-
ceeding his authority.[10]

The rookie lawyer was face to face with some powerful foes.
Prominent El Paso attorney and civic leader Theodore (Ted) Andress represented the organized lumbermen. Nearly twenty-three
years older than Calamia, Andress had been practicing law in El
Paso for almost twenty years. Andress also represented Sheriff
Campbell in the lawsuit. Likewise, Judge Mulcahy carried similar
baggage considering his statements about Texas sovereignty some
years earlier. The armed sheriff, who was in the courtroom, tapped
his sidearm in response to the accusations of the "young lint-faced
lawyer." Calamia instinctively donned a boxer's stand, ready to
fight. Judge Mulcahy quickly restored order and granted the temporary restraining order on both grounds. A month later, the judge
modified the order, ruled that reciprocity of licensing requirements
could not be allowed without an agreement between the State of
Texas and the State of Chihuahua. Several months later, Mulcahy
issued a permanent injunction on both grounds—after all an
agreement between Texas and Chihuahua was now in existence.

The permanent injunction was an agreed judgment strictly
based on the points of law in the restraining order and not quite a
winner-take-all arrangement. The injunction applied specifically
to forty-one drivers and their licensed vehicles. Outside the courtroom, the question of corruption was not addressed except for a
short *El Paso Herald Post* newspaper editorial. The editorial outlined
the money laundering scheme and expressed amazement that the
county court and sheriff "should let their offices and themselves
be used to restrict the imports of the United States in behalf of a

small group and to the damage of many."[11] Among those many people were the popular World War II veterans returning and being honored by a grateful American public. In a separate note, *Herald Post* editor Ed Pooley, who had acquired a reputation of going after certain interests in El Paso in his "Juan Smith" column, wrote tongue-in-cheek, listing the benefits of having a private deputy sheriff. He concluded, "Commissioners Court could use a private deputy to scare their opponents into withdrawing from the primary campaign."[12] Pooley and Calamity Joe shared a common fear, a retraction of the U.S. Constitution's promise to "establish justice, insure domestic tranquility, provide for the general welfare and secure the blessings of liberty to ourselves and our posterity." Still, the organized lumbermen did not give up easily. They sought emergency adoption of a weight limit ordinance by the City of El Paso. Calamia warned the city council that "any such legislation enacted be done for the benefit of the general public and not to serve special interests." Unspoken, but understood, was the fear that if such an ordinance were to be applied without discrimination, a large number of El Paso drivers would become law-breakers. A few weeks later the El Paso city council refused to enact an ordinance concerning load limits on city streets.[13]

Joseph Calamia's reactions were reminiscent of the actions of that romantic fighter of windmills from the desert plains of La Mancha in Spain. The passion to undo a perceived wrong was similar. But in Calamia's case, the immediate reaction to right a wrong was tempered by a cerebral process. This process, which matured with time, was one based on the law as well as on what could realistically be accomplished. Some fifty-five years later, Calamia recalled: "Some chided me as being a Don Quixote. But I told them 'The big difference is that my demons were real.'"[14] About two years after the lumbermen's case, another demon appeared, this time in the court of lowest jurisdiction where minor offenses were routinely dispensed without fanfare and seemingly summarily.

Victor De la Peña was a taxi driver whose livelihood depended on his cab driver's license. In 1952, El Paso police gave him a ticket for reckless driving while on the job in the downtown area. El Paso was a city that occupied about one-tenth of the 250 square miles that covered El Paso in 2005. Major business activity was in the downtown area. Corporation court (today's municipal court) was where minor offenses were prosecuted with fines ranging from $5 to $30 in most cases. De la Peña faced a $10 fine, but this was at a time when one could buy a pound of baloney for thirty-nine cents and a dozen eggs for thirty cents. De la Peña's $10 fine was about one-half his week's pay.

De la Peña was brought before corporation court judge Charles M. Lanier, found guilty and fined. Offenses handled in corporation court in the early 1950s included drunkenness, disturbing the peace, loitering, theft under $5, driving without an operating license, running a red light and reckless driving. In view of these circumstances, most defendants choose to pay their fines.[15] De la Peña, however, asked for Calamia's help, knowing that this citation would put an end to his livelihood. Calamia, in practice only a couple of years, had an intrinsic understanding of the dilemma, given that not too many years before, he had worked as a taxi driver. Beyond the driver's livelihood, Calamity Joe saw an injustice, "The man was fined $10 in corporation court and couldn't appeal the case beyond the county court at law which upheld the lower court's ruling. De la Peña would lose his license. It just didn't seem right."[16]

More importantly, Calamia's thoughts went back to law school and those classes on constitutional law. He had learned that the Bill of Rights called for specificity when it came to the rights of an accused person. Calamia studied the contents of the charge in its broad nature. The offense contained in the 1947 Texas statute was that of "driving an automobile without due caution and at a speed and in a manner endangering persons and property." To Calamia, the offense was stated in a very broad manner, the public had no notice of the definition and police could apply it in a very subjective manner.[17] Calamia was convinced that he had a good argument. However, the case had already been unsuccessfully appealed to the county court at law. There had to be a way to bring this issue before a higher court.

Calamia looked at the personal liberty guarantees of U.S. and Texas constitutions and found refuge in habeas corpus, that great guarantor of personal liberty. "This guarantee goes back to rights in England's Magna Carta," Calamia continued to stress some five decades later. "This writ directs a person detaining another to produce the body of the person. It is a matter for the government to show cause for detention. It orders the lower court to produce the entire record. It can order a lower court to explain."[18] For his client to petition successfully for a writ of habeas corpus, De la Peña had to be in custody. Calamia told his client not to pay the fine even though this meant De la Peña would be placed under arrest. He filed a petition for a writ of habeas corpus before the Texas Court of Criminal Appeals alleging that the vagueness of the statute violated De la Peña's constitutional rights and restrained his liberty. The writ was granted and De la Peña was released on bond pending a determination by the appeals court (*Ex parte De la Peña*, 251 S.W. 2d 890 [Tex.Cr.App. 1952]).

Six months after the incident, the Texas Court of Criminal Appeals agreed that the statute was unconstitutional and ordered the defendant free from further restraint. The court observed that, three years earlier, the 1947 statute had been declared unconstitutional in part and had been amended by the Texas Legislature in 1951. In its earlier ruling, the court established that, "A statute which forbids or requires an act in terms too vague that men of common intelligence must guess as to its meaning and differ as to its applications lacks the first essential of 'due process of law.'" (*Ex parte Chernosky*, 217 S.W.2d 673 [Tex.Cr.App. 1949]). Calamia recalled, "Chernosky opened the issue and De la Peña sealed the point of law."

Habeas corpus victories are not necessarily of a "they lived happily ever after" nature. The freed victim has the opportunity to move on with his or her life. In the case of De la Peña, however, the end was tragic, a fatal car crash involving alcohol. The City of El Paso did take care to instruct its peace officers on the proper applicable law. The attorneys went on to their next cases, with the decision in hand and a challenge to apply that lesson learned in future cases. To Calamia, though, the judicial victory was not final. He knew that there would be more diligence by the enforcer (Calamia's term for the executive branch) and more action by the lawmaker (Calamia's term for the legislative branch). But believing his demons to be real, Calamia would view their actions with caution. The enforcer would often take a cavalier approach to enforcement when dealing with those who were not among the educated, politically powerful and wealthy. If necessary, Calamity Joe would resort to that third component of the Constitution's system of checks and balances, the judiciary. He found himself continually questioning whether the enforcer's actions would be consistent with the Bill of Rights.[19]

For years, El Paso, like many other communities, used the city's jailed prisoners on chain gangs. The city defended the system, arguing that prisoners volunteered to do chain-gang chores of cleaning alleys and streets. The city believed that this gave prisoners a chance to get away from the small jail tanks. The city gave the chain-gang prisoners three meals a day, compared to two for those who remained in their cells. Calamia saw the practice as reprehensible. "It was awful," he recalled some fifty years later. "It was degrading to have human beings in chains in public display." His love for constitutional law at SMU had instilled in him an ardent belief that the Sixth Amendment prohibited cruel and unusual punishment. Without question, he believed that this protection extended to the states and their subordinate jurisdictions.

In 1954, Calamia saw his opportunity to challenge this practice. He represented three Hispanic individuals with little education and no money who had been jailed for drunkenness, loitering and vagrancy. They had not paid a $100 fine, roughly equivalent to a month's rent and groceries. Calamia petitioned for a writ of habeas corpus seeking their release or a prohibition against their use in a chain gang. "In this day and age," the petition stated, "such conditions of laboring persons who only have been convicted of misdemeanors is cruel, degrading and unusual punishment."

Forty-First District Judge Mulcahy dismissed the claim. Mulcahy reasoned that the practice was consistent with the Texas constitution. Further, legislation had been passed at a time when the use of prisoner labor was common. He found that there was no prohibition against using balls and chains. Not one to give up, Calamia vowed to continue the fight once he found a city prisoner willing to challenge the practice. "I still believe working chain gangs is cruel punishment," he said after the decision.[20] Calamia's unsuccessful search for a willing city prisoner lasted for several years, but was finally over when Mayor Raymond Telles took the lead in city council action terminating the chain-gang practice.[21]

Calamity Joe got a quick start in his law practice, going against practices he considered corrupt and attitudes that he considered to be cavalier. These first cases showed a young lawyer who asserted an unguarded and unsophisticated passion, which had developed in his youth, to undo a perceived wrong. Yet these cases seemed to be moving Calamia's character to one that would become more refined. There would be an evolution of this youthful lawyer beyond a mere instinct for championing and protecting the constitutional rights of the underdog. Calamia would grow into an experienced lawyer who was well aware of how organized and individual interests could adversely impact law contrary to the constitution. He would be characterized as one who delved into the constitutional foundation of those laws and practices that he perceived were often used to the detriment of the undereducated and the working class. In short, Calamity Joe evolved into a fighter of windmills whose immediate impulse to right a wrong was tempered by a mature and realistic cerebral process.

Setting Precedents
The Early Cases

—⁓⁓⁓—

THE EARLY CASES: SEEMINGLY
INNOCUOUS, BUT . . .

More cases came to Calamia in the next few years, many of which made the headlines in the local press. These were years in which El Pasoans relied on the daily newspapers and the weekend movie theater newsreels for their news. Television news was in its infancy. There were murder cases with all the notoriety that went with news of that sort. There were the drug cases and the theft cases and other headline grabbers. Some cases went to trial. Some never got to trial. At times, the defendant pled guilty. At other times, the cases were dismissed for lack of evidence. Often in the news media's rush to meet a deadline for publication, the story was simply a catchy phrase uttered by attorneys, witnesses, and judges.

The points of law argued by Calamia, while not always printed, remained inscribed in the court record. He learned to argue his case not only to a jury but also to an appellate court. In preparation for the former, Calamia studied the law and applicable precedents raising those specific points of law in the pre-trial and trial stages. In preparation for the latter, he often challenged not only the various aspects of the testimony itself but also the adequacy and application of procedures and the validity of the law. Issues arose over unlawful detention and the right to counsel. Some of Calamia's cases seemed innocuous, but upon closer analysis, a pattern began to emerge of a probing legal mind intent on clarifying and upholding the true spirit of a specific constitutional issue.

What about unlawful detention? A man arrested in El Paso on a California parole violation appeared before Judge Jackson in the Thirty-fourth District Court. He waived extradition and Judge Jackson ordered him turned over to California authorities "forthwith." To Calamia, "forthwith" meant quickly. But the man had been in jail for nineteen days, was slated to stay there longer, or, as the sheriff assumed, until the California authorities came for him. Calamia mused over the sheriff's assumption. In the eyes of a lawman, the man had been convicted and had been spared from doing time; now he had blown it and would likely go back to the slammer. But Calamia thought that the man was still entitled to a speedy public trial on the elements of the incident alleged as a parole violation. He believed an open-ended confinement amounted to unlawful detention, and thus he sought the man's release through a writ of habeas corpus. After review, Sixty-fifth District Judge Galatzan granted the writ.

What about a defendant's state of mind? A client was faced with a life sentence for a fatal shooting outside a Socorro cafe. Calamia concluded that a conviction hinged on the matter of intent. Moreover, a verdict of guilty would require a decision of all the jurors; they would find that the verdict was beyond a reasonable doubt and based solely on the evidence presented in court. Such being the case, Calamia's strategy focused on presenting testimony that would create reasonable doubt in the minds of jurors as to whether the shooting could have been accidental. Expounding on the defendant's testimony, Calamia painted a scenario of a victim fumbling in the pocket of his coat while the accused—believing he was reaching for a weapon—reacted accordingly. The jury returned a verdict of murder without malice, a lesser-included offense and assessed a five-year suspended sentence.

By now, El Paso had a new sheriff in Jimmie Hicks. Hicks had come to El Paso from southern Arizona where he developed an ongoing friendship with Calamia's father. The two met on the baseball field where they played in a semiprofessional league. Calamia's seven-year-old son, J. R., became fascinated with Hicks whom he came to know while visiting his grandfather. J. R. was fond of dressing up as a police officer in a costume made by Grandma Calamia. Hicks would turn on the siren and flash the red light to the delight of the little boy who stood there with an imaginative gaze and wished, "I want to be a cop!"

While Hicks was sheriff, a near-fatal shooting by a jealous husband took place along the international boundary. The husband admitted to the shooting but swore that the incident took place on the Mexican bank of the Rio Grande. The man's father hired Calamia to defend his son. Meanwhile, the sheriff's deputies were driving the suspect along the banks of the Rio Grande. Calamia waited impatiently for his client in the downtown courthouse some thirteen miles away. What about an accused person's right to an attorney?

With little convincing evidence, Calamia believed there would be no cause for formal detention. More than three hours elapsed and the deputies had not brought the accused downtown for booking. Calamia grew concerned that the lawmen were "confession riding" his client—interrogating a suspect with the explicit intent of obtaining a confession before the suspect had secured legal representation. Calamia's mind went back to the Constitution. "The man has a right to have assistance of counsel for his defense." While the extent of this protection was not quite definitive at the time, the courts seemed to be moving toward making this protection more qualitative. Calamia thought, "Surely, a person should not be questioned indefinitely without an attorney present while he is being questioned by police." At the same time, Calamia recognized that local and state law enforcement officials were slow in recognizing the extent of the application of this constitutional right to criminal law. In defense of his deputies, Hicks insisted that the investigation was still at a general inquiry stage and that his deputies were on a fact-finding mission. Calamia argued that the inquiry had focused on his client and that he had a right to have a lawyer present. Calamia also pointed to the matter of jurisdiction, contending that the shooting took place in Mexico. The now-more-seasoned attorney was successful in obtaining a writ of habeas corpus before Sixty-fifth District Judge Galatzan. Judge Galatzan ordered the man to be released immediately without having to post bond even though Hicks questioned Calamia's assertion that "immediate" meant "instantaneous." Calamia recalls, "The sheriff finally complied and fortunately the shooting victim recovered."[1] This incident took place in 1955, nearly one decade before the U.S. Supreme Court clarified the distinction in *Escobedo v. Illinois* (378 U.S. 478, 84 S.Ct. 1758, 12 L.Ed.2d 977 [1964])[2] and eleven years before the landmark ruling establishing that a defendant must be warned of his rights in *Miranda v. Arizona* (384 U.S. 436, 86 S.Ct. 1602, 16 L.Ed.2d 694 [1966]).[3]

DRUG LAWS: TOUGH BUT
WITH RESERVATIONS

In the 1950s, there was a growing national concern over an increase in the use of narcotic and other illegal drugs. However, there were those who worried that in the haste to attack a perceived clear and present danger, some constitutional protections might be overlooked. Congress held hearings over the health threat. Startling statistics emerging from Washington alarmed an unsuspecting public that drug addiction was spreading to the school-aged population.[1] The federal government's ensuing assault was based on a series of drug laws that had been enacted since 1909.[2] Careful to avoid a major conflict over the rights reserved to the states, federal laws were based on a clear-cut federal jurisdictional issue—the regulation of imports. These acts made it illegal to import opium for non-medicinal purposes and were enforced under the assumption that possession of the drug was sufficient evidence that the drug was smuggled and thus ensured conviction unless the defendant explained "the possession to the satisfaction of the jury." The U.S. Supreme Court determined that this smuggling assumption did not violate either due process or self-incrimination protections (*Yee Hem v. United States*, 268 U.S. 178, 45 S.Ct. 470, 69 L.Ed. 904 [1925]). This holding motivated Congress to assert it as a rule of evidence in future antidrug legislation.

In El Paso's federal court, the Jones-Miller Act (National Narcotics and Drug Importation Act) of 1942 and the marijuana[3] tax law enacted in 1937 (26 U.S.C. § 4741) seemed to be the Fed's best weapon in the war on drugs. However, by the mid-1950s, national sentiment favored greater law enforcement and harsher penalties to stem this epidemic, and the National Drug Control Act of 1956 called for mandatory imprisonment. Under the Act, a first offense carried a penalty of two to five years' imprisonment. The Act required drug addicts and persons convicted of narcotics violations to register with U.S. Customs before leaving the United States. It also authorized the Immigration and Naturalization Service to deport alien drug users and drug law violators. The Act specifically prohibited illegal importation of marijuana, including knowingly receiving, concealing, purchasing, selling and facilitating the transportation of marijuana. As with the marijuana tax statute, the 1956 law established that possession was sufficient to prove that the marijuana was smuggled.

In El Paso, there was easy access to drugs from Juárez. La Nacha's marijuana and heroin business had been in operation in Juárez since the 1920s and it operated with impunity.[4] But in El Paso, there was concern that drugs were being used by school-aged youth supplied by these dealers in El Paso who smuggled the drugs from Juárez. Texas and El Paso adopted laws that forbade the possession and sale of narcotics drugs. As a result, police undercover operations led to roundups of suspected drug dealers. Arrests were many. Some of those arrested came to Calamia to defend them. In many cases the evidence against the client was overwhelming, and it was in the client's best interest to have Calamia plea bargain with the district attorney for a lesser charge and a lower penalty recommendation to the court. In others, the government's case was weak, and Calamia focused on possible pretrial actions. He prepared his case for the eyes and ears of the jury and set the groundwork for an appeal in the event of a conviction.

Calamia found himself on the wrong side of a popular cause —the crusade to put druggies and pushers off the streets and behind bars. However, his firsthand experience revealed that too often those "baddies" were characterized as Hispanics who lived south of the tracks. As a lawyer, he had learned to expect the risk of defending the accused since a lawyer must represent his client without regard to a potential social cause. In America's criminal justice system, a defendant is presumed to be innocent until proven guilty. This protection, inscribed in the Bill of Rights, applies regardless of how heinous the criminal charges or how psychopathic the defendant. Calamia also understood the risk in dealing with difficult defendants. In some cases, the defendant could become the enemy of the lawyer, or even his victim. The public threat was also a reality.[5] Still, in this rather hostile environment, Calamia chose to take on several drug-related cases precisely because they challenged the constitutionality of drug control laws. Still, he did not see himself as a social reformer but rather as a protector of the constitutional rights that apply to all individuals, even the underdog.

In 1956, the City of El Paso made it a misdemeanor for a person to be in a public place while under the influence of a narcotic drug. It was also a misdemeanor to throw away or dispose of a narcotic drug in the streets or in a public place. Hundreds were jailed upon conviction in corporation court, which was not a court of record. The only appeal was to the El Paso county court at law. Before corporate court Judge Woodard, Calamia argued that, "The charge of being under the influence is a serious one. It should be handled by a higher court than Police Court because a state law makes conviction a felony." In consideration of Calamia's arguments, Woodard dismissed the case against one defendant, but fined the second $51.00. This positioned Calamia to file a petition for writ of habeas corpus before County Court at Law Judge Ward to review the constitutionality of the city ordinance.

At the habeas corpus hearing, the very experienced City Attorney Travis White argued that there was no precedent for the argument and Judge Ward upheld the conviction. Not one to give up, Calamia patiently searched for an applicable Court of Criminal Appeals ruling, a new defendant and another hearing before Judge Ward. A few months later, the opportunity arose, and Judge Ward declared the ordinance unconstitutional.[6]

In a different twist on the city's drug ordinance, Calamia challenged the manner in which police obtained evidence based on a person's behavior. This raised the question of warrantless searches and seizures. Police often approached a suspected heroin user along a south El Paso street curb. Their experience and their knowledge of the criminal element in the area seemed sufficient to suspect that the individual, upon seeing the officers, had placed some folded papers containing heroin in his mouth. One officer inserted his finger in the suspect's mouth, opened it and disgorged three papers of heroin. Calamia challenged the possession charge and argued that the suspect was not acting in a suspicious manner as required by the ordinance. He contended that a police officer's knowledge that a person is a drug user did not meet that test and that extracting the drug from the suspect's mouth constituted a search without a warrant. The district attorney dismissed the charges.[7]

In the mid-1950s, the State of Texas successfully incarcerated habitual criminals under a "three strikes" statute that could impose a life sentence if the defendant had three prior convictions. Calamia and his new Asian-American partner, Dan Y. Garbern, took on a case that involved a defendant who had had three convictions since 1948.

A jury found the defendant guilty in a trial before District Judge William E. Ward (1916–1986). Ward, the son of county court at law Judge M. V. Ward, had been appointed district judge in 1955 after the death of Thirty-fourth District Judge Jackson. Judge Ward received his law degree from the University of Texas. He served in the European theater during World War II. He continued as Thirty-fourth District Judge until 1969, when he was appointed to the Eighth Court of Civil Appeals. He served on the Court until his death in 1986. District Attorney William E. Clayton (1916-1986) represented the State. A native of El Paso, Clayton was a graduate of the University of Texas and its law school. He served in the Texas House of Representatives from 1933 to 1936. He served as district attorney until 1961 when he was named to the Eigth Court of Civil Appeals. He retired in 1969.[8] Assisting Clayton was assistant district attorney Edwin F. Berliner. Berliner was a graduate of Texas Western College and the University of Texas Law School. He succeeded Clayton and served as district attorney until 1965 when he was appointed to the newly created 171st District Court.

During the trial, Calamia and Garbern alleged that the State's evidence supporting three prior convictions by the defendant was not convincing, but the judge refused to throw out the evidence. Calamia wondered about the vagueness of the law itself, but understood that the courts had upheld its constitutionality. He also understood that application of a vague statute requires the elements to be precisely stated in an indictment and supported by evidence in the trial. In view of the court's decision, Calamia and Garbern appealed their client's "three strikes" conviction to the Texas Court of Criminal Appeals. Calamia agreed that evidence was clear and convincing on two of the prior convictions, but argued that it was questionable that a third conviction occurred, if it even occurred at all. The high court reversed the conviction, and remanded the case to the trial court. (*Armendáriz v. Texas*, 294 S.W. 2d 98 [Tex.Cr.App. 1956]).

The federal government was indeed tough on drug smugglers. A conviction was almost a certainty if a suspect was caught entering El Paso from Juárez with any amount of narcotic drug. A conviction in cases of failing to register as a drug addict or a person convicted of a narcotics charge was fairly certain. An addict was required to register with U.S. Customs upon his return from Mexico. Few bothered to register. The smuggling and registration laws, along with the marijuana tax law, were great tools for law enforcement to keep habitual criminals behind bars. Conviction in most cases meant a prison term. From a civil rights perspective, however, something seemed to be amiss.

Federal District Judge Thomason sometimes found himself apologizing for having to assess a long prison term based upon possession of a small amount of drugs. On the other hand, there was an occasional temptation to enhance the penalty. In one instance, Calamia recalled his client's disgust over such a sentence. "My client was mumbling something as he was being taken out of Judge Thomason's courtroom," Calamia related. "Judge Thomason called the man with an authoritative voice, 'What did you say? Repeat it so I can hear it?'" Calamia went on, "My client just turned

around and said, 'Just this Judge. You sure are free with my time!'"
In another instance, Calamia remembered the sentencing of a
client with a long criminal record. Judge Thomason, in possession
of the presentencing report, asked for a presentencing statement.
The client said, "Justice, just give me justice." In this case, there
was little reason for leniency. Thomason replied, "Just be careful
what you ask for."

Calamia became concerned that in the prosecution of federal
drug cases, the government may be too quick to assume that the evidence was sufficient for conviction without considering whether a
suspect's rights were violated by the manner in which the evidence
was obtained. Calamia again looked to the protection in the Fifth
Amendment that no person "shall be compelled in any criminal
case to be a witness against himself, nor be deprived of life, liberty,
or property, without due process of law."

In 1956, at the height of the get-tough-on-drugs period,
Calamia gained support in his belief that expediency in curbing
drug-related crime should not lead to convictions based on pure
speculation. (*Durán v. United States*, 234 F.2d 932 [5th Cir. 1956]).
Durán and two other men were convicted of importing and concealing bulk marijuana and were sentenced to three years' imprisonment. Calamia filed for a motion for judgment of acquittal due
to insufficient evidence. The arresting officers testified but the defendants did not. Durán's two codefendants, traveling in Durán's
car, were stopped for a routine inspection as they entered El Paso
at the international bridge. A search yielded seventeen packages
of marijuana. One defendant claimed the drugs and denied that
any other person was involved. Federal agents also found a locker
key on one of the men and followed up with a search of a public
locker in an El Paso bus station. The locker was found to be empty,
but there were witness accounts that Durán had removed two suit-
cases from it. Durán admitted that he owned the car and that he
had been in Juárez with the other defendants. But he swore that he
had disassociated from them long before he returned to El Paso. In
urging his motion, Calamia focused on the adequacy of the circumstantial evidence. Judge Thomason denied the motion and that
issue would have to wait.

Calamia thought he had that opportunity less than a year later in a case challenging the test required to prove possession. His client was charged with failing to pay tax on marijuana. Like the drug-smuggling laws, the marijuana tax law presumed that possession of the drug was sufficient for conviction. The defendant was convicted for failing to pay tax on fifty marijuana cigarettes in his possession.[9] Calamia argued that the presumption required self-incrimination. He also argued that the evidence did not prove that his client knowingly possessed the marijuana cigarettes found on the floor of his car. Indeed, the government's evidentiary case was simple. U.S. Customs had laboratory proof that the substance in the cigarettes was marijuana and the defendant had no proof that he paid the marijuana tax.[10] The government called on an El Paso policeman who provided what the jury accepted as circumstantial evidence to prove beyond a reasonable doubt that the defendant was in possession of marijuana. After all, evidence showed that the marijuana was near a club owned by the defendant. On the other hand, Calamia argued this was a matter of a policeman tailing the defendant after he got into his unlocked car. The marijuana was found on the passenger seat side.

Calamia appealed and a three-judge panel reversed. (*Guevara v. United States*, 242 F. 2d 745 [5th Cir. 1957]). Indeed, the court focused on the ambiguity of the term "possession." The opinion observed that:

> no term is more ambiguous than the word 'possession,' and this is especially true when it occurs in criminal statutory provisions. It is so fraught with danger that the courts must scrutinize its use with diligence, and the jury must be carefully instructed in order to prevent injustice. (*Id.* at 746–47.)

The court reiterated that the test to be applied is whether the jury might reasonably find that the evidence excludes "every reasonable hypothesis except that of guilt." (*Id.* at 747, *citing Vick v. United States*, 216 F.2d 228, 232 [5th Cir. 1954]). Emphasizing that the defendant's car was unlocked, the court concluded that there was no connection between ownership of a car and possession of a substance found in the car since it was possible that someone else could have placed the marijuana in the car. The court did not address the constitutionality of the marijuana tax law, and it remained a contentious issue for a number of years. It was not until 1969 that the U.S. Supreme Court declared the marijuana tax law unconstitutional (*Leary v. United States,* 395 U.S. 6, 89 S.Ct. 1532, 23 L.Ed.2d 57 [1969]). Unlike the environment twelve years earlier, conditions in the United States had changed.

The country was in the midst of a social revolution marked by demonstrations and antiwar sentiment. A civil rights law had been enacted, and its provisions were being tested to advance a wide spectrum of minority rights, extending beyond that of the African-American community. Timothy F. Leary (1920–1996), an advocate of psychedelic drug research, was associated with the drug counterculture of the 1960s. By 1969, the *Leary* case had some strong precedents leading to the Supreme Court's decision. In one case, the high court held that an occupational tax on wagering—which included a requirement that those liable for the occupational tax register each year with the director of the local internal revenue district—implicated the protection of the Fifth Amendment self-incrimination clause (*Marchetti v. United States,* 390 U.S. 39, 88 S.Ct. 697, 19 L.Ed.2d 889 [1968]). In two other cases, the court had held that an excise tax on wagering proceeds and a presumption of ownership in a firearms registration law had a similar effect. (*See Grosso v. United States,* 390 U.S. 62, 88 S.Ct. 709, 19 L.Ed.2d 906 [1968]); *Haynes v. United States,* 390 U.S. 85, 88 S.Ct. 722, 19 L.Ed.2d 923 [1968]).

As with the marijuana tax law, something also seemed to be amiss in the addict registration law. The law carried maximum penalties of two years in prison and fines of up to $5,000. Like the marijuana tax law, this statute was a strict liability offense. Mere possession presumed guilt. Was this contrary to the Fifth Amendment protection against self-incrimination? Was the provision contrary to Fourth Amendment protection against unreasonable search or seizure? Calamia needed a test case. The opportunity came in early 1958.

A known addict was found guilty in federal court for failing to register as a drug addict. Government testimony in a non-jury trial revealed that in April 1957, the defendant returned to the United States without registering with U.S. Customs before going to Juárez. There were eyewitnesses. In Calamia's view, the addict registration law was unconstitutional because it placed a defendant in a position of incriminating himself. Based on this argument, Calamia claimed that his client was being restrained illegally. He sought his client's release under a writ of habeas corpus. Judge Thomason did not buy the argument. Calamia then sought acquittal on grounds that the charge was unconstitutional. Thomason did not buy that argument either and sentenced the defendant to prison.

On appeal, Calamia challenged the constitutionality of the statute on multiple grounds. He claimed that the law compelled his client to incriminate himself and to subject himself to an unreasonable search and seizure; it deprived his client of his right to personal and civil liberty; it was arbitrary, vague and indefinite; it did not provide prior notice; and it constituted cruel and unusual punishment. He argued that the addict registration law had not fulfilled the intent of Congress "to facilitate effective control of international traffic in narcotic drugs and to prevent the spread of drug addiction." The government relied on similar federal cases in California—*Reyes v. United States* and *Pérez v. United States*, 258 F.2d 774 (9th Cir. 1958)—and a Supreme Court case involving a gaming tax (*United States v. Kahriger*, 345 U.S. 22, 73 S.Ct. 510, 97 L.Ed. 754 [1953]). Nine months after the conviction, the Fifth Circuit held that the registration statute was not subject to constitutional attack. (*Palma v. United States*, 261 F.2d 93 [5th Cir. 1958]).

There was no victory in 1958. As with the marijuana tax challenge, Calamia had touched on constitutional issues that eventually would bring an end to the addict registration law. For now, it had the opposite effect. Even as late as 1969, the Supreme Court used *Palma* as a principal precedent in defense of the addict registration law. (*See Leary v. United States*, 395 U.S. 6, 89 S.Ct. 1532, 23 L.Ed.2d 57 [1969]). After *Leary*, it was only a matter of time before the addict registration requirements were removed from the books. In 1970, the U.S. Congress enacted a comprehensive drug control law that repealed the addict tax requirement.

CONSTITUTIONALITY: THE FOURTEENTH AMENDMENT AND THE STATES

To some, perhaps, Calamia seemed to quibble over insignificant evidentiary and procedural matters overlooked by the government. But to the appellate courts, the nit-picking was significant in that these omissions were at times sufficient grounds to reverse a conviction in favor of a new trial or outright dismissal. To Calamia, these were issues that involved a person's liberties guaranteed in the Bill of Rights and the Fourteenth Amendment. In his mind, the Fourteenth Amendment applied the entire Bill of Rights to the State of Texas. The Sixth Amendment guarantees that the accused shall be informed of the nature of the accusation and shall be entitled to confront witnesses. In part, this was a process of discovering the evidence that the government had against the accused. In one case, Calamia found himself involved in a discovery dispute involving a man convicted of a crime of passion. The issue was newly discovered information as a basis for reversal of a harsh sentence.

Calamia and his partner Wellington Chew, joined by attorney George Rodríguez, Sr.,[1] stepped in posttrial to represent an El Paso man found guilty of murder with malice in the shooting death of his wife. The jury heard testimony that the killing took place in a fit of passion but the evidence was not convincing. Under Texas law at that time (Vernon's Ann. P.C. art. 1256), the statute recognized a lesser included offense of murder without malice. Sudden passion arising from an adequate cause could justify murder without malice.[2] The State argued that there was no evidence of infidelity on the part of the dead woman. It further argued that a letter written to the woman by her alleged lover, now in a New Mexico hospital, did not indicate the existence of an intimate relationship. The tone of the letter, however, was open to a different interpretation. The trial attorney had not sought discovery either pretrial or during trial. Calamia suspected that there was more to the relationship.

Calamia did some detective work and traveled to New Mexico where he had a long conversation with the man his client believed to be the wife's lover. Calamia obtained admissions that the couple had indeed engaged in an intimate relationship. The man explained the mysterious tone of his letter; he was conciliatory because he feared for his life. Calamia argued that the prosecutor had possessed similar information but had disregarded it. "This was a breach of ethics by the State," Calamia recounted. "I still question why there was no sanction against the prosecutor." In considering a motion for new trial, Judge Jackson asked, "Mr. Calamia. You say the State did this. [. . .] Give me your three best cases." Calamia provided three cases, resulting in a conviction of murder without malice, the lesser-included offense.

Calamia had touched on two significant points of law: (1) that of a lesser-included offense involving a crime of passion, and (2) that of the government withholding information supporting the lesser offense. Calamia viewed sudden passion as a potential defense, considering that it is a common instinct among human beings. At the same time, he recognized that sudden passion would have to arise from an adequate cause, which at that time was defined as that which "would commonly produce a degree of anger, rage, resentment, or terror in a person of ordinary temper sufficient to render the mind incapable of cool reflection." Just how far could one take this definition? "Depends on the circumstances," Calamia reminisced fifty years later. Recalling some successful cases involving a defense of sudden passion, Calamia suddenly asserted in a loud voice, "How about the 'law of the barrio'?" This was a case involving the stabbing death of a gang member. "My client had been roughed up by gang members, one of which he confronted later and stabbed," Calamia recalled. "I told the court that in a barrio infested with gangs, the law was simple; if you don't kill this man then he'll kill you."[3]

Calamia viewed the second point with significant concern. He believed that the withholding of information that could result in a lesser sentence or acquittal had no place in the criminal justice system. In his mind, the prosecutor should be ever mindful of the defendant's constitutional rights. Remarkably, after his victory, a similar sudden-passion case was argued before the U.S. Supreme Court. One month later, the high court held that a prosecutor who urged a witness not to volunteer information about a sexual relationship with the murder victim denied the defendant due process of law (*Alcorta v. Texas*, 355 U.S. 28, 78 S.Ct. 103, 2 L.Ed.2d 9 [1957]).[4] In *Alcorta*, the high court relied on general Fourteenth Amendment due process of law principles arising in cases concerning perjured and suppressed testimony. (*See Mooney v. Holohan*, 294 U.S. 103, 55 S.Ct. 340, 79 L.Ed. 791 [1935]; *Pyle v. Kansas*, 317 U.S. 213, 63 S.Ct. 177, 87 L.Ed. 214 [1942]). As in Calamia's earlier case, the Supreme Court reasoned that "suppressed testimony, taken as a whole, gave the jury the false impression that his relationship with petitioner's wife was nothing more than that of casual friendship." The high court concluded that the sudden-passion defense might have been accepted by the jury had the witness not been allowed to testify falsely. *Alcorta*, 355 U.S. at 32. "[H]is offense would have been reduced to 'murder without malice,' precluding the death penalty now imposed upon him." (*Id.*)

Concerning these and other similar cases, the local press often wrote that a criminal was being let loose on a technicality. Perhaps this concern was to be expected. The communist conspiracy theory proposed by Senator McCarthy seemed real. Now there was the Korean War and the arrest, trial and execution of Julius and Ethel Rosenberg over the passing of nuclear weapon secrets to the Soviet Union. Adding to the concern was the proximity of Mexico, the vice associated with Ciudad Juárez and the easy access to illegal drugs added. There were cases of stolen cars winding up in Juárez with little or no chance of recovery. There were cases of fugitives finding a safe haven across the border.

In Calamia's mind, a violation of the Bill of Rights was hardly to be considered a technicality. His credo was to "believe in your case and research with an open mind." Perhaps a technicality is a simply rule of law that the court or the prosecutor forgot. Calamia continued to be appalled at the lack of understanding that in the American system of justice, "a defendant is presumed to be innocent. The burden of proof is on the government. And the test of that proof is one of beyond a reasonable doubt."[5] To Calamia, it is the prosecutor's job to see "that justice is done, not only to win a case. If the evidence is weak and the defendant's rights are being violated, then the case should not be prosecuted."[6]

Calamia remembered a state district judge's puzzled look when he mentioned the Bill of Rights. "Why do you mention the federal bill of rights in a state court?"[7] The issue was the extent to which the protections under the Bill of Rights extended to state action. There were those like U.S. Supreme Court Justice Felix Frankfurter who argued that the Fourteenth Amendment did not fully incorporate the Bill of Rights. Instead, it only honored its basic principles (*Adamson v. California*, 332 U.S. 46, 67 S.Ct. 1672, 91 L.Ed. 1903 [1947]). Then there was the extreme view of Justice Hugo Black that every provision in the first eight amendments is applicable to the states (*Betts v. Brady*, 316 U.S. 455, 62 S.Ct. 1252, 86 L.Ed. 1595 [1942]). There would be a middle of the road or selective application approach during the Warren Court years.

Nevertheless, for Calamia there was the satisfaction of a job well done—a prize for the many hours of searching and researching in what at times seemed like endless nights. El Paso chiropractor Oliver R. Smith, who had an office in the same building as Calamia, once recalled: "Fifteen, maybe twenty years ago I remember coming to my office sometimes at odd hours when I needed something for a house call and seeing [Calamia] in [his] office studying during those wee hours of the morning. I was greatly impressed with [his] intelligence along with [his] determination to succeed."[8] Calamia donned a sheepish grin and exposed a characteristic twinkle in his eyes as his mind wandered back to the 1950s. His father had interrupted him on one of those long nights and said, "Joe. Put that stuff away. Get some sleep." With no reaction from his son, the elder Calamia shook his head and uttered, "There is no rest for the wicked!" He sighed, "Or for their lawyers!"[9]

In the first five years of Calamia's legal career, few criminal cases from El Paso had proceeded to the Texas Court of Criminal Appeals. This phase of Calamia's career was more than a "fight City Hall" attitude. He was sincere in his view of strict adherence to the Bill of Rights. At the same time, he had entered the legal profession during a period when, for a number of reasons, the average person would pretty much consider a lower court's decision as final. Calamia had brought attention to the fact that lower courts, for whatever reason, did make mistakes and that every American, regardless of wealth or standing in the community, was entitled to challenge those mistakes under a rule of law that had as its bedrock the presumption of innocence. Little did he know that in the second five years of his career, he would be thrust into important precedent-setting cases where defendants and their causes were under close scrutiny by the U.S. Congress—cases in which many perceived that the leftist leaning of the defendants was a threat to the American way of life.

Light in a Dark Period

THE COMMIES ARE COMING
MINE-SMELTER AND HOLLYWOOD

The anticommunist sentiment that preoccupied the United States at the beginning of the Korean War in 1950 continued to be felt in El Paso throughout most of the decade. The threat of communist infiltration in centers of influence, including the government and key industries, seemed real. There was reaction to one's expression of anti-capitalist ideas. There was reaction to ideas that seemed contrary to the American way of life. Many Americans truly believed there was a clear and present threat of a communist overthrow of the U.S. government. Others kept their opposing views to themselves, fearing reprisals. Still others pushed the envelope, standing up for their unpopular beliefs, regardless of the price they had to pay. After all, they asserted, the Bill of Rights also protects the freedom of expression for all Americans.

Enter Joe Calamia, a World War II veteran with strong anti-communist views. He was not necessarily an advocate of labor unions. He was just a lawyer with a love of freedom, the rule of law and the Bill of Rights. Little did he know that his legal mind would be tapped in support of freedom for left-leaning and communist defendants or that he would be in the company of nationally recognized leftist lawyers from Washington, New York and Hollywood who advanced mysterious legal maneuvers in support of their clients' social causes. The commies,[1] so it went, were coming to El Paso. Their flamboyant lawyers would blatantly challenge the arcane Washington-motivated Communist prosecutions in El Paso's federal district court. The notoriety of the commie trials was perhaps summed up by a key character, a commie, then not a commie, and then a commie supporter. That character, Harvey Matusow, made an equally outrageous claim that he was "the greatest thing to happen in El Paso since Pancho Villa."[2]

Indeed there was a Washington-led effort to halt this perceived communist infiltration. The Smith Act (18 U.S.C. § 2385), on the books for some fifteen years, outlawed anyone in the United States from advocating, abetting or even teaching the desirability of overthrowing the U.S. government. The law was constitutional. In 1951, the Vinson Supreme Court upheld the conviction of American Communist Party members under the Smith Act (*Dennis v. United States*, 341 U.S. 494, 71 S.Ct. 857, 95 L.Ed. 1137 [1951]). In that case, the court ruled that merely teaching communist philosophies and advocating such ideas created a clear and present danger that threatened the U.S. government. In some circles, advocacy of workers' rights was also seen as part of an international communist conspiracy that sought to overthrow American democracy. To be sure, organized labor had made significant gains during the Roosevelt administration following widespread unrest in the midst of the Great Depression (29 U.S.C. § 151 *et seq.*, National Labor Relations Act "Wagner Act," Public Law No 198, 74th Congress, July 2, 1935).

During this period, the International Union of Mine, Mill and Smelter Workers (Mine-Mill), a union with a militant reputation, was active in El Paso. The federal government was convinced that Communists had infiltrated the top leadership of Mine-Mill. In spite of anti-communist opposition in the community and anti-communist campaigns by El Paso's sheriff in the 1940s, Mine-Mill was successful in unionizing the copper smelter and refinery in El Paso.[3] The Wagner Act had guaranteed workers the right to join a labor union without fear of reprisal by management. As a result, several industries became unionized. By 1945, more than one-third of the U.S. work force was unionized. But opponents feared the movement had gone too far. With a shift in political power and fear of a Soviet- and Chinese-led communist infiltration of organized labor, Congress weakened the Wagner Act in 1947 by outlawing mass picketing and secondary boycotts (Taft-Hartley Act, 61 Stat. 136 [1947]).

Importantly, Section 9(h) of the Taft-Hartley Act required officers of labor unions to sign affidavits indicating that they were not members of the Communist Party, supporters of that party, or advocates of the violent overthrow of the government. The Vinson Supreme Court in *American Communications Assn. v. Douds* (339 U.S. 382, 70 S.Ct. 674, 94 L.Ed. 925 [1950]) found this provision to be constitutional and not an infringement on the First Amendment right of freedom of speech. Still, not all union leaders were willing to comply with these provisions. It was in this climate that Clinton Jencks (1916–2005) achieved notoriety. In 1950, Jencks was president of the Amalgamated Bayard District Union, Local 890 of Mine-Mill. Jencks was a Colorado Springs native and a decorated Army Air Corps veteran. While in Colorado, Jencks earned a reputation as a militant organizer with Mine-Mill. *El Palomino*, as his strong base of Hispanic workers called him, set his sights on leading Local 890 in Bayard, New Mexico. Jencks chose to comply with the noncommunist affidavit requirement in the Taft-Hartley Act. However, it was suspected that he had done so under false pretenses.[4]

Mine-Mill was one of several radical unions in the Southwest. The union had just been expelled from the Congress of Industrial Organizations (CIO) because Mine-Mill espoused positions that were parallel to those of the U.S. Communist Party. Mine-Mill favored the Russian plan for rebuilding postwar Europe and opposed the U.S.-led Marshall Plan. The early 1950s were characterized by recession, shortages of raw materials and the controversy of guns over butter as the Korean War continued. There was widespread unemployment in the metals industry. This was not a good time for Mine-Mill to open controversial labor contract negotiations with the Bayard, New Mexico Empire Zinc Company. A principal issue was discriminatory wages for Hispanic workers. The fifteen-month-long strike was divisive and violent, and it resulted in acrimony that lasted long after the strike ended in 1952.[5] Perhaps the notorious communist trials in El Paso and Calamia's intervention in this sensation-riddled episode may not have occurred had Mine-Mill not taken the matter a step further. Mine-Mill decided to team up with Hollywood writers and directors who had been blacklisted by the movie industry on suspicion that they were Communists. Both parties were being hounded for their unpopular beliefs. The partnership was ideal. Hollywood would document the Empire Zinc strike and the story would be shown to American audiences everywhere. At least, this was their hope.

Known for its liberal views, Hollywood was an easy target for the anticommunist movement. Beginning in 1947, the House Un-American Activities Committee opened investigations into movie industry personalities whom they suspected of having left-wing views. The committee's suspicions were fed further by former Communists who were now working for the FBI as government witnesses. The investigations resulted in the McCarran (Internal Security Act of 1950, Public Law 831, 64 Stat. 1016). In passing this law, Congress was in effect warning America of a global communist threat to the American way of life. It characterized Communists as working in cells as part of an organization that used treachery, deceit, espionage, sabotage, terrorism and infiltration of government and key industries to achieve an overthrow of the U.S. government. The McCarran Act excluded Communists from admission to the United States. They were portrayed as anarchists or affiliates of the Communist Party that advocated economic and other doctrines of communism and an overthrow of the government by force. The law required Communist and Communist-action organizations to register with the U.S. attorney general. The law also established oversight by the Subversive Activities Control Board, a board that played a key role in the investigation of Mine-Mill. The House Un-American Activities Committee had already provided some red-cleansing, "red" being a term for Communists since the Russian Revolution. Red-baiting referred to the legislative practice of asking a witness to declare that he was not a Communist. Should such a person take the bait and incriminate himself? Of course not. He or she should refuse to answer the question. There was, after all, a protection in the Bill of Rights against self-incrimination in criminal matters. However, these were Congressional hearings. Many of those summoned by the committees simply refused to bite and faced contempt charges. Forty-one persons were initially investigated. Some confessed and left the country. Others gave names of suspects to the committee. Still others stood by their Fifth Amendment protection against self-incrimination.

These reluctant individuals, among them a group of directors and writers known as The Hollywood Ten, were found guilty of contempt of Congress and were sentenced from six to twelve months in prison. Mainstream Hollywood, in an effort to reassure Congress, refused to hire any of these pink or red individuals in their productions. Some of those blacklisted fought back. Three of the film industry personalities, director Herbert Biberman (1900–1971), screenwriters Paul Jarrico (1915–1997) and Michael Wilson (1914–1978), formed a blacklistee's company. The Mine-Mill strike against Empire Zinc provided them with the perfect theme. Moreover, Mine-Mill came up with the funding to produce the movie.

The strike had all the elements of a film designed to stir social conscience if not class warfare. There was a company-dominated community afraid of change from the outside. There was a reluctant management. There were Mexican workers earning lower wages than non-Mexicans. There was police brutality. There were women jailed for being on the picket line while their men were under injunction or in jail. In short, the strike afforded an opportunity to show America a case of unjust exploitation of workers. The film was to be shot on location, where emotions still ran high a year after the strike ended. Anticommunist and antiunion sentiments ran strong in the Silver City area. The name of the movie was *Salt of the Earth*, a term taken from the parable of Jesus (Matthew 5:13-16) about the indispensable nature of salt in which Jesus calls his disciples to activism. The cast was comprised of Local 890 officials and other members, including former local leader Jencks. The lead female role went to Mexican actress Rosalva Revueltas (1909–1996). A native of Durango, Mexico, Revueltas had appeared in four films in Mexico since 1946 and was also well-known as a dancer, teacher and writer. More importantly, Revueltas was a member of the chic leftist artistic circles in Mexico City, whose elite included Communist muralists Diego Rivera and Alfaro Siqueiros as well as Rivera's wife, Frida Kahlo. In *Salt of the Earth*, Revueltas was cast in the role of a strong-willed wife of a striking mine worker. Filming began in January 1953 at a ranch located some eight miles from Bayard, New Mexico, near Silver City, setting the stage for a confrontation that would soon move the action to El Paso's federal district court.

FIRST COMMIE TRIAL: *SALT OF THE EARTH*

Just as filming began, there were rumblings among the local populace that a subversive movie was being filmed near Silver City. This was a bad time to be associated with anything Communist or anything that had a tinge of red. For the Mexican actress, it was a bad time to be an outspoken alien doing film work in the United States. Anticommunist Washington had all bases covered. Another anticommunist law would play into this developing drama. It became effective on Christmas Eve and appeared as an amendment to the Immigration and Nationality Act of 1924. Congress approved still another antiterrorist law over President Truman's objection. The law explicitly authorized the exclusion or deportation of any alien who engaged, or purported to engage, in activities prejudicial to the public interest or subversive to national security.[1]

At the end of 1952, Calamia's practice had expanded into various aspects of immigration law, but little did Calamia know that his knowledge would be tapped in defense of the leftist Mexican movie star. Outside his seventh-floor office at the onset of 1953, El Paso was consumed with the seesaw battles of the Korean War. There was soon-to-be-inaugurated President Eisenhower's promise of peace. There was a murder trial in federal court of two Fort Bliss soldiers who had killed a taxi driver and set his cab on fire. Water shortages, water district irregularities and annexation woes were the big issues at City Hall. The mayor married a twenty-year-old model only to have her leave him for a Hollywood career. El Paso got its 50,000th telephone and 3-D movies hit the Plaza Theater. But a storm was brewing in the not-too-distant Silver City area in southern New Mexico.

Filming began on *Salt of the Earth*, and there were reports of film crew confrontations with the locals. Farther away in Washington, California Congressman Donald Jackson delivered a long speech on the House floor in which he predicted that the film would be "a new weapon for Russia." Jackson emphasized that the Hollywood Ten directors and writers had not been cooperative with Congress, invoking the Fifth Amendment when asked about their affiliation with communist organizations. Jackson vowed to do everything in his power to prevent the movie from being shown in public theaters. Hollywood Ten director Jarrico fought back, calling Jackson an unmitigated liar. The next day, the Mexican movie star was detained at the filming site. U.S. immigration officials questioned her legal status under provisions of the recently enacted McCarran-Walter Act. Filming was nearly complete. Mine-Mill leader Jencks, film director Jarrico and their Hollywood lawyer, Ben Margolis, cried foul. To them, it was too much of a coincidence that Revueltas's arrest came the day after Congressman Jackson's alarming speech. Thus, the first of the commie trials came to El Paso. Margolis needed local counsel to guide him through the legal maneuvers before Federal District Judge Thomason. Margolis found Calamia and Chew, attorneys whom no one would associate with communism.

To Calamia's thinking, communism was something associated with a foreign power's insidious conspiracy to win the hearts and minds of the American people, ostensibly in a crusade for equality of all working people. Yet the goal of equality seemed to contradict communist Russia's and China's stifling of personal freedoms at home and illusions of world conquest by force. Only a few years earlier, Calamia had served his country in that dark period when the personal freedoms, if not the existence of the Western world, were threatened. In the early 1950s, the poster boy was not the mad-man from Nazi Germany or the ambitious emperor from Japan. Rather it was Soviet Union leader Josef Stalin, who had a record of atrocities against human freedom. "The foundation of American's personal liberties," Calamia ruminated, "was formed from the lessons of ideological conflict and uncontrolled freedom in eighteenth-century Europe. However, with the Bill of Rights, the foundation of American's personal freedom was now established as a rule of law." Some fifty years later, an older and wiser Calamia mused over the delicate balance between absolute freedom and dictatorship. He raised his voice, flailed his hands as if to begin his opening argument in a criminal case. "It is often said that a Supreme Court's decision on constitutionality is the final word. In my opinion, there is one last word. That last word is the will of the people." He went on to warn that the will of the people should not be absolute, citing the Prohibition experiment (U.S. Constitution, XVIII Amendment, 1919) as an example of an unreasonable assertion of the will of the people. "It led to serious lawlessness," Calamia continued. "But it was corrected by the will of the people to repeal Prohibition, convinced that the law could not be enforced" (U.S. Constitution, XXI Amendment, 1933). Calamia asserted that the framers of the Constitution were acutely aware of the dangers of absolute freedom. They remembered the mob justice in the reign of terror in revolutionary France. On the other hand, the framers had also experienced the other extreme of restraints on personal freedom inherent in a monarchy. "There must be a balance between an unbridled will of the people and unbridled rule of man," Calamia concluded. "That balance is the rule of law." Calamia would hold steadfast to that principle throughout his career, even if it meant asserting the Bill of Rights protections for some unpopular clients.

It was clear to Calamia that the Bill of Rights applied to everyone in America, including ideologues from either political extreme. This included their right to representation by competent counsel. The young lawyer's unalterable tenet of "Believe in your case and read the law with an open mind"[2] was not something that a flashy Hollywood lawyer like Margolis expected in local counsel.

In contrast to Calamia, Margolis was a big-time lawyer with a national reputation. At age forty-two, he was a seasoned labor and civil rights attorney. He began his practice in the 1930s in San

Francisco. Among his triumphs was the late 1930s defense of Harry Bridges of the International Longshoremen's and Warehousemen's Union against charges that Bridges was a Communist. In Los Angeles, Margolis also led the successful appeal of twenty-two men, most of whom were Mexican American, convicted of murder in a trial that set off the acclaimed 1940s Zoot Suit Riots in Los Angeles. He was instrumental in a landmark decision concerning the right of a defendant to unimpaired access to counsel during a criminal trial (*People v. Zamora*, 152 P.2d 180 [Cal. App. 2nd Dist. 1944]). In the 1940s, Margolis represented Los Angeles's Communist Party leaders charged with violations of the Smith Act. In 1945 he took up the cause of the Hollywood Ten in hearings before the House Un-American Activities Committee. Only one year before coming to El Paso, Margolis had appeared before that committee telling the Congressmen he would "fry in hell before they got any information out of me about my clients." A few years after his El Paso appearance, Margolis successfully argued to have his clients' conviction under the Smith Act set aside (*Yates v. United States*, 354 U.S. 298, 77 S.Ct. 1064, 1 L.Ed.2d 1356 [1957]).[3]

Once in El Paso in early March 1953, the suave and well-dressed Margolis made sure that Revueltas, the dark-skinned, dark-eyed actress, appeared before the press wearing the full-skirted peasant dress she wore when arrested in Silver City the previous week. Revueltas had been placed under house arrest in El Paso's Gateway Hotel, a block east of Calamia's office. Her black hair was slicked back and tied with a bright ribbon, uncovering heavy gold earrings. The "Mexican Bette Davis" delighted the press with her excellent English expressed in a deep throaty voice. She said all the right things. She praised the United States as a "warm haven for all who love liberty." In the same breath, the actress expressed surprise that she had lost her liberty while working in a movie that depicted "the working people, their struggles, their sorrows, their loves and their joys." Margolis accused immigration officials of making the arrest for the sole purpose of stopping the filming of *Salt of the Earth*. Immigration officials denied any conspiracy. They insisted that the arrest was routine.[4] Margolis masterfully handled the "show and tell" and photo opportunities as he presented his case before the press. Courtroom trials were big news items in those days. Lawyers often staged photo sessions with the defendants and offered press conferences to the news media. Calamia thoroughly studied the case and the law. He was familiar with high court rulings on immigration law and with the new McCarran-Walters Act. He recognized that the law accorded wide discretion to immigration officials in excluding aliens. Revueltas's case was administrative in nature. She could face deportation, or she could return voluntarily to Mexico. Unfortunately, she had entered the United States with a local crossing card that was issued to Mexican citizens for short term visits to American border cities. This permit did not allow a Mexican citizen to work in the United States, although it was a practice that had not previously been fully enforced. At best, Calamia considered that he could seek a delay that would allow the actress to finish filming, which was about a week or so from completion. A second avenue was to seek her release under a petition for writ of habeas corpus. Calamia understood that the writ would be difficult to obtain while the administrative process was still under-way. One could challenge the speed of the process, but this might not be to the defendant's advantage. Calamia recalled that his goal was to delay the process. However, he felt that one could readily question whether immigration authorities had abused their discretion.[5]

This was not a good time in Federal District Judge Thomason's professional life. He had just sentenced two soldiers to die in the electric chair for the torching death of a taxi driver (*Austin v. United States*, 208 F. 2d 420 [5th Cir. 1954]). He later admitted he lost sleep over the mandatory death sentence and the thought that he had the defendants' blood on his hands.[6] His troubled state of mind was obvious as he closed the sentencing hearing for the two soldiers with this comment. "This court will be very liberal to permit you to get your appeals fully and fairly presented."[7]

The petition for writ of habeas corpus for Revueltas's release was filed with Judge Thomason. It focused primarily on a claim that the district director of Immigration and Naturalization had abused his powers. The government was represented by assistant

U.S. attorneys Francis C. Broaddus and Holvey Williams. Margolis's behavior before Judge Thomason portended the boisterous conduct of California and New York lawyers who would soon be performing in the upcoming trials. Margolis eloquently argued against the statute. He contended that Congress had usurped a person's right of habeas corpus by passing draconian immigration laws. He lauded the character of Revueltas. He argued with sarcasm that immigration officers detained Revueltas after reading about Congressman Jackson's declarations against the movie the day before. Continuing his attack on the Immigration Service's intentions, he blared out, "This country is not going to be destroyed or damaged or injured by her. She is not going to place a bomb under some building."

Williams relied on Immigration Service District Director Joseph Minton's testimony. They argued that Minton acted within his authority, that provided him significant discretion in application of the law.

Thomason listened patiently to Margolis, and Williams and then he denied the request. First, he ruled that immigration officials were proceeding with dispatch. Second, the facts of the case did not establish that the government had abused its wide discretionary powers. Meanwhile, Calamia was able to get a five-day delay in the deportation hearings at which time Revueltas agreed to return to Mexico voluntarily.

Depending on how one looked at it, the delay may have helped. In time, the film was completed. While Revueltas sought to have the movie finished in Mexico, this would be a difficult task. Mexico's government in the 1950s, while engaged in hostile rhetoric against the United States, quietly followed the same anticommunist line. Mexico was still seeking to ameliorate the extreme socialist reforms of the 1930s born out during its Revolutionary Constitution in 1917. Mexico needed tourism income and U.S. investment. This was no time to upset an angry U.S. Congress. In short, Mexico's official censor would have to review the script. Disapproval was imminent. In the Silver City area, the locals were threatening "to carry out movie crews in black boxes." Jencks had been attacked at a fill-ing station. The state and local governments were weary of having some one hundred troopers and local police attempting to maintain order. Chants of "We don't want communism" dominated a loyalty parade. Jencks insisted that the film would be completed with Revueltas in it. Finally, the film crew packed their equipment and left the Silver City area.[9] In the end, some of Revueltas's scenes had to be voiced over in the processing stage.

There were other difficulties in getting the film out to the public as it was blacklisted by mainstream Hollywood. The movie received accolades abroad. Revueltas received the *Academie de cinema de Paris,* Best Actress Award for her role. She went on to live in Germany through 1960 when she returned to Mexico. She did not make another movie until 1976, and she died in 1996 in Cuernavaca, Mexico. Except for a New York City premiere in 1954, *Salt of the Earth* was not shown to the rest of the American public until 1963.[10] The film was restored in the 1990s and was placed in the U.S. National Film Registry of the Library of Congress.[11] In 2003, *Salt of the Earth* was the highlight of a conference in Santa Fe, New Mexico that revisited the trials endured and triumphs achieved in making the film.

THE FIRST JENCKS'S CASE: QUICK AND SIMPLE?

It did not take long for the long arm of the federal government to reach Jencks. Jencks had been Mine-Mill's coordinator for *Salt of the Earth* and was an actor in the movie. In April 1953, one month after filming, Jencks was indicted by a federal grand jury in El Paso for violating the noncommunist affidavit provision of the Taft-Hartley Act. The two-count indictment charged that on April 28, 1950, Jencks falsely declared in a noncommunist affidavit that he was not a member of the Communist Party and was not then affiliated with the Communist Party. It would be another nine months before the second of the "commie" trials would open in El Paso in January 1954. The Jencks trial brought the national spotlight to Thomason's federal district court, complete with local and national news reporters and large numbers of courtroom spectators. And yes, there would be more Margolis-like defense attorneys disrupting the usually calm decorum in Thomason's courtroom.

December 1953 was a difficult month in El Paso. The area had been hit by snowstorms, one so bad that it was blamed for the fiery crash of a B-36 into the west side of El Paso's Franklin Mountains. El Paso's chief of police had declared war on gangs after the city was plagued by a two-week streak of beatings and robberies. He promised to enforce curfews and make greater use of vagrancy laws. There was also some political change. County Attorney Guinn decided to enter private practice after twenty years of politics.

This was also a period when strong gusts of a mighty wind of civil rights were blowing in the nation's capitol. The U.S. Supreme Court, under recently appointed Chief Justice Earl Warren, was hearing oral arguments in several school segregation cases involving future Supreme Court Justice Thurgood Marshall and Spottswood William Robinson III on behalf of the National Association for the Advancement of Colored People (NAACP). Signaling the start of an intense civil rights movement, the pair argued that the Fourteenth Amendment was passed to prohibit states from maintaining "caste systems predicated on race." They added, "Candor requires recognition that the plain purpose and effect of segregated education is to perpetuate an inferior status for Negroes which is America's shoddy heritage from slavery." The central issue was the degree to which the Fourteenth Amendment extended the Bill of Rights to the states, a question that Calamia answered with a resounding "Yes, absolutely!"

The chilling snowstorms that were battering El Paso also had their effect on the compassionate Thomason, who had just given suspended sentences to 168 illegal aliens. Concerned that the men would be left out in the street in the bitter cold, the judge offered them a short jail time. He told them, "The jail will give you a hot lunch." The Mexican men broke out in applause.[1]

At the end of 1953, assistant U.S. attorney Williams was quite proud of his 100 percent conviction rate, mostly on narcotics and Dyer Act violations. The Dyer Act (18 U.S.C. 2312) had been on the books since 1919 as a means to help state law enforcement authorities overcome car thieves' ability to transport stolen vehicles into another jurisdiction. Like the narcotics laws, this federal offense carried harsh sentences of up to ten years' imprisonment. Williams reported only one reversal out of ten cases that were appealed to the Fifth Circuit. That case involved the death sentence against the two Fort Bliss soldiers in the burning death of the taxi driver (*Austin v. United States*, 208 F. 2d 420 [5th Cir. 1954]). The case was remanded for a new trial that Thomason scheduled for February. Williams recalled, "At the time we were commended for the speed with which we brought Austin and Button (defendants) to trial and got them sentenced." He added, "Perhaps that speed was a mistake."[2] As it turned out, the two soldiers pled guilty. Thomason gladly gave them life sentences, and with that he erased his concern of sending the men to the electric chair.[3] As the new year began, federal court observers turned their attention to the January 1954 trial of Clinton Jencks.

The U.S. government was more than adequately represented by assistant U.S. attorneys Broaddus and Williams with assistance from the Western District of Texas headquarters and the Department of Justice in Washington. The out-of-state defense team brought memories of the Margolis episode in the Revueltas case. Into the spotlight came Nathan Witt, Jenck's lead attorney, along with John T. McTernan (1911–2005) of Los Angeles. Both had leftist tendencies. Witt (1903–1982) worked for the National Labor Relations Board from 1936 to 1941 before becoming full-time counsel for Mine-Mill. McTernan was an associate of Margolis in Los Angeles and, like Margolis, had a record of defending minorities and unpopular clients. Witt hired El Paso lawyer Edmund B. Elfers (1890–1958). He had to, for Judge Thomason required an out-of-town lawyer to have local counsel. A native of Ohio County, Indiana, Elfers studied law in Indiana and was admitted to the State Bar of Texas in 1907.

The trial began with an unsuccessful attempt by Jencks' lawyers to change the venue to a friendlier Southern California. They charged that statements by Texas Governor Allan Shivers and Texas Attorney General Ben Shepperd prejudiced their client's case. Shivers told the press that there was "no place in Texas for Communists." Shepperd had warned Texans that unions were engaged in a master plot from Moscow to get a stranglehold on Texas minerals, port and petroleum centers. The lawyers also argued that there were no women on the jury since Texas law excluded women from jury service.[4] As this drama unfolded, the U.S. attorney went after a guest list at the San Cristobal Guest Ranch near Santa Fe. The government suspected that this ranch was a meeting place for Communists. There was fear that it was located too close to the Los Alamos government laboratories and the atomic bomb secrets they held. The ranch owner refused to turn over the list and Thomason found him in contempt. Jury selection proceeded with the empanelment of an all-male jury.

Testimony opened with the FBI and two Silver City area residents as witnesses. One told of the violence during the filming of *Salt of the Earth*. Others told of Jencks's close dealings with Communists in 1946. Then came the testimony of the government's star witness, Harvey Matusow, a former Communist turned government witness. Dressed in a dark suit and bow tie, Matusow related his own experience with, and expulsion from, the Communist Party in January 1951. Matusow met Jencks at the San Cristobal Guest Ranch. With an arrogant assurance, he told jurors that Jencks had advised him of plots by the U.S. Communist Party to hamper the war effort by crippling metal production. Matusow's most damaging testimony related to Jencks's Communist Party activities occurring at the time Jencks had signed the non-communist affidavit. McTernan, Jencks's Los Angeles attorney, confronted Matusow in a number of heated exchanges over his role as a paid informant.

About ten days after testimony began, the defense rested without calling any witnesses. Throughout the trial, however, Jencks's attorneys raised objection after objection and concluded with a motion for dismissal. In closing arguments, McTernan called the government's witnesses "people who have no moral sense whatsoever." He chided the government's case: "If the prosecution did not have the scare words, communism and Moscow, plotting and night meetings, this case would be laughed out of court." Assistant U.S. attorney Broaddus summarized the government's case. "Since 1946 Clinton Jencks had only one goal, one aim, the Communist Party." The next day the jury returned a verdict of guilty after less than thirty minutes of deliberation. Thomason assessed a five-year sentence and released Jencks on a $10,000 appeal bond.

The appellate record comprised more than one thousand typewritten pages, most of which covered defense motions and objections. There were some ten points of error that could be categorized into four major areas. Jencks's attorneys claimed that there was insufficient evidence to support the conviction. They alleged that Thomason erred in denying a bill of particulars and in failing to caution the jury about the credibility of informers. Finally, the defense asserted that the judge erred in denying a motion for the inspection of certain FBI records. Was this likely to be another unsuccessful appeal? That appeared to be the thought in El Paso. Matusow seemed quite credible. After all, he had much courtroom experience. He had identified 245 Communists in several courts and other forums. He had worked closely with Senator McCarthy in his anticommunist crusade. No one in El Paso, least of all Calamia, would have imagined that this government witness would be back in El Paso fourteen months later, having proclaimed himself as the greatest thing to happen in El Paso since Pancho Villa. Strangely enough, Matusow would be represented by none other than the staunchly anticommunist Joe Calamia.[5]

MATUSOW AND JENCKS: FALSE WITNESS, CONTEMPT AND DISCOVERY

Harvey Matusow, a New York native and a self-proclaimed actor in left-wing plays,[1] was about five years younger than the thirty-four-year-old Calamia. Soon after his twenty-first birthday, Matusow appeared before the House Committee on Un-American Activities, telling all on his former Communist colleagues. Before long he became an aide to Senator McCarthy, assisting the government in identifying Communists. As a paid FBI informant in the Jencks trial in El Paso, Matusow's testimony concerning his interactions with Jencks in New Mexico seemed credible. Matusow had quite adroitly defended his testimony when bombarded with pointed questions by defense attorney McTernan. McTernan had managed to get Matusow to admit that he had provided periodic oral and written reports to the FBI, something that the press and courtroom observers failed to notice. The reports were included as part of the "other information" that McTernan had asked the government to produce in one of his many motions. Thomason denied that motion and many others.

In the second half of 1954, however, Matusow's situation began to change. The clout of McCarthyism was not what it used to be. McCarthy's list of some two hundred Communists in high government positions was just that—a list of accusations lacking support and documentation. These accusations had struck a nerve in the American public that feared a Communist takeover of the American way of life. Still, McCarthy's actions came into question when he aimed his attacks at President Eisenhower and his cabinet secretaries. The Senate became concerned over its reputation. At the end of 1954, the Senate censored the junior senator from Wisconsin for his abuse of legislative powers.[2] With McCarthy's imminent downfall, Matusow prepared himself for another abrupt shift. He claimed that he had had a religious experience. A religious leader told the public in a number of speeches that Matusow confessed that he had lied in identifying the 245 purported Communists and that he now wanted to tell the American public the truth. These poor fellows had either faced charges or were imprisoned in part due to Matusow's testimony about their communist affiliation.[3]

Not surprisingly, just as he declared himself a liar, Matusow was also swearing before the House Committee on Un-American Activities that he had told the truth at the Jencks trial. Quickly, Jencks's attorneys seized upon the information and embarked on a number of activities with a view toward seeking a new trial. Witt learned that Matusow needed financing for his manuscript titled *Blacklisting Was My Business*, which told of his experiences as a false witness. A sub-rosa scheme was conceived in September in which Mine-Mill would cover the publishing costs. In this scheme, the publisher would secretly work directly with Matusow. Supposedly unknown to Matusow, the publisher also worked with Witt and Mine-Mill. The scheme intended to show that Matusow was not in cahoots with Witt. In early 1955, the manuscript was nearly complete. The book received its final name, *False Witness*, with a new chapter entitled, "Witness for the Prosecution." There, Matusow admitted that he did not know or care whether Jencks was a Communist. In February 1955, while Jencks's conviction was pending before the Fifth Circuit Court of Appeals, his lawyers filed a motion for a new trial with Judge Thomason. The motion contended that newly discovered evidence existed, supported by an affidavit signed by Matusow only days before. Matusow had reversed his double cross of the Communist Party. Now he was double-crossing the government to perfect a triple cross. He recanted parts of the testimony he gave in the early 1954 trial.[4] It was now up to Thomason to consider this bizarre situation.

By the beginning of 1955, much had happened in El Paso and in the United States. A civil war continued in China. What remained of America's Chinese ally controlled only the island of Formosa off of mainland communist China. There were dogfights between American jets and Russian-made MIGS over the Yellow Sea. There was also a change in Soviet Russia's leadership. That post would soon go to Nikita Khrushchev. In El Paso, the city council was about to increase the city's population and land area by annexing the township of Ysleta and other communities southeast of town. Nearby Hudspeth County got its first woman juror. El Paso's federal prosecutors were on their way out as President Eisenhower appointed sixty-year-old Robert Wine as the U.S. attorney for the Western District of Texas.

Matusow's recantation caused quite a stir. Mine-Mill began a campaign to discredit Matusow's testimony at the first Jencks trial. The chairman of the House Un-American Activities Committee was convinced that Matusow was a Communist Party plant. It didn't help that the publisher of Matusow's book had been found in contempt in New York for failing to produce records. Matusow then said he intended to turn over book sales proceeds to scholarship programs. At the same time he admitted: "I was a perpetual and habitual liar." It seemed as if everyone wanted a piece of him. The State of Texas considered charging Matusow with perjury. In El Paso, District Attorney Clayton also gave thought to trying Matusow on perjury charges. This was possible under Texas law even if the perjury occurred in connection with federal proceedings. However, Clayton figured that the government had a better chance to convict him as Texas had a more severe test. Thomason convened a grand jury to deal with the Matusow matter a month before the start of the March 7, 1955, hearing on a new trial for Jencks.

The Jencks camp was quite content to have a turncoat government witness to help their cause. For this new hearing, Jencks was represented by New Mexico attorneys A. T. Hannet (Governor of New Mexico 1924–26) and Harry L. Bigbee. McTernan was unavailable. Witt remained as cocounsel and Elfers remained as local counsel. Once on the witness stand, Matusow, dressed in a dark-grey sports jacket, dark trousers and a black-and-white striped tie, loudly asserted "I do" as he took the oath. Portion by portion, Bigbee went over the parts of Matusow's testimony that had incriminated Jencks. At the end of each statement, Matusow declared "False." Matusow said he lied out of fear from the anticommunist hysteria that enveloped the country during this period. He added "greed and need." Matusow wanted to clear his conscience by telling the truth.

The government focused on Matusow's "greed" by reviewing the sub-rosa plot between Matusow and Mine-Mill, brokered by Witt. The government's case also revealed Witt's influence in the rewriting of the chapter dealing with Matusow's testimony at the first Jencks trial. Matusow repeatedly denied that money was an incentive for his sudden turnaround. Thomason listened patiently, but concurrently he reconvened a grand jury concerning Mine-Mill's role in the publication of *False Witness,* resulting in a number of Mine-Mill witnesses asserting Fifth Amendment claims.

Meanwhile, Jencks's attorneys pressed for discovery of Matusow's oral and written reports to the FBI. By the end of the workweek, Jencks's attorneys had sought, on several occasions, to have Judge Thomason force the government to allow the defense to inspect these documents. Thomason repeatedly denied the discovery motions. The hearing was recessed until Saturday to allow for closing arguments.

Courtroom observers had come to expect that Thomason would take the matter under advisement. Apparently they were misreading his patient demeanor throughout the hearing. At Jencks's trial nearly one year before, he had heard objection after objection and motion after motion on many points that he considered irrelevant. The loud verbal confrontations between Jencks and Matusow were still fresh in his mind. Now Matusow had switched sides. He knew he was in real trouble with Thomason.[5] He needed a good defense lawyer, one that did not have any communist leanings. Matusow turned to Calamia and Chew.

On Saturday morning, El Paso's federal courtroom was packed with news media and other observers. The hearing began with a summation by both sides. In closing argument, the government described the recantation as part of a communist conspiracy. Bigbee pleaded that hysteria and accusations not take the place of justice. Thomason once again listened patiently and then denied the motion for a new trial. Hearing over? Not quite. Thomason was not going to stop there. He had witnessed too much. Evidence had convinced him that the Communist lawyer Witt and the turncoat witness Matusow were in cahoots with each other. Thomason placed Witt on the witness stand. He asked Witt why he did not follow the ethical practice of first sharing Matusow's information with the government. Thomason considered Witt's actions to be a subversion of the legal system. Witt answered that it was the Department of Justice that was subverting the legal system by withholding information. Thomason then looked at Witt with disbelief and pointedly asked him, "Are you a member of the Communist Party?" After some argument over the nature of the question, Witt took the Fifth. Thomason then disbarred Witt from practice in his courtroom, stating, "Any lawyer who takes the witness stand and invokes the Fifth Amendment on grounds that it might incriminate him cannot practice in my court." Witt had no reply. He would remain Mine-Mill's general counsel until the 1960s when Mine-Mill merged with the United Steel Workers of America. He stayed on as Mine, Mill and Smelter division associate counsel under the merger until his retirement in 1975. He died in 1982 in New York.

Back at the defense table, Matusow's face paled. Thomason asked Matusow and Calamia to approach the bench. Looking directly at Matusow, his voice controlled, Thomason declared firmly:

> After listening attentively to your testimony and the other testimony and proceedings in this court on this motion, I am thoroughly convinced that you are in contempt of this court in that you, alone or in conjunction with others, deliberately and maliciously and designedly schemed to obstruct justice in this court, and in furtherance thereof have caused the filing of the affidavit in this cause and thereby obtained the hearing in this court on the motion for a new trial which has just been completed.

Thomason then told the astonished Matusow that he considered his original testimony to be true in substance and that he recanted for his own personal gain.

Calamia was equally surprised to see this normally calm federal judge suddenly burst out with such a statement. Was this the same judge who at times had told Calamia, "You're making some unusual points, but I'll give your defendant a fair trial"? Was this the same judge who had told Calamia, "Your points are beyond those for this court, but I'll give your defendant a chance to appeal"? Perhaps in this era of secrecy, lest the commies get sensitive information, the judge had more information than what was presented in court. Calamia regained his composure and asked Thomason to clarify the basis for the contempt charge. Thomason interrupted, "Those details would be in the contempt charge document." Calamia was not about to upset the judge any further. He only asked for a hearing to show cause why Matusow should not be held in contempt. Thomason agreed to give Matusow an opportunity for an immediate hearing. Calamia asked for additional time, and the judge set the hearing in three days.[6]

Judge Thomason's actions in "cutting through the legal fog" without any "dilly dally on the business of taking the matter under advisement" were greeted favorably by the El Paso press as a message against Communists. In *Herald Post* editor Ed Pooley's words, "Judge Thomason talked American to the Reds." Timing was everything for the clever Matusow. *False Witness* was fresh off the presses and would be available to El Paso bookstores in the next week. But the bookstore owners had little enthusiasm to carry it on their shelves. Maybe a copy or two would find their way to the local public library.[7] Meanwhile, in their small office a few blocks from the federal courthouse, Calamia and Chew planned Matusow's defense strategy in the company of Jencks's lawyers.

Calamia's interaction with Witt and Bigbee was necessary. The Jencks and Matusow cases were intertwined. Jencks's appeal of the January 1954 conviction was still pending before the Fifth Circuit. Calamia sensed that Thomason would rule against Matusow and that he would have to appeal the decision. One of Jencks's appellate theories was that the jury was not instructed on the reliability of a government informant. Or perhaps Matusow's false testimony would open the door to the discovery of FBI documents that contained the reports from Matusow and other informers.

Some fifty years later, Calamia reflected on the points of law in the Jencks and Matusow appeals. "I offered advice to Jencks's lawyers. Some they took. Others they did not." Like Thomason, Calamia saw Witt's relationship with Matusow as unethical. He recollected saying, "People believe that you paid Matusow yourself. You should have gotten Matusow's recantation in the office of the U.S. attorney. Don't you ever do that again 'cause I won't associate with you!" Calamia made it clear that he was only representing the client and not his cause. He added, "Witt was a smart lawyer. Only problem was he was too involved in his client's cause."

Calamia also considered McTernan and Bigbee to be brilliant civil rights lawyers. Calamia understood their tenacity in going after government documents that the prosecution may not want the defense to see. But he also understood the government's reluctance to release them. Always one to insist on full disclosure of particulars that the government had against any of his clients, Calamia believed that a defendant had a right of inspection under the Sixth Amendment. It was not that long ago that he had faced a district attorney who had not fully disclosed evidence in a murder case, leading to a reversal of that ninety-nine-year conviction.

Calamia knew that Thomason was upset with the Jencks case. Calamia surmised that if one looked at the issue objectively and untainted by public hysteria, there was a case to be made for requiring the government to allow the defense access to the informant's reports. The propriety of disclosure rested on whether the request constituted an "extraordinary circumstance." The defense argued that the FBI had reports that would impeach Matusow's testimony. Thomason believed that it was within his purview to decide whether the documents were relevant. It would be another seven months before the Fifth Circuit would hear oral arguments. And it would not be until December 1955 that the Fifth Circuit would make a decision.

Focused on Matusow, Calamia needed to convince Thomason to dismiss the contempt charge. He did not expect such relief. In an acute understanding of the mood in that far-west Texas courtroom, Calamia's thoughts turned to points of law he would have to make on appeal. The Fifth Circuit was an uncertain venue for success. First, it was likely that the same three-judge panel that was reviewing Jencks's conviction would hear the Matusow appeal. That panel had made rulings consistent with a philosophy of strict constitutional construction. Second, there would soon be new faces on the court.

The issue in Matusow's appeal was different than that in the Jencks case. Matusow was held in contempt of court. Calamia had unsuccessfully sought clarity on the applicable federal criminal contempt rule. "The test on the law of contempt rested on the circumstances under which it occurred," Calamia recalled. "If the contempt occurred in the presence of the court, the judge can act summarily, if he can certify that the actions in contempt occurred in the court's presence. On the other hand, if the contempt occurs by actions outside the judge's presence, the defendant is entitled to a hearing with all the protections of the Bill of Rights." Thomason did not define the applicable rule, but he had agreed to give Matusow a hearing.[8]

There was quite a scene at El Paso's international airport on March 15, 1955. The first passenger out of the airplane was the stocky, dark-haired Matusow. He spoke in "self-assured and self-righteous tones." He proclaimed to the press that if sentenced to jail for contempt, "I'll go proudly, because I know I'll go to jail for telling the truth." A few hours later, the twenty-eight-year-old was before Judge Thomason. The hearing opened with Calamia taking the stand and announcing "for the world to know" that "I am not a Communist, never have been one and never intend to be one." Why such display? Thomason's disbarment of suspected communist lawyer Witt was still fresh in Calamia's mind. Chew was prepared to do the same, but Thomason told him it was not necessary.

Assistant U.S. attorney Williams argued that Thomason had correctly concluded that the contemptuous conduct had occurred in his presence.[9] Williams continued, "But some of the (appeals court) judges have intimated that you should give them a hearing to rebut those inferences that you drew, and that is what we have done here today." Calamia asked the court, "Is it your ruling that unless we proceed (with the hearing) that your verdict will remain as it is?" Thomason replied, "Yes." Calamia then objected to proceeding in the absence of a certification of facts and conclusions that Matusow's acts of contempt occurred in his presence. He was overruled. Williams then retracted his earlier statement. Thomason replied, "Well, the Court hasn't said it, but the Court thinks you are proceeding under both sections," referring to then-Rule 42 (a) that allowed a summary proceeding and then-Rule 42 (b) that required a hearing with all the protections of the Bill of Rights.[10]

Calamia presented case law requiring a trial under the due process clause. Williams argued that Matusow had lied for personal gain and "to humiliate the whole jurisprudence of government." Calamia then put Matusow on the witness stand: "Did you ever conspire to deliberately, maliciously and designedly scheme to obstruct justice." Matusow responded, "No" to this and other questions. He denied conspiring with the publishers of *False Witness* and Mine-Mill. He denied receiving money to get his book published. He admitted seeking a new trial for Jencks' but explained that this was to undo the harm he had caused.

Calamia argued that if the criminal contempt charge was based on actions occurring in open court, Judge Thomason could act summarily without a hearing. But the court had not certified that the contemptuous conduct occurred in his presence. Calamia demanded that the government be required to go forward with its evidence and assume the burden of proving guilt beyond a reasonable doubt under then-Rule 42(b) of the Federal Rules of Criminal Procedure. At the close of the two-hour hearing, Thomason sentenced Matusow to three years in prison on the contempt charge. Calamia gave notice of appeal. Matusow was taken to the county jail where he remained until Calamia and Chew arranged for the publisher to post an appeal bond.

On November 16, 1955, Calamia was joined by Stanley Faulkner of New York in presenting oral arguments on the Matusow appeal before a three-judge panel. As it turned out, this was the same panel that had heard arguments in the Jencks case. It consisted of Judges Benjamin Franklin Cameron (1890–1994)[11], Warren Leroy Jones (1895–1993)[12] and Elbert Parr Tuttle (1897–1996).[13] Jones had been appointed by President Truman while Tuttle and Cameron had been appointed by President Eisenhower.

Faulkner opened the presentation, but it soon became obvious that he was not well prepared. Earlier in the day, Calamia was upset that Faulkner had not fully read the briefs Calamia had written nor had he discussed them with him. Just before the argument began, Faulkner told Calamia that his briefs were not written "in the King's English." Calamia responded, "All I want to know is if they are enough to get a reversal." Now before the three-judge panel, Faulkner hesitated when asked to explain the law. Calamia got up to explain. Judge Cameron ordered Faulkner to sit down and let Calamia continue. Calamia reiterated his arguments in support of the motions that were overruled by the trial court. He added that perjury in itself is not contempt. Criminal contempt, he argued, must be committed in the presence of the court, which was not the case here. And a three-year sentence amounted to cruel and unusual punishment considering that in similar cases, the courts had assessed six-month sentences. Calamia emphasized that Judge Thomason and assistant U.S. attorney Williams had interpreted Matusow's actions as "an overt and fraudulent attempt to make the court his tool for personal achievement." It would be another two months before the appellate court would issue its decision. In the meantime, the panel ruled on the Jencks's appeal.

Jencks found little sympathy with the Fifth Circuit. On December 1, the court affirmed the conviction (*Jencks v. United States,* 226 F.2d 540 [5th Cir. 1955]) (*Jencks I*). Two key points were directed at Matusow's behavior. One argued that Judge Thomason should have instructed the jury concerning the reliability of government witnesses. The court rejected this argument. The second point addressed discovery issues. Citing *Gordon v. United States,* (344 U.S. 414, 73 S.Ct.369, 97 L.Ed. 447 [1953]), the court ruled that it was

Jencks's burden to establish that the government had records of Matusow's oral and written reports.

In a companion opinion, the panel addressed whether Judge Thomason had erred in denying Jencks's motion for a new trial on the basis of Matusow's recantation (*Jencks v. United States*, 226 F. 2d 553 [5th Cir. 1955]) (*Jencks II*). The court emphasized that other witnesses named persons who participated in the activities Matusow attributed to Jencks, but Jencks had not tried to challenge or refute any of this testimony. In most instances, others were present when Jencks made the statements ascribed to him by Matusow. Jencks had the burden to bring forward witnesses to refute the otherwise undisputed testimony or at least to give a satisfactory explanation of his failure to do so. (*Id.* at 559–560.)

In late January 1956, Calamia was awakened by a telephone call from *Herald Post* reporter Cliff Sherrill, who exclaimed, "The Fifth Circuit has reversed Thomason." (*Matusow v. United States*, 229 F.2d 335 [Fifth Cir. 1956]). Indeed, the court had ruled that Matusow was entitled to a fair hearing, even if the trial judge thought Matusow was not telling the truth. Matusow was not allowed to confront witnesses against him, he was not given an opportunity to cross-examine his accusers and he was not presumed to be innocent at the hearing. One by one, the court found merit in Calamia's arguments. Calamia later reiterated the point of law in *Matusow*, "It lays the law that a judge's order must comply with the Bill of Rights. There must be due process of law."

The appeals court focused on the question of whether Matusow's actions were committed in the presence of the court such that Thomason could act summarily under federal procedural rules. "Any consideration of a proceeding which brings a man's liberty into jeopardy begins with the assumption that he is entitled to the full protection of the Bill of Rights" (*Id.* at 338). The opinion reads like a treatise on the law of contempt. The court observed that only Matusow's testimony at the 1954 Jencks trial and the 1955 motion for a new trial hearing occurred in Judge Thomason's presence. Everything else that he considered occurred outside his presence. Even if there was proof of perjury in Matusow's testimony, "proof of perjury alone will not sustain a conviction for contempt, but misbehavior constituting obstruction of court must also be established" (*Id.* at 341). The reversal brought immediate reaction from Texas and Washington. Not surprisingly, most comments were in favor of Thomason's tough stand.

There was not much interest in pursuing perjury charges against Matusow in El Paso. Back on the East Coast, Matusow and Jencks were facing perjury charges. Matusow had been charged in New York with perjury in connection with statements he had made in a trial of thirteen Communist Party leaders.[14] In September 1956, he was convicted and sentenced to five years in prison. After his release, Matusow moved to England where he worked in the broadcasting industry. He returned to the United States in the 1990s. Calamia remembered having met with him while he was in Tucson with his son Mark around 1993. Matusow was working with public television's children's shows. "Something like Captain Kangaroo, I believe," Calamia recalled. Matusow was living with his wife and children in a trailer. "He asked me to join him in writing a book about my handling of his case," Calamia recalls. He sighed at the thought, "Not a good idea. Not a good idea."[15]

AFTERMATH: JENCKS, MINE-MILL
AND NO CALAMITY IN JOE

It was now October 17, 1956. The Supreme Court had already issued its landmark ruling against school segregation (*Brown v. Board of Education*, 347 U.S. 483 74 S.Ct. 686, 98 L.Ed. 873 [1954]) (*Brown I*). It had delivered implementing instructions of integration "with all deliberate speed." (*Brown v. Board of Education*, 349 U.S. 294, 75 S.Ct. 753, 99 L.Ed. 1083 [1955]) (*Brown II*). In the years to come, the high court would extend desegregation to public transportation in a case arising from the civil disobedience of Rosa Parks (*Browder v. Gayle*, 142 F. Supp. 707 [D.C. Ala. 1956]), *aff'd.* (*Gayle v. Browder*, 352 U.S. 903, 77 S.Ct. 145, 1 L.Ed.2d 114 [1956]). Indeed, the mood of the nation was changing. This raised the question of how the Warren Supreme Court would rule on Jencks's appeal of the Fifth Circuit's 1955 decision.

Before the high court, Assistant Attorney General John V. Lindsey (later mayor of New York City) argued the government's case. McTernan argued for Jencks. Simply stated, the threshold question was: Did the lower court err in denying production of Matusow's reports to the FBI for purposes of impeachment? The government had argued that the defendant had not laid a sufficient foundation as required by *Gordon v. United States*, (344 U.S. 414, 73 S.Ct.369, 97 L.Ed. 447 [1953]).[1] McTernan would have been satisfied with an *in camera* review by the trial judge, but the Supreme Court went further in reversing the Fifth Circuit's decision (*Jencks v. United States*, 353 U.S. 657, 77 S.Ct. 1007, 1 L.Ed.2d 1103 [1957]). Not only was the existence of the reports sufficient to require their production, the defense was entitled to inspect the reports and decide whether to use them. "The practice of producing the documents to trial judge for determination of relevancy and materiality without hearing the accused is disapproved. Only after inspection of the reports by the accused must the trial judge determine admissibility" (*Jencks*, 353 U.S. at 668). Finally, the court held that "the criminal action must be dismissed when the Government, on the ground of privilege, elects not to comply with an order to produce, for the accused's inspection and for admission in evidence, relevant statements or reports in its possession of government witnesses touching the subject matter of their testimony at the trial" (*Id.* at 672). In short, the Supreme Court enunciated a new standard for discovery and government production of evidence, much to the chagrin of Justice Clark in his dissenting opinion:

> Unless the Congress changes the rule announced by the Court today, those intelligence agencies of our Government engaged in law enforcement may as well close up shop, for the Court has opened their files to the criminal and thus afforded him a Roman holiday for rummaging through confidential information as well as vital national secrets. (*Id.* at 681-82.)

The FBI refused to give Jencks full access to its records. This forced the government to dismiss the case and perhaps abandon prosecutions under anti-communist legislation of the 1940s and 1950s. Congress took Justice Clark's dissent so seriously that three months later, it passed a new law designed to close the door to discovery opened by the Supreme Court's decision. The Jencks Act, (18 U.S.C. § 3500), provides that the government cannot be compelled to disclose the statement of a government witness before he or she testifies on direct examination at trial.

Soon after the *Jencks* decision, the Supreme Court reversed a federal conviction of fourteen individuals on Smith Act charges of conspiracy to overthrow the U.S. government (*Yates v. United States*, 354 U.S. 298, 77 S.Ct. 1064, 1 L.Ed.2d 1356 [1957]). In a change from the "clear and present danger" principle, the Supreme Court ruled that the actions of the defendants were an advocacy of ideology, observing that the difference between speech and action was significant. The ruling took the sting out of the Smith Act, even though the law remains on the books. Jencks's troubles with the government continued. He was blacklisted from foundation jobs. He eventually became a professor of economics at San Diego State University until his retirement in 1988. Jencks died in 2005.

Jencks's challenge and eventual victory did not sit well with the government. It was around this time that Calamia's marriage to his college sweetheart would end in divorce. His wife, Geraldine, took custody of young J. R. and went to work at the Los Alamos National Laboratory for a few years before remarrying and returning to El Paso. While at Los Alamos, she was questioned by two men in black suits. The FBI agents demanded to know if she knew Harvey Matusow. "No!" she replied. "My ex-husband defended him." The men in black then asked her if Joe Calamia was a Communist. "I had to laugh," she recalls. "Joe a Communist? Come on!"[2] Joe Calamia would also remarry. He married Hortencia Saenz Medina in 1956 in a marriage that bore two children, Mark Anthony in 1957 and Virginia in 1960. Hortencia's father, José Medina and her mother Epifania Saenz, were natives of the La Boquilla area of the Mexican state of Chihuahua, the largest of four states that border Texas.

The government continued its feud with Mine-Mill. In some cases, those affiliated with Mine-Mill were targeted for investigation. In one such case, Manuel Gonzalez Jasso, former vice president of El Paso's Mine-Mill Local 509 and a U.S. citizen, was arrested on illegal entry charges. Immigration and Naturalization Service district director Marcus Neeley asserted that Jasso might have been born in El Paso, but that he had renounced his American citizenship when he allegedly voted in an election in Mexico. Neeley had recently replaced former district director Minton, following a Washington-led shake-up of the local immigration office. Mine-Mill hired Calamia to defend Jasso against the charges filed under McCarran-Walter Security Act of 1952.

Calamia recalled his intervention in the week-long deportation hearings in late February and early March 1956. "Mine-Mill was under federal investigation and the government seemed to be taking these actions in retaliation for what was occurring in the *Jencks* case. The government's evidence on voting was very weak. No witnesses. No direct evidence. Only circumstances that he was seen with other persons near a ballot box. It was just a case of retaliation." Immigration officials told the deportation officer that Jasso admitted to inspectors in 1945 that he had voted in a Mexican election. Jasso responded that he had been pressured into lying. The hearing officer overruled Calamia's objections to the officer's statements that Jasso had returned to Mexico to dodge the draft and that Jasso had worked for the Chihuahua state government. The hearing officer ordered Jasso deported. Calamia appealed the deportation order to the U.S. Board of Immigration Appeals in Washington. Five months later, the Board confirmed the hearing officer's decision. "The case was then brought to a district court in Washington instead of in El Paso," Calamia mused. "It seemed that we would have a better chance of obtaining a declaratory judgment there as there was no clear and convincing evidence to justify removal of citizenship." The district court denied the petition. The case was appealed to the Court of Appeals for the District of Columbia Court, which, in March 1959, reversed the decision (*Gonzalez-Jasso v. Rogers,* 264 F.2d 594 [C.A.D.C. 1959]). Expatriation is a matter of grave concern. Jasso's admission was insufficient. The government was required to corroborate it by other evidence.[3] (*Id.* at 587.)

As the 1950s decade came to a close, Calamia had established a reputation of being an outstanding criminal defense lawyer in both the state and federal courts. The objections and motions introduced by "Calamity Jose" in the course of hearings were not to be taken lightly. Calamia, court officials understood, knew the law and studied it continuously. And, they were beginning to understand that in Calamia's thoughts and actions, there was a clear and necessary distinction between the Enforcer (executive branch) and the

Interpreter (Judiciary). Calamia's suspicion that the distinctive line separating the Enforcer and the Interpreter was often too blurred in the eyes of the police, prosecutors and judges, and the rights of the individual were being ignored for the sake of expediency. The "commie" trials had shown this tendency. It took decisions by higher courts to remind officials of the separation of powers and the rights of the accused. With the red hysteria no longer dominating thinking in Washington and across the country, the United States would soon find itself consumed by intensified social, legal and political struggles to extend civil rights to minorities and other disenfranchised groups. The 1954 desegregation ruling by the Warren Supreme Court would extend to a number of areas and causes much to the vexation of the protectors of the status quo. Congress, even in the face of resistance, would ensure that this extension of civil rights would be codified in the law.

For Calamia, the challenge continued. Mindful of Thomas Jefferson's reaction to an omission of people's rights in the ratification of the U.S. Constitution, to Calamia there was always the unrecognized "peoples' branch," the rights of the people in the Bill of Rights.

Tenacity Calamia Style

―∞―

THE 1960S: JUDGE THOMASON
PASSES THE TORCH

The struggle occurring in the conscience of a nation was evident in the decade of the 1960s. The United States was now
a country of nearly 180 million people with a racial mix of
about 10.5 percent African American and less than 5 percent Asian
and Hispanic combined. El Paso's population had grown by nearly
50 percent in the last ten years to 314,000 in the city and some
144,000 in the rest of the county. El Paso's legal community had
also grown considerably. Calamia was now one of nearly two hundred attorneys who practiced in El Paso. His office remained at
the Caples Building until 1964 when he relocated to the new
Southwest National Bank Building. The building was modern, and
its offices were roomier. Its large open glass windows, hallways, automatic elevators, semi-automated telephones and piped in music
were in tune with the architectural style of the times. There was less
noise, more privacy and seemingly less individual contact than in
the 1930s style Caples Building. At Caples, people mingled in the
first floor area, waiting for the elevator that was operated by a real
person who greeted and chatted.

This shift from this personal to the impersonal was a metaphor
of the changing times. Nevertheless, Calamia retained a personal
touch. It was his quixotic nature to correct a perceived wrong. One
might sense a degree of caution and sophistication in the manner
that Calamia attacked his demons, but perhaps this was merely a
perception. His courtroom arguments were still assertive, if not ag-
gressive, as if delivered not in a legal contest, but in the boxing

ring. His approach was quite conservative compared to the iconoclastic one that the courts were about to experience, led by those eager to see rapid change in America's social structure. Tempting as it may be to go after a radical cause, Calamia chose to keep his idealism while never losing sight of the perception that, in his words, "My demons were real." Near the end of his first ten years of practice, Calamia had a well-earned reputation as the go-to criminal defense attorney.

As the 1950s came to a close, Fifth Circuit Judges Hutcheson, Rives and Brown took the unusual step of intervening in what at first appeared to be a frivolous appeal by three San Antonio defendants. They sought an appointed counsel in form *a pauperis*, that is, they were without funds to cover normal costs of their criminal defense. The trio had been convicted in Judge Thomason's federal court in Del Rio, Texas, on March 27, 1957, on charges of smuggling, concealing and transporting marijuana and were given prison terms. The men claimed that their San Antonio lawyer had failed to follow through with their appeal. Thomason denied the appointment, ruling that the appeal was frivolous. In turn, the defendants wrote to the Fifth Circuit, which surprisingly overruled Thomason's decision. In an even more unusual move, the court appointed Calamia to represent the men in the appeal, a fitting recognition as the decade drew to a close.[1] Calamia thought that there was substantial trial error in the admission of testimony concerning marijuana found in the automobiles following a high-speed chase. He unsuccessfully argued that there was a short lapse when the officers did not see the marijuana and that the judge failed to instruct the jury on the meaning of "possession." The Fifth Circuit affirmed the conviction (*Ketchum v. United States*, 259 F.2d 434 [5th Cir. 1958]).

In 1960, the mood of the nation was indeed changing. The Cold War was heating up with the downing of a U.S. spy plane over Soviet air space. The space race now factored in the arms between the Soviet and Western blocs. The Russians had launched four Sputniks, and they even sent a dog into space. America was playing catch-up as the young President Kennedy set a goal: "Be-

fore this decade is out, of landing a man on the Moon and re-
turning him safely to the Earth."[2] The fear of a Soviet colony in
Fidel Castro's Cuba escalated. The Fourth of July was special. The
U.S. flag debuted with fifty stars to include Alaska and Hawaii. In
El Paso, the political landscape was changing. The elections of two
Mexican Americans—Raymond Telles as mayor in 1957 and
Mauro Rosas as a state legislator in 1958—portended a future His-
panic political clout.

In 1960, however, El Paso voters still had to pay a poll-tax. For
all intent and purposes there was one political party that had a
chance of winning partisan elections—the Democratic Party. Candidates were required to pay a filing fee designed to cover the cost
of the primary election. Elections for city officials were nonparti-
san, and candidates ran at-large. Local king-makers determined
the slates for the mayoral and city council elections. Texas Senate
and House candidates ran in districts that covered the county, essentially making these at-large districts. County commissioners and
justices of the peace were elected by precinct. The Midland-
Odessa area congressmen had represented El Paso's Sixteenth
Congressional District since Judge Thomason left that post in 1947.
But with El Paso county's large population growth and the congressional redistricting mandated by the constitution, this situation
was about to change.

Big changes were also coming to El Paso's federal court system. With a Democrat as president, there would be an opportunity
for the appointment of Democrats as federal judges. There would
also be a new U.S. attorney for the Western District of Texas headquartered in San Antonio. That presidential appointee was Ernest
Morgan. In turn, Morgan would appoint two new assistant U.S.
attorneys for the El Paso office. The first was Fredrick (Fred) Morton, a young twenty-six-year-old native El Pasoan and recent University of Texas law school graduate. "I'm glad to see so many
distinguished friends of this 'defendant' here," Judge Thomason
said upon administering the oath of office to Morton, his former
law clerk. A staunch Democrat, the judge continued, "I notice we
have some Republicans present here, and this also is a pleasure."

After Morton left the U.S. attorney's office, he later returned to the federal courthouse as U.S. commissioner, the federal court's general counterpart to a state justice court. Before Morton, Colbert Coldwell and Henry Clifton held the part-time commissioner's post. The commissioner was the judicial officer that presided at arraignments and set bond. The U.S. commissioner also had the power to hold preliminary hearings under the Criminal Justice Act of 1964. Morton would remain the U.S. commissioner until that post was upgraded and renamed U.S. magistrate with expanded responsibilities designed to reduce the pre-trial workload of federal judges.[3] Morris Raney, also a native of West Texas, would become the other assistant U.S. attorney. Raney left the U.S. attorney's office to work for the U.S. Section of the International Boundary and Water Commission (IBWC) in its Chamizal Boundary Relocation Program. The program involved the relocation of some five thousand residents, and demolition of a large number of tenements, houses and businesses to allow the transfer of nearly one square mile of land to Mexico in settlement of a one hundred-year-old boundary dispute (Convention between the United States and Mexico, Solution of the Problem of the Chamizal, signed in Mexico City, August 29, 1963, TIAS 5515). Three assistant U.S. attorneys, Harry Lee Hudspeth, Jaime Boyd and Raymond Caballero, would prosecute federal cases until about the end of the decade. Hudspeth would later be appointed to the El Paso federal bench. Boyd would later serve as district attorney and become El Paso's first U.S. magistrate. He eventually moved to the San Antonio division of the Western District of Texas. Caballero would go into private practice in El Paso and California. Years after his return from California, Caballero would be elected mayor of El Paso. In 1960, U.S. District Judge Thomason was eighty-one years old, but he still had the stamina to preside over a couple of significant cases that, like the commie trials of the 1950s, would bring the national spotlight to El Paso's federal court.

One of these cases was a first for the United States that grew out of the strained political relationship between the United States and Fidel Castro's communist Cuba. On August 3, 1961, Leon

Beardon, a Chandler, Arizona ex-convict, and his juvenile son, Cody, ordered the pilot of a Los Angeles to San Antonio Continental Airlines flight, with sixty-five passengers on board, to fly to Cuba. The pilot, ironically a victim of the first ever hijacking in 1931, convinced the hijacker that he needed to land in El Paso to refuel. It took some twelve hours of negotiating with the FBI to get the Beardons to release the passengers. The older Beardon was convicted in October 1961 on charges of kidnapping, obstruction of interstate commerce by robbery and interstate theft. He was sentenced to life in prison on the first charge, with concurrent twenty five-year terms on the other two charges. A few years later, the Fifth Circuit set aside the life term (*Bearden v. United States*, 320 F.2d 99 5th Cir. [1963]). Perhaps a sign of the changing times, the El Paso hijacking incident set the tone for air travel security that was to come in the increasingly popular world of air travel. It became fashionable to hijack airplanes to Cuba, and the U.S. government would seek to put an end to this behavior. Just like in the old days of protecting stagecoaches from marauding gangs in the Southwest, U.S. marshals now rode shotgun on certain flights. No joking was allowed. Now an airline passenger had to take care not to address John, his fellow passenger, with "Hi, Jack!" for fear that a secret lawman may take his remarks the wrong way. The Spanish-speaker also had to be careful not to greet his buddy with *"cuvo,"* Spanish for "How ya doin'," lest he be thought to have the aim of rerouting the plane to Cuba.

The second important case was that of West Texas millionaire Billie Sol Estes, whose ammonia fertilizer tank empire existed only on paper. He had managed to obtain millions of dollars in proceeds from promissory notes guaranteed by that fictitious entity. Estes went on trial in April 1963. It took the jury two days to reach a guilty verdict. Judge Thomason handed Estes a fifteen-year sentence. The judge just could not resist rebuking the defendant. Reminiscent of his statement to the turncoat witness in the commie trials of the 1950s, Judge Thomason remarked: "The record shows that you were author and perpetrator of one of the most gigantic swindles in the history of our country." No reversal this time around. The Fifth Circuit not only affirmed the rulings, but had high praise for the judge as his distinguished career came to a close:

> From beginning to the end, this case was hard fought. The ingenuity of counsel was matched only by the skill of the trial judge and his patient endeavor to avoid error and to insure appellant a fair trial. In each he succeeded well. *Estes v. United States*, 335 F.2d 609, 619 (5th Cir. 1964).

Judge Thomason retired in June 1963, assuming senior status or in his words, "they'll call me when they need me." With Thomason on senior status, two federal judges, Adrian Anthony Spears (1910–1991) and Ben Rice (1889–1964) remained on active status. It would be another six months before Judge Thornberry, Thomason's successor, would take over the El Paso docket after he moved from Austin. Judge Suttle would succeed Judge Rice in 1964 and take over the El Paso and Del Rio dockets. In 1966, Judge Guinn assumed the new judgeship that was created for El Paso. Thomason's successors would be considerably different in personality and judicial and public temperament.

Suttle was a country lawyer from the cattle grazing lands between San Antonio and the Mexican border. Quite studious and detailed in conducting court proceedings, Suttle often exhibited a large degree of independence from the influence of law enforcement and prosecutors. Suttle demanded and adhered to strict decorum in his courtroom. He also strictly adhered to the law and, much to the dislike of lawmen, prosecutors and a law-and-order-oriented public, Suttle applied it equally to defendant's rights. At the same time, though, he was not the darling of defense lawyers. Judge Suttle was aloof with local politicians and community leaders, recognizing the independent role of the judiciary.

In contrast to Suttle, Guinn was a longtime local attorney. He had been a tough-minded city and county prosecutor with a brilliant law school record. He had tired of the stress associated with politics in 1954 and had been in private practice with his wife. The judge knew his stuff and did not rely much on the work of law clerks. Like Suttle, Guinn also maintained his distance from local politicians and community leaders. He also adopted strict court-room decorum, but he followed an expedient application of the law.

The era of a personable federal judge involved with community leaders and politicians had come to an end. Calamia was conscious of the change, quick to recognize it and quick to adjust. There had been challenges in having a trial judge with a conservative law-and-order orientation. But in the latter, Calamia found an opportunity to apply what he had learned so well—preservation of trial error. The U.S. Supreme Court's landmark civil rights rulings were making their way to the Fifth Circuit Court of Appeals. Recently, the late Scott Segall of the El Paso County Public Defenders Office wrote:

> What Mr. Calamia had done was to change the focus of the criminal trial from trying to win in spite of the law, to using the law to compel a win. Prior to Mr. Calamia, lawyers tried the case to the jury, with a hope of obtaining an acquittal. What Mr. Calamia did was to try the case not only to the jury, but also to the Court of Criminal Appeals.[4]

Calamia was not one to dabble in party politics. When the temptation came, a certain built-in resistance tempered any further involvement. To Calamia, there was a sense of respect for elected officials; yet, there was a certain distrust that influenced his thinking stemming from his experiences as a taxi driver working his way through college and as a young lawyer fighting against local government practices. Call it caution. Call it cynicism. Whatever the term, the distrust was one that paralleled Calamia's thinking when it came to the separation of powers in the U.S. Constitution. In his words, "Unbridled power leads to tyranny." Calamia limited his civic involvement to the work of the El Paso Bar Association. He took on an inordinate amount of indigent cases at a time when lawyers were appointed from the local bar without compensation.

While Calamia had pretty much proclaimed himself as a champion of the Bill of Rights, he was not a member of activist organizations. His attacks on any perceived inequities through actions or inactions of the government were made where the case warranted them, depending on the impact on his client, and then, in the appropriate judicial forum. The idea of helping the under-represented had been ingrained in him by his beloved philosophy professor, Joe Ross. The mandate of rushing to help a fellow human being, especially the many returning World II and Korean War veterans, had become second nature.

In February 1966, Calamia was traveling along a west El Paso thoroughfare when he witnessed a two-car collision. One of the vehicles struck a utility pole and then veered into the path of an on-coming car. The gasoline tank of the second car ruptured and caught fire, ignited by sparks from the collision. Calamia did not think twice. He rushed out of his car and ran toward the burning vehicle. One by one, he pulled out the driver and two passengers as flames continued to consume the car. A week later, the El Paso Bar Association honored Calamia for his heroic act. On the day of the incident, however, Calamia had experienced a fear that he had not felt before. He had saved the lives of three persons, but his own life might have ended had the automobile exploded while he at-tempted the rescue. A nominal Catholic, Calamia did what his fa-ther, a nominal Catholic, and his mother, a devout Catholic, might have done. He went to the peaceful confines of a church and re-flected on his life. There, he contemplated just how fragile human existence could be and just how unpredictably one's life could end. The thought was terrifying, but once he was strengthened spiritu-ally, he understood that one must go on with one's life.[5]

Calamia continued to be a fitness fanatic. The family manor in El Paso's rural and verdant upper valley had an area set aside for exercise machines, weights and the always-present speed and punching bags. More than a boxing enthusiast, he was now into English-style horseback riding. At one time, five thoroughbred horses milled around the Calamia's two-acre homestead. Hunting also became his passion. As the 1960s drew to a close, the El Paso Bar Association honored Calamia by temporarily naming him judge of the Sixty-fifth Judicial District at a time when El Paso's legal community was beset with complications stemming from the prolonged absence of the incumbent district judge.

The Texas judiciary faced an unusual situation. The illness of Sixty-fifth District Judge Jack Fant had kept him from performing his duties. The office could not be declared vacant, but the business of the court had to go on. To deal with this unusual situation, the State ordered the local sheriff to call for a special election of a "special judge" to serve for the next thirty days without vacating Judge Fant's elected position. In the first election, former corporation court Judge R. P. Langford was chosen. Two weeks later, Langford resigned. The Bar, in a second election, chose Calamia by an overwhelming margin of votes. To the surprise of many, Calamia accepted the short-term appointment with no pay. After all, Calamia had a heavy caseload in his private practice.[6]

CLANAHAN: EVEN "LA MIGRA" DESERVES A FAIR TRIAL

I t the start of the 1960s, El Paso was becoming a big city with big-city issues. Outside the city limits, it was a different story. A largely rural community had developed a vast expanse to the east and southeast of El Paso, which seemed to stretch forever through several large and sparsely populated counties along flat desert highlands and rolling grasslands. There were the irrigated farmlands along the floodplains of the Rio Grande, along valleys near the Mexican border separated by some of the largest mountains in Texas. The contrast between the big-city dwellers and the mostly Anglo rural landowners and farmers was startling. The rule of law dominated the criminal justice system in the city of El Paso. But in the rural areas east of El Paso, there were significant vestiges of the old "Law West of Pecos," with some horsemen still sporting shooting irons and rifles. A man's land was his own, and no trespassing meant just that. At first sight, these open lands seemed barren and unproductive. However, on closer inspection, these rangelands supported a multimillion dollar cattle-growing industry. There were also sheep and goats grazing in Presidio County. Cotton was king in thousands of acres irrigated by wells or waters from the Rio Grande. Both the livestock and irrigated agriculture industries needed ranch hands and farm labor. Nearby Mexico provided this.

Use of immigrant labor was a fact of life since the early development of agriculture and livestock grazing in El Paso, Hudspeth, Culberson and Presidio counties. World War II had brought an influx of workers under a 1941–1960 U.S.-Mexico guest worker undertaking known as the Bracero Program. "Braceros," from the term meaning hand laborers, were brought in primarily to work the fields. More than 4.5 million Mexican braceros were legally contracted in the twenty-two years that the program was in effect. At the same time there were also an estimated one million undocumented Mexican workers, not only in agricultural but also in industrial jobs largely in the Midwest. There were concerns by organized labor over "wetbacks" taking the higher-paying industrial jobs. "Wetback" was a pejorative term used to refer to Mexicans who crossed the Rio Grande into the United States without benefit of documentation. Those farmers who followed the rules complained of unfairness by some growers who hired "wetbacks" to bypass strict wage, housing and other Bracero pact regulations. This situation lead to a tough law enforcement effort called Operation Wetback in 1954.

Operation Wetback, led by retired General Joseph Swing, drastically reduced Mexican illegal immigration by 1960.[1] By that time, the Bracero Program was winding down, but in far-west Texas some of the "braceros" remained. Other undocumented workers from Mexico filled the void. With their status now undocumented, these workers were now the Rio Grande "wetbacks"—or "wets" in the vernacular—of the ranchers, farmers and indeed the U.S. Border Patrol. The Border Patrol, or "la migra" as they are called by undocumented Mexican workers, was now on the front line. Their job was to enforce laws that had been on the books for some forty years but enforced only sporadically. Although la migra's enforcement effort was not as intense as during Operation Wetback, this renewed government effort was still tough on the migrant worker. The Border Patrol rounded up the undocumented aliens in the fields. Their employers were left untouched. It was not customary to charge the employers under the federal harboring statutes. Courthouse observers referred to the practice as the "south Texas clause." However, under a ten-year-old law, the Border Patrol could conduct warrantless searches on lands but not in dwellings, so long as they occurred within twenty-five miles of the international boundary (Act of March 20, 1952, 66 Stat. 26).[2]

Farmers and ranchers complained of Border Patrol vehicles going after "wets" destroying their property and leaving cattle fences opened. In one case, a Hudspeth County rancher shot at a Border Patrolman's horse and was prosecuted. In 1963, veteran *El Paso Times* reporter Art Liebson described the rugged individualism of the ranchers and farmers:

> Smoldering underneath is the battle of the rugged individualistic West Texas ranchman to be a law unto himself.
>
> Through the years the ranchers rode herd over their lands without any governmental interference—a tacit agreement that they would respect the government, pay any necessary taxes, providing the law officers kept their distance. They were kings of their domains, and you risked your life any time you went inside their fences without permission.
>
> Grudgingly, ranchers have come to accept benefits from their government, soil conservation payments to build water storage and other assistance, but on their terms. Unlike the cotton farmers, they could not be told what to plant and when or take any official tip from anybody on how to run their business.
>
> They are a clannish group, loyal to each other. Any time a rancher was put on trial, a large number of friends would gather in the courtroom to shake his hand and gently remind the judge and jury that they were on his side.
>
> Along the Rio Grande they used labor wherever they could find it, and they never could see any logic in the immigration and naturalization telling them who they could hire or in Washington dictating how much they were to pay their Mexican workers.
>
> Then came the Border Patrol, under orders to enforce the immigration laws, and the resentment grew stronger. It burst into the open with the trial and conviction of Moody Bennett who came out of his car to shoot a horse from under a patrol inspector [. . .].
>
> Since Bennett's conviction, the resentment has burned deep in the minds and memories of ranchers who also do some cotton farming close to the river. They have been waiting for a chance to put the government on the defensive.[3]

The ranchers got their chance on November 20, 1962. On that day, Border Patrol Agent Dudley Clanahan flew his aircraft too low and struck a presumed undocumented alien mounted on horseback, apparently heading toward Mexico. He told his superiors that it was an accident. The twenty-eight-year old Clanahan had been with the immigration service for five years. During the last year, Clanahan's job had included tracking undocumented Mexican aliens from the air. The federal air jockeys would work as spotters in the spacious, desolate and treacherous terrain in Presidio County. Their information was passed on to motorized units on the ground. In turn, these units used the information to attempt round-ups of undocumented aliens. Aliens that were not able to evade the lawmen were taken to detention areas and most were released to Mexico after administrative hearings. Many returned to the United States resuming their "wetback" status. Once news of the horseman's death was made known to Texas authorities, Presidio county district attorney Shelby H. Blades easily obtained a murder with malice indictment against Clanahan from a grand jury in Marfa, Texas, the Presidio county seat.

Back in El Paso, assistant U.S. attorney Raney filed a motion before Judge Thomason to remove the case to U.S. district court. The action was considered to be a sure thing since the officer was on duty at the time of the incident. But neither Texas nor the Presidio County ranchers were about to let the government off so easy. The Texas attorney general named former assistant U.S. attorney Frank Hunter as a special prosecutor for the State of Texas. His first task was to bring the case back to Marfa state court for a "fair law-west-of-the-Pecos River" trial and suitable conviction.

Texas was tough on liberals. The Kennedy brothers were not exactly loved by the Texas right wing. Those Texans had little trust of federal judges. One would think that they would consider Thomason to be an exception. After all, this was the same fellow who, from 1931 to 1947, had campaigned in rural Texas, shook hands with many of these ranchers, gotten their contributions and their vote while a Congressman for the Sixteenth Congressional District. In 1962, many a highway sign called for the impeachment of Supreme Court Justice Earl Warren due to public distress over the Warren Court rulings that were extending the Bill of Rights to the states under the Fourteenth Amendment. These rulings had thrown out white-only practices in public schools and other public accommodations. Now in early 1962, that liberal court had the gall to rule on legislative district composition (*Baker v. Carr*, 369 U.S. 186, 82 S.Ct. 691, 7 L.Ed.2 663 [1962]). In the minds of many a person in power, this portended more liberal court rulings that, "Lord forbid" would create a dramatic change in political power.

The death took place about thirty-five miles southwest of Marfa on the Love Ranch. The owner went out seeking funds from area ranchers to cover Special Prosecutor Hunter's fees. Associations of cattle, sheep and goat raisers made a strong appeal to ensure justice in state courts. Flyers distributed by the groups claimed the pilot repeatedly dove at the mounted horseman, eventually striking him with the aircraft and killing the man. "This tragic and utterly useless fatality was the logical and inevitable culmination of a long series of incidents proving the ruthless and complete disregard of due process of law by some Border Patrol officer pilots," the protestors charged. They complained of other incidents of low flights over trucks, corrals, animals and horsemen, that disrupted ranch operation and terrorized the locals. At the same time, the ranchers assured that they did not condone the harboring of illegal aliens.

Texas tried again to get the case back in state court before the end of 1952, citing federal cases in which negligence by a federal officer may trump an automatic removal of a state murder charge to federal court. In early 1963, Thomason denied the motion.[4] The State decided not to appeal, taking its chances in El Paso's federal court. The United States was faced with the unusual case of its prosecutors having to act the part of criminal defense lawyers. To remedy this, Deputy U.S. attorney general Nicolas Katzenbach went directly to Calamia, appointing him as an assistant U.S. attorney to defend Clanahan. U.S. district judge Reynaldo Garza of the Southern District of Texas (1915–2004) was in El Paso to administer the oath of office to Calamia. President Kennedy had appointed the visiting judge from Brownsville, Texas, in 1961. He served in that post until 1979 when appointed by President Carter to the Fifth Circuit Court of Appeals, replacing Judge Thornberry.[5]

Trying a state murder charge in federal court and defending a federal agent was quite an anomaly. The government needed Calamia. The substantive charge, murder with malice, was found in the Texas Penal Code. Calamia had tried a case or two of murder with malice in the state court system with considerable success. Calamia had also tried a case or two in the federal court system, again with much success. The government understood that one like "la migra" could not be assured of a fair trial if his job and tactics were held in low esteem by so many. Finally, the government understood that rascal Calamia's emphasis on preserving error for appeal in case of an unfavorable verdict.

Calamia reviewed the substantive matters in the case. Defense and prosecution witnesses had provided much information at the hearings to remove the case from state to federal court. Observation aircraft used in surveillance of persons and vehicles tended to fly at low altitudes. The terrain in this part of Presidio county was hilly in part. There were caves and canyons to be concerned about. It was conceivable that the pilot did not see the horseman. The incident had received considerable press coverage during the State's attempts to convict the Border Patrol agent in the friendly confines of Marfa and its unsuccessful attempts to keep the case out of federal court. At these hearings, there was also testimony as to what the ranchers had seen on the ground. Yet, Calamia wondered, "Just how much did the prosecution witnesses really see?"

Calamia also focused on procedural matters. His overriding concern in defending Clanahan was the attitude of the ranchers and the general rural populace. Their antigovernment sentiment was not just confined to Presidio county. It extended to adjoining Culberson, Hudspeth, and parts of El Paso county. This was the area from which the federal jury pool would be selected. Calamia recalled thirty or so tough-looking ranchers who took up a couple of benches of Thomason's courtroom when the Texas attorney general's special prosecutor sought to have Clanahan face the murder charge in Marfa. Then there was the exchange between Special Prosecutor Hunter and Thomason at the January 1963 removal hearing. "Clanahan will get a fair trial in El Paso, where the case is not controversial," Thomason told Hunter. Hunter responded that that issue was irrelevant, observing that the agent had killed a mounted ranch hand by making a low pass with his aircraft without regard to federal flight regulations. Finally, Calamia wondered about the funds put together by the ranchers to pay the special prosecutor's fees. Calamia became suspicious of any potential jury pool member who may even look as if he contributed to the special prosecutor's fund. A fair and impartial jury would be difficult to find. But that would have to wait another year.

By the middle of 1963, Judge Thomason had retired. For the next few months, El Paso's federal district court docket was handled by visiting judges. And near the end of the year, El Paso and, indeed, the entire United States was in shock over the assassination of President Kennedy in Dallas on November 22, 1963. Continuity in government was the first priority after the death of the president. Vice President Lyndon B. Johnson was sworn in as president aboard Air Force One. U.S. District Judge Sarah Tilghman Hughes (1896–1985), one of three federal judges in the Northern District of Texas, was brought on board to administer the oath of office to President Johnson. A native of Maryland, Hughes was a George Washington Law School alumnus. Hughes moved to Dallas in 1922 where she practiced law until her election to the Texas House of Representatives. As a legislator, Hughes was instrumental in the passage of the 1953 Texas constitutional amendment allowing women to serve as jurors. Appointed to the Fourteenth District Court in Dallas as Texas's first woman district judge in 1935, she was re-elected six times until her appointment as a federal judge by Kennedy in 1961.[6] In just a couple of months, U.S. District Judge Hughes would be in El Paso to preside over the Clanahan trial.

Jury selection began on January 6, 1964. Calamia remained every bit as skeptical about his client's chances of a fair trial. He wanted to know which jury panel members had answered the call for contributions to cover Special Prosecutor Hunter's fees. Five prospective jurors were quickly excused upon admission that they would be prejudiced against the defendant. One complained that it was not fair to allow an officer to kill. Others simply did not like "la migra." Calamia referred to a letter written by the owner of the Love Ranch soliciting funds to cover Special Prosecutor Hunter's fee. Judge Hughes ordered Calamia not to read the letter. Calamia attempted to rephrase the question. Judge Hughes directed him to not refer to the letter again. Calamia then asked, "Have any of you contributed." Judge Hughes interrupted, "I instruct you not to ask that question." Calamia stopped. One more attempt and the judge would hold him in contempt.

"I just could not understand her position," Calamia reflected some forty-three years later. "The defendant was despondent over the accidental death of the horseman. He even threatened to commit suicide. It was necessary to raise those questions. It was a perfectly good question based on the law. The judge in a similar case had allowed similar questions concerning who was paying for the Puerto Rican's defense." Calamia was referring to the March 1, 1954, shooting in the U.S. House of Representatives by four Puerto Rican nationalists (*Labron v. United States*, 229 F.2d 16, [C.A.D.C. 1955]). Back in El Paso in 1964, Calamia offered the case for the record. He was obviously preparing for the worst case scenario and was cognizant of potential trial error.[7]

Judge Hughes seemed appalled at the large size of El Paso's federal courtroom and the large number of observers. "I'm used to a very small courtroom in Dallas," she told the audience in a loud voice. She found the case to be unusual in that the State of Texas was the prosecutor.[8] Special Prosecutor Hunter opened with the argument that the pilot was negligent and that the killing was intentional. Assistant U.S. attorney Raney insisted that the death was accidental. Calamia followed with assertions that Hunter was paid by the ranchers and not by the State of Texas. Hunter placed the ranch foreman and his wife on the stand. They testified that a Border Patrol airplane made several low passes at two men on horseback headed toward Mexico. The foreman also told of his conversation with the Border Patrol agents who were chasing the horsemen in a jeep and who stopped pursuit when their jeep got a flat tire. No one saw the Mexican horseman get hit by the airplane. Then there was a question over the nationality of the dead man. After the prosecution rested, Calamia said he was preparing a motion for an instructed verdict of acquittal. Judge Hughes quickly responded, "I will overrule that motion."

Calamia's trial strategy was now one of convincing jurors that the death was accidental and that the prosecution witness accounts were not credible. The Border Patrol agents in the jeep told of an uncooperative ranch foreman who denied harboring aliens and commented, "I bet you fellows don't catch 'em (the horsemen)." Clanahan told jurors his task was that of surveillance and spotting trails from the air. He told of following the horsemen into a canyon area but did not see the victim, only a horse's head as he attempted to pull out of the canyon area. He told of his aircraft being caught in a downdraft and described his attempts to stabilize the craft.

Calamia had done his homework. He had traveled to the Love Ranch area and understood the terrain and the climate. What appeared to be a sandy-brown blanket with few features suddenly appeared to be dotted with canyons of varying widths and depths caused by the eroding force of the infrequent but sudden desert flash floods. Flying in this treacherous terrain with sudden-changing weather patterns was risky business. Calamia needed an expert witness, and he found a bush pilot from Alaska. The expert flew the Marfa area and worked with the FBI to develop a flight simulation film that was played for the jury. It showed the difficulties in maneuvering out of a canyon when caught in a downdraft. While at work on the defense, Calamia also pulled another card from his back pocket. In need of an expert who knew about the accuracy of viewing from a distance, Calamia called a local optometrist to testify that the prosecution witness accounts were likely distorted because of their distance from the accident scene.

It took the jury fifteen minutes to acquit Clanahan. The not-guilty verdict was a triumph. And Calamia knew that he had prepared meticulously, fearing that his client may not get a fair trial. In Calamia's mind, even "la migra" has a right to a trial by a fair and impartial jury.

Little Joe in sailor suit at five years of age (El Paso, Texas, 1926).

Joe (center) with mother Laura Calamia and father Joseph Calamia, Sr. (Monterrey, Mexico, 1934).

Young Joe the sailor with rank of U.S. Navy Aviation Machinist Mate
Second Class (Petty Officer) following service in the Aleutian Campaign
of World War II (El Paso, Texas, 1943).

Joe's graduation from Southern Methodist University Law School,
(Dallas, Texas, August 26, 1949).

Joe, the boxer (El Paso, Texas, ca. 1950).

Joe lifting weights in his mother's back yard (El Paso, Texas, 1952).

Joe as temporary Judge for Texas State Sixty-fifth District Court (El Paso, Texas, 1966).

Joe (standing left) with his second son Mark (middle); daughter Virginia (front, second from left); father Joseph Calamia, Sr. (far right); mother Laura Calamia (to left of Joseph Calamia, Sr.) and other family members.

Joe at the height of his career (El Paso, Texas, 1975).

Joe seated left with his son Mark, second wife Hortencia and daughter
Virginia (El Paso, Texas, 1976).

Joe, the equestrian, riding his favorite thoroughbred horse (El Paso, Texas, 1979).

Joe receiving the "2002 Calamia War Horse Award" and title of "Magnum War Horse" from the El Paso Criminal Law Group, Inc. for recognition of his many years of service and legal wizardry for the criminally accused and for his positive impact on the Texas and Federal criminal jurisprudence systems (Ruidoso, New Mexico, October 4, 2002).

Joe during target practice using a 243 caliber rifle (Fort Bliss Rod and Gun Club, Ft. Bliss, Texas, ca. 2002-2003).

Joe hitting his speed bag (El Paso, Texas, ca. 2003).

Left to right: Hortencia Calamia, Joe, daughter Virginia and husband Johnny Lechuga (Chambarino, New Mexico, July 19, 2003).

Joe (center) with sons Mark (left) and Joseph Robert (right) (El Paso, Texas, Christmas Day, 2003).

Joe's civil rights work recognized at an El Paso Bar Association Luncheon. Joe (seated) with attorney friends and colleagues Maria Salas-Mendoza (former assistant county attorney and currently judge of the 120th District Court), and standing behind her left to right attorneys Clinton Cross, Fred J. Morton and David J. Ferrell (El Paso, Texas, October 12, 2004).

Joe (seated far left end) El Paso Bar Association Salute to Attorneys for 50 years of distinguished service (El Paso, Texas, December 14, 2004).

Joe and his wife Hortencia Calamia at his 87th birthday celebration
—his last birthday party (El Paso, Texas, June 5, 2008).

A frail but smiling Joe (center) with his wife Hortencia and their son
Mark five days before his death (El Paso, Texas, February 15, 2009).

NAGELL: DISCOVERY, INSANITY, CLEAR AND CONVINCING EVIDENCE

T he entire episode was bizarre. The defendant's actions on the day of the attempted bank robbery were not those expected of a person acting with full knowledge of what was right and what was wrong. The man insisted that he did not intend to rob a bank. He only wanted to be arrested. His hints that he knew, in advance, of a plot to kill President Kennedy did not appear to be those of a rational person. The defendant was sometimes his worst enemy. He insisted he was mentally competent. Sometimes he wanted a lawyer. Other times he did not. Some of the things he asserted in and outside of the courtroom made sense. Other things that he uttered did not. He launched several outbursts at his trial and at pretrial hearings. Several lawyers later, Calamia was the only one willing to stick it out. Calamia thought that crucial evidence, discovered after the trial, was clear and convincing evidence that the man was insane. El Paso's new federal judge, and former Austin Congressman, Homer Thornberry, was not buying any arguments about insanity or about newly discovered evidence. More important, jurors found the man guilty. Not once, but twice, his mental competency facts notwithstanding.

The United States was going through a difficult period. The "red menace" had moved into Southeast Asia, and it was now close by in communist Cuba. The United States had been increasing its military advisory presence in South Vietnam. There was controversy within the Kennedy administration over whether to pull back from this military commitment. It had not been long since October 1962. During those tense days in October, the entire world stood at the brink of nuclear war as the United States and Russia quarreled over Russian missiles in Fidel Castro's Cuba. At home, President Kennedy was getting the Democratic Party's ducks in a row in preparation for a second term campaign. He was coming to Texas to try to unite a divided Democratic Party. In a speech Kennedy planned to deliver on November 22, 1963, he wrote:

> Today [. . .] voices are heard in the land—voices preaching doctrines wholly unrelated to reality, wholly unsuited to the sixties, doctrines which apparently assume that words will suffice without weapons, that vituperation is as good as victory and that peace is a sign of weakness.[1]

In the South, only weeks after the famous "I Have a Dream" speech by Dr. Martin Luther King, the Kennedy administration was going head-to-head with Alabama Governor George Wallace's resistance to federal school desegregation orders. There were injuries. There were deaths. Wallace had called on the Alabama National Guard to stop the integration attempt. Kennedy trumped him by federalizing the Guard. Texas wasn't integrating its public schools quickly either, with the exception of El Paso where public schools were integrated in 1955. San Antonio started with integration of half of its schools and then phased in the remainder. Others were completing the go-slow effort. In 1963, fifty-five Texas school districts, including one in neighboring Fabens, finally moved towards desegregation.

In El Paso, the big news was that the Kennedy administration was giving back to Mexico nearly one square mile of south El Paso land, Calamia's childhood turf. The Texas attorney general considered a legal challenge over the U.S. government giving away a portion of Texas, in settlement of the dispute over the movements of the international Rio Grande that had lasted nearly one hundred years. El Paso's mayor and county judge along with business and other El Paso leaders sought to make the best of the Chamizal Settlement. They got the government to pay for a border highway, a memorial park, land for a new high school, relocation of a canal, and special compensation for families who would lose their south El Paso homes to Mexico. All this was the price Washington would pay for Senate ratification of the treaty and congressional funding to carry out the massive relocation project. El Paso might have gotten more had it not been for the Senate Foreign Relations Committee chairman's opposition to the Vietnam War and his use of that power to curtail spending in other foreign affairs areas.[2]

The bizarre bank robbery episode exploded on September 20, 1963, about two months before the Kennedy assassination. Richard Case Nagell, a thirty-three-year-old decorated Korean War veteran, walked into the State National Bank in downtown El Paso and asked a teller for $100 in traveler's checks. As the teller moved to get the checks, Nagell pulled out a .45 caliber pistol and told the teller, "Lady, this is a real gun." The teller ran away. Nagell fired two shots at the wall near the ceiling, well above the teller's head. Then he ran out of the building. Nagell voluntarily surrendered to El Paso police officer James Bundren who followed him outside the bank. The young traffic officer arrested Nagell before he could get into his illegally parked car. Bundren was in the bank at the time of the shooting, guarding a display of special U.S. currency and diamond jewelry. To witnesses, cops and the government, the case was simply one of a man who was caught attempting to rob a bank. At that time, the State National Bank bragged about being "In El Paso Since 1881." That was a year for frontier justice; four men were shot to death during a five-second gun battle just around the corner from the bank. In 1963, Nagell only shot up a wall of that historic bank, but it would take the wheels of justice five years before his case was settled.

Up until his arrest, Nagell, police and witnesses had the same story. Then, the discrepancies began. Nagell said he wanted to be arrested. Later, he said he had considered a shooting caper in the spacious downtown El Paso post office where he was mailing letters with notes and money. He changed his mind for fear he might hit someone in a crowded building. Nagell was having marital problems with his Japanese-born wife over custody of the couple's children. He was angry with the government over the amount of his military disability pay. He had been in a Florida veterans' hospital and a Los Angeles veterans' clinic a few months earlier, apparently suffering from personality disorders. Nagell was not about to admit it. He told arresting officer Bundren, "I'm glad you caught me. I really don't want to be in Dallas." Later he told the FBI, "I'd rather be arrested than be tried for treason." Much later, he claimed the money he mailed at the downtown post office was destined for Kennedy assassin Lee Harvey Oswald to cover Oswald's Mexico City airfare. Long after he was tried, Nagell still spoke as a spy coming out of the cold. He claimed that it was the prior knowledge of a Kennedy assassination plot that caused his bizarre behavior on September 20, 1963.[3]

Some forty-six years later, Nagell's comment about Dallas is still buried in Officer Bundren's memory.[4] At the time of Nagel's arrest, Bundren found a loaded revolver in the suspect's pocket and a suitcase in the trunk of his car. In the suitcase were Nagell's 1959 Army discharge as a captain and his military honors, including three Purple Hearts and a bronze medal he received while in the Korean combat zone. The military papers also revealed Nagell was an army intelligence school graduate with service in the army's counter-intelligence corps. There was also a camera, a few notebooks and *Fair Play for Cuba* leaflets. Local detectives couldn't get any information. He "refused to give us the time of day." Now in jail, Nagell attempted to cut his wrists with a tin can used as an ashtray and refused to eat his breakfast. He told police he would kill half of them. The jail physician recommended a psychiatric examination for Nagell. The government charged Nagell with entering a federally insured bank with intent to commit robbery and attempting to commit robbery in violation of 18 U.S.C. § 2113(a).[5] Nagell pled not guilty and assistant U.S. attorney Raney asked Judge Thomason for a mental competency determination. Dr. R. J. Bennett, a qualified El Paso psychiatrist, had no luck in examining Nagell. The would-be robber wasn't talking to anyone. At least that's what Nagell believed. Now appearing before Judge Thomason at a habeas corpus hearing, Nagell told the court, "I had a motive for doing what I did. But my motive was not to hold up the bank. I do not intend to disclose my motive at this time." Thomason was minding El Paso's federal court in senior status awaiting the arrival of his successor in early 1964.

Nagell's court-appointed lawyers received limited, if any, cooperation from the defendant. On the other side of the coin, Nagell was not satisfied with their services. Nagell accused James E. Hammond, his first court-appointed lawyer, of divulging confidential information. Hammond, an experienced and highly qualified attorney, denied the claim and was quite satisfied to be excused from the appointment. John Langford, another veteran attorney, was appointed to represent Nagell. Soon, Nagell was again dissatisfied. At a December habeas corpus hearing before Judge Thomason, Nagell ranted about his unwillingness to cooperate with psychiatrists at prison hospitals. He would cooperate, however, if the examination were held at a non-prison hospital. Then he put forth a caveat. "I will not tell him my motive for going into the bank." Nagell went on, "I have always acted in principle of love for my country and this same principle actuated my conduct on September 20, 1963, however inappropriate or incomprehensible it may appear. God and I, and also the FBI, know that I am not guilty." Nagell talked at random about a notebook and other items seized from him when he was arrested. Judge Thomason granted Nagell's request that the items be returned to him. Nagell's mysteriously worded statements were opening the door for strange stories about his involvement in espionage and prior knowledge of a plot to assassination President Kennedy.[6]

The assassination of President Kennedy and the events in the weeks that followed overshadowed most local news. The quick capture of Lee Harvey Oswald was welcome news to America. However, Oswald's connection with the Soviet Union, his marriage to a Russian citizen and his reported visits to the Soviet embassy in Mexico City elicited fears that a communist conspiracy might be behind the assassination. Then, just two days after his capture, Oswald was shot to death while in transit from the Dallas county jail. An entire television audience witnessed the shooting by Dallas nightclub owner Jack Leon Ruby (formerly Jacob Rubenstein).

Ruby was charged with murder in state court. His nightclub was a private burlesque club, and Ruby had close contacts with the criminal underworld, including organized crime in Chicago. Ruby had moved to Dallas in 1947 from Chicago where he had been a labor organizer and a runner for Al Capone's organization.[7] Ruby was upset over how his nightclub clients seemed to be gloating over the president's assassination. He felt bad that Oswald shot a Dallas policeman. So Ruby shot the man who killed Kennedy. At least that's what the nightclub owner with a shady reputation said.[8] Case over? Not quite. The Oswald assassination only added more fodder to conspiracy rumors in the Kennedy assassination.

One would think Nagell's statements might raise national attention. After all, both Nagell and Oswald were found to have *Fair Play for Cuba* literature. Not so. After just a few days in office, President Johnson called for a commission headed by Supreme Court Chief Justice Warren to investigate the Kennedy assassination. When the commission's report issued in 1964, there was no mention of Nagell.[9] Calamia had no clue that some of the Kennedy assassination conspiracy fodder would be coming out of the mouth of a client he never expected to be representing, Richard Case Nagell.

At the end of 1963, Calamia was at work on a number of cases. He had just arranged a compromise with City Hall to permit the stabling of horses on city property. Horse owners, Calamia among them, could now keep one horse on one-third acre (instead of one-half acre), and the stalls could now be at least fifty feet (instead of one hundred) from a residential dwelling. He was also preparing a defense for an El Paso policeman accused of the shooting death of his wife who was driving away from their residence in the officer's car. El Paso policeman Shelby East told detectives that he had mistaken his wife for a car thief.[10] For the most part, the activities between Nagell and lawmen were not before the public. Nagell remained behind bars in the El Paso county jail. Through no one's fault but his own, Nagell had no lawyers with whom to consult.

By January 1964, U.S. District Judge Thornberry was presiding over El Paso's federal court. He granted assistant U.S. attorney Morton's request that Nagell be taken to the federal hospital in Springfield, Missouri to determine whether he was mentally competent to stand trial. Nagell contested any claim of treatment by a psychiatrist or any evidence of psychosis. He told of being questioned by the FBI concerning subversive activities. He told of questions by the U.S. Secret Service concerning his connection with Oswald. Nagell claimed that not all his seized property had been returned.[11]

The doctors in Springfield received no cooperation from Nagell. However, they had the benefit of the records from the Florida and Los Angeles veterans' facilities. In January 1963, the Florida hospital's chief medical officer diagnosed Nagell as suffering from brain trauma, which showed passive-aggressive and paranoid behavior. Nearly five months later, the Los Angeles outpatient clinic in which Nagell had been confined diagnosed him to be suffering from depression and nervousness. Regardless of the previous findings, the Springfield doctor concluded that Nagell understood the proceedings against him and that he was able to assist in his defense. Back in El Paso in March 1964, Nagell changed his mind. He wanted a court-appointed lawyer after all. Judge Thornberry decided it best to appoint two lawyers from the El Paso Bar Association's list of attorneys. The next two in line were Gus Rallis and Richard B. Perrenot.

A rather bizarre hearing took place before Judge Thornberry on April 10, 1964. Nagell filed a motion to have the court subpoena all of the FBI's records relating to him, including material seized from him. He wanted this information for use in his trial. Assistant U.S. attorney Raney opposed the subpoena because it was "far reaching and broad." Judge Thornberry denied the motion, telling Nagell that introducing irrelevant material would not be in the best interest of his defense. Nagell mentioned material taken from him and statements he made to FBI agents E. Murphy and Thomas White in November 1963 and January 1964. White testified that Nagell had made a statement to justify his actions, to which Nagell interrupted, "I am being railroaded because I am a Communist and an accused spy." Judge Thornberry restored order and denied the subpoena request.

As Nagell's trial was set to start in April, there were basic disagreements between Nagell and Perrenot. Perrenot was allowed to withdraw. Next on the El Paso Bar list was Joe Calamia. On April 20, Calamia complained that he could not prepare a defense without a complete psychiatric examination. Judge Thornberry then allowed Rallis and Calamia to withdraw, concluding that Nagell would prepare his own defense. The next day, Nagell changed his mind. Calamia went right to work. He had Nagell examined by El Paso psychiatrist Dr. Manuel Hernández and had Dr. Hernández review Nagell's Veterans' Administration clinic records. Trial began on May 4, 1964.

"Nagell was his own worst enemy," Calamia recalled more than forty years later. "He kept insisting on his mental competency. He refused a psychiatric examination. He refused to acknowledge that there were psychiatric findings that would render him mentally incompetent. Unfortunately, the Springfield report had reached a conclusion recommending a finding of mental competency to stand trial. Yet, there were unanswered questions over factual knowledge and rational knowledge." Calamia was relying on the test for mental competency set by the Supreme Court in *Dusky v. United States* (362 U.S. 402, 80 S.Ct. 788, 4 L.Ed.2d 824 [1960]):

> whether he [the defendant] has sufficient present ability to consult with his lawyer with a reasonable degree of rational understanding—and whether the accused has sufficient present ability to consult with his lawyer with a reasonable degree of rational understanding and whether he has a rational as well as factual understanding of the proceedings against him.

To Calamia, the unanswered question concerning factual and rational knowledge raised a more serious issue. Specifically, did the conviction of a person who is incompetent to stand trial deprive that person of his life or liberty without due process of law? This Fifth Amendment protection was perhaps only a matter to keep in his back pocket given that Judge Thornberry had already ruled that Nagell was competent to stand trial. An appeal of that ruling at this point seemed out of the question since Nagell was not co-operating and continued to insist that was mentally competent.[12]

In Calamia's mind, he was a defense lawyer, not a Kennedy assassination investigator. The only way to keep his client out of prison was to convince jurors that Nagell was insane. Calamia focused on defending a war hero. Espionage and assassination conspiracies were outside this framework. Calamia figured that such information might distract the jury from an insanity defense. Nagell still talked about the seized property and accused the FBI of retaining it. He accused the FBI of knowing more about his secretive life than what they told the prosecution. He talked about a secret motive. Even with an insanity defense, it would still be an uphill battle. Calamia felt assured that the government had provided all the information in its possession concerning Nagell's sanity. Calamia mused, "After *Jencks,* trial by surprise was to be a thing of the past." Nagell's insistence on his sanity compounded the matter. Indeed, Nagell seemed to understand the charges. He seemed to understand the workings of the court, the prosecutor and investigators. He had drafted a number of fairly decent legal petitions.

Calamia now looked at the points of law, as if with a magnifying glass. He viewed evidence as if through a microscope. Maybe Nagell's insistence that he did not intend to rob a bank was a good defense after all. Nagell's only statement at the bank was that he had a real weapon. He did not demand money. He seemed to be seeking attention. It was the government's obligation to prove that Nagell specifically intended to rob the bank. Surely, the government's evidence must show a requisite intent beyond a reasonable doubt.

Nagell's trial began with testimony by the bank clerk and police officers who described the September 1963 incident. Any mention of "insanity" by prosecutors, witnesses or counsel prompted Nagell to call them liars. He constantly interrupted testimony despite Judge Thornberry's best efforts to control him. Nagell would jump from his chair and demand that he was not insane. Government witnesses supported Nagell's contention that he was sane. Dr. Hernández's testimony did not help Calamia's strategy. Dr. Hernández concluded that while Nagell's schizoid personality would keep him from controlling his behavior at the bank, Nagell could nevertheless distinguish right from wrong. When another El Paso psychiatrist testified that Nagell was suffering from a paranoid condition, Nagell angrily jumped to his feet and objected. He quieted down when the same witness said Nagell could distinguish right from wrong. The government brought in another psychiatrist who had some knowledge of Nagell's stay at the Florida veterans' hospital. He testified that Nagell had not shown bizarre behavior and concluded that he could have known right from wrong the day of the attempted bank robbery. The staff psychiatrist from the Springfield hospital offered the same conclusion.

It was time for Nagell to take the stand. Calamia's questions were designed to show Nagell as a person who suffered a difficult youth but who bravely fought for his country. Nagell was to be seen as a Korean War hero, thrice wounded and highly decorated. This was a hero who had advanced to the rank of captain. He was the sole survivor of a 1954 military plane crash in Maryland. After a short stay at Walter Reed Army Hospital, Nagell was honorably discharged with a medical disability not related to a mental condition. In 1958, Nagell had married a Japanese woman, and the couple had two children. But by 1963, the marriage had soured, and Nagell was having a difficult time holding down a job.

Still looking to bolster the argument for insanity, Calamia questioned Nagell about his travel to El Paso and his plans to permanently leave the United States for Mexico. Nagell volunteered information about assignments with the army's counter-intelligence corps. He talked about having dealt with the FBI and secret things that go on behind the scenes in law enforcement circles. Nagell admitted that he went into the bank and fired two shots but insisted that he just wanted to be arrested.

It took the jury a little more than two hours to reach a guilty verdict. Judge Thornberry deferred sentencing. Nagell was led out of the courtroom by U.S. marshals. Abruptly, he shouted, "Why weren't the real issues brought out in this court? They will be sometime!" Was Nagell being railroaded? Nagell considered that the efforts to declare him insane were part of a plot to discredit his espionage activities. Calamia was thoroughly convinced that Nagell was insane. At this point, Nagell began to talk freely with Calamia, in part about his Korean War injuries. Nagell told of suffering a wound in combat and eluding medics to return to combat only to get wounded again. Then, there was the 1954 plane crash. Calamia questioned whether there could have been a brain injury that affected Nagell's personality. The conversations then turned to Nagell's stay at Walter Reed Army Hospital following the plane crash. Nagell told about being diagnosed with a chronic brain injury problem by Dr. Edwin A. Weinstein, a highly-respected neurology and psychiatry consultant for Walter Reed Hospital and the Veterans Administration. Nagell said he had told the FBI about Dr. Weinstein. Surely there was a report of his findings. Calamia contacted Dr. Weinstein.

Calamia was impressed with Weinstein's credentials. The man was a foremost expert on behavior changes following brain injuries. One of Weinstein's areas of expertise concerned denial of illness following brain injury. To Calamia's surprise, Weinstein was quite familiar with a brain injury case study involving Nagell. Nagell apparently suffered a brain fracture in the plane crash that damaged his brain and some of the cranial nerves. Weinstein remembered Nagell's violent behavior at the hospital and his potential for committing suicide. Nagell's denial of illness and attempts to hide information stood out among the observations. Nagell, according to Dr Weinstein, could not "completely and accurately differentiate between right and wrong."

Did a report of these findings exist? Yes! And it was in the hands of the FBI and federal prosecutors. It turned out that the FBI had interviewed Dr. Weinstein not long after Nagell told them about the psychiatrist and his Walter Reed hospitalization. The government had not provided this information to Calamia, Rallis, or the other court appointed lawyers before them. An angry Calamia filed a motion for a new trial based on crucial newly discovered evidence. Judge Thornberry ordered a full evidentiary hearing.

Calamia's mind returned to the 1950s and the incident in which the State of Texas had concealed crucial information concerning the intimate relationship between his client's dead wife and her lover. He also recalled the reluctance of the U.S. government to allow a mining and smelting labor union leader and accused Communist access to FBI reports. The appalled Calamia wondered. "It was now 1964!" Trial by surprise should no longer exist. The Supreme Court had issued a landmark ruling in May 1963 that suppression by the State of Maryland of an accomplice's confession violated the defendant's Fourteenth Amendment due process protection (*Brady v. Maryland*, 373 U.S. 83, 83 S.Ct. 1194, 10 L.Ed.2d 215 [1963]). Precedent was good to have, but Calamia was well aware that the federal courts had set extremely high standards for granting a new trial. There was significant discretion given to a trial judge.

The June 1964 evidentiary hearing got right into the heart of the matter. Calamia declared that he and cocounsel Rallis "discovered that Dr. Weinstein had taken part in observing Nagell in Walter Reed Hospital. There is no greater authority in the world on the subject of brain injury." Dr. Weinstein testified about his intensive study of Nagell at Walter Reed from November 1954 to April 1958 and his more recent June 1964 interview. He described Nagell's brain injuries and his behavior. Of Nagell's behavior, Dr. Weinstein said Nagell showed sufficient intelligence most of the time, but that Nagell also had episodes of violence, denial and suicidal gestures. Then he declared that unless a psychiatrist had knowledge of Nagell's history, that doctor would be at a loss and confused by Nagell's behavior. He asserted that Nagell's denial of an illness and practice of concealing information were characteristic of his illness. As to Nagell's behavior at the bank, Dr. Weinstein made two important points. Nagell was out of touch with reality on September 20. The bank shoot-out was directly associated with his mental illness. In Dr. Weinstein's expert opinion: "I would say that this was a symptom or manifestation of disturbed brain function and during this period his judgment and perception of reality was seriously disturbed so that he could not accurately differentiate right from wrong."

The other psychiatrists had just heard this from the country's top expert. One by one, the government psychiatrists said they would change their earlier testimony. They were now of the opinion that Nagell was not able to distinguish right from wrong. The government tried to impeach Dr. Weinstein, contending that his statements at the hearing were inconsistent with what he told an FBI agent in an interview soon after the bank-shooting incident. Weinstein stood by his testimony observing that the FBI agent, not being a doctor, may have misunderstood him. Outside the courtroom, Weinstein told reporters, "We predicted just such things as this (attempted robbery) when we had Nagell at Walter Reed Hospital."[13]

Judge Thornberry denied the motion and sentenced Nagell to ten years in a federal institution. "There is no doubt that you need treatment." He added that a ten-year sentence was best "not only for your own protection and welfare but also for society." After sentencing, Calamia expressed concern. "This hero, who fought for his country and nearly paid with his life twice on the battlefront and who by all qualified evidence is insane, should not be subjected to the stigma of a prison sentence." Then he declared, "We are confident that this judgment will be reversed on appeal." Just one week later, Nagell swallowed several tranquilizers while in the county jail in a suicide attempt. He was sent to the hospital ward at La Tuna Federal Correctional Institute, some twenty miles north of downtown El Paso near the Texas-New Mexico state line. From there he would be sent to a public health service hospital in Fort Worth, Texas. Then he would be locked up at Leavenworth Federal Penitentiary for about eighteen months until February 1966 when he would be returned to El Paso county to face a new trial.

In 1964, however, Nagell was still behind bars. His case was appealed to the Fifth Circuit. Joining Calamia and Rallis in the appeal was Edward F. Sherman, who had been Judge Thomason's law clerk before the judge retired. It had not been long since Sherman had graduated from Harvard Law School.[14] U.S. attorney Morgan and assistant U.S. attorney Harry Lee Hudspeth joined Raney and Morton in defending the conviction. The appellate record included some eight hundred pages. There were seven issues for review. Calamia argued that the government did not prove Nagell's intent to rob the bank or his sanity beyond a reasonable doubt. He complained of procedural errors, evidentiary errors and a charge error. Another point alleged that the court appointed lawyers were "lulled by erroneous representations by the government that all available evidence" concerning Nagell's mental state had been disclosed. The appellate court dismissed these six without extended discussion, and focused primarily on the seventh claim, that a new trial should have been granted on the basis of newly discovered evidence. One year and eight months after Nagell was found guilty, the Fifth Circuit reversed Judge Thornberry's decision and ordered a new trial (*Nagell v. United States*, 354 F.2d 441 [5th Cir. 1966]).

The opinion emphasized that reversing the denial of a new trial was a rare event. In a case of newly discovered evidence, the decision is left to a sound discretion of the trial judge. In this case, however, the trial judge had not prepared findings of fact or conclusions of law in support of his decision. The appellate court reiterated the hurdles an appellant must clear, all of which had been met. New evidence was discovered after the trial. The new evidence was not cumulative in nature. The new evidence impeached the government's evidence. It was material. The new evidence could produce a different outcome. A final test was whether counsel was diligent in discovering the evidence. Calamia's untiring effort to gain Nagell's confidence and pursuing any and all clues that would support his case for insanity certainly met this requirement. The opinion took a sound bite from Calamia's fundamental tenet that doing justice is the final end of the court system. The court said, "The whole purpose of the courts is to do justice and prevent injustice" (*Id.* at 448.) The court specifically avoided ruling on the merits of an insanity plea. This was a matter to be left to another jury. The opinion only strengthened Calamia's belief that withholding critical information is tantamount to shifting the burden of proof to the defendant. "This goes against the very bedrock of human liberty, the presumption of innocence." Calamia raised his voice in firm declaration four decades later. "While the U.S. Constitution does not specifically cite presumption of innocence in the Bill of Rights, this right is at the core of an accused's rights in the Fifth and Sixth Amendments."

The government did not appeal to the Supreme Court. Calamia was convinced another jury would find Dr. Weinstein's testimony to be clear and convincing evidence that Nagell was not capable of distinguishing right from wrong.

Nagell was now back in the El Paso county jail. And again there were differences over defense strategy. There was an opportunity for voluntary commitment and a good chance that the government would dismiss the bank robbery charges. Nagell would have none of that. He had been in touch with his sister who was seeking a new lawyer for her brother. In early April, Judge Suttle ruled that any new lawyer would serve under Calamia's strict supervision. Suttle ordered Nagell back to Springfield for yet another psychiatric examination. The judge wanted to ensure that Nagell was mentally competent for his second trial. Nagel's sister changed her mind about hiring another attorney. Nagell yelled as he was being led out of the courtroom. "This is a mockery of justice." Before he could be sent to Springfield, Nagell barricaded himself with blankets and sheets attached to his cell door. He threatened to slash his throat if anyone tried to remove him. Somehow he had acquired some razor blades. Nine days later, Nagell gave up.[15]

At Calamia's prodding, Nagell submitted to the mental examinations at Springfield, and in June he was found to be mentally competent to stand trial.[16] He was returned to the El Paso county jail in July. Nagell again differed with Calamia's defense strategy. Judge Suttle would not wait forever for Nagell to change his mind on a voluntary commitment possibility. Calamia was prepared to go with the insanity defense, but Nagell would not accept that he was insane. He wanted "the truth to come out." What truth nobody knew. Finally, Calamia struck a compromise with Nagell on a defense of temporary insanity at the time of the bank shoot-up.

Nagell's second trial began about three years after the shooting at the bank. During jury selection, Judge Suttle went through a detailed explanation of the law. In one instance, he told jurors that in the case of an insanity defense, the government had burden of proof to show that Nagell was sane at the time of the offense. Assistant U.S. attorneys Hudspeth and Boyd represented the government. Their strategy was to present eyewitness testimony to prove that Nagell attempted to rob the State National Bank on September 20, 1963. The government would then let the defense attorneys present Dr. Weinstein's testimony and that of the other psychiatrists who had changed their opinions as a result. Through cross examination and rebuttal witnesses, the government would seek to convince jurors that Nagell was sane at the time of the shooting.

Calamia and Rallis relied upon their principal witness, Dr. Weinstein, who repeated his testimony from the hearing on the motion for a new trial. He told of Nagell's Korean War injuries and of the brain injury Nagell suffered in the 1954 plane crash. He explained his ten-year research involving the effects of brain injuries on behavior. He referred to letters from Nagell concerning severe headaches, blackouts, repeated dreams of falling and hitting the ground, and reliving the plane crash. He told of nightmares about Korean combat in which Nagell, "smelled phosphorous and the dead." The government introduced testimony of two other psychiatrists who said that based on their limited information, Nagell likely could tell right from wrong on the day of the incident. The psychiatrist who performed Nagell's most recent examination at Springfield reported a similar, but qualified, conclusion. This time, jury deliberations lasted several days but it found Nagell guilty of the two-count indictment. Judge Suttle sentenced Nagell to ten years, giving him credit for the three years he had already been behind bars. Once again, Nagell was in Leavenworth. And once again, Calamia was prepared to appeal the decision to the Fifth Circuit.

Appeals had now become an important part of Calamia's practice. Many lawyers sought his advice. Chicago lawyer and civil rights activist William Kunstler (1919–1995) was representing the Jack Ruby family and hunting for an appellate lawyer. San Francisco criminal defense attorney Melvin Belli (1907–1996) had represented Ruby during the trial at no cost. Belli chose to go with an insanity defense, rather than a defense of sudden passion, but the jury found Ruby guilty of murder with malice. Kunstler approached Calamia about handling the appeal. Calamia hesitated because of Kunstler's radical reputation. But Calamia had worked with radical lawyers in the 1950s. "I said I would do the work for a fee of $3,000," Calamia recalled some forty years later. "Kunstler said the fee amount was acceptable, but he would make it contingent on the sale of a book. Not a good idea." The case was just too high profile. Austin attorney and Texas AFL-CIO general counsel Sam Houston Clinton[17] (1923–2004) was hired as the Ruby family's appellate lawyer. In November 1966, the Texas Court of Criminal Appeals reversed the conviction and granted a new trial. One month later Ruby was in a Dallas hospital, and in early January 1967, he died of a pulmonary embolism.

A few months later, word was out that New Orleans District Attorney Jim Garrison had arrested New Orleans businessman Clay Shaw on conspiracy charges related to the assassination of President Kennedy. Shaw was acquitted in a 1969 trial. Garrison's later books added more ammunition to assassination theories. What an opportunity for Nagell to get his story out!

Back at Leavenworth following his second conviction, Nagell was soon taken again to the Springfield prisoner's hospital. He apparently made contact with one of Garrison's investigators. Nagell had prepared, but apparently did not file, a habeas corpus petition in federal district court in the Western District of Missouri on June 6, 1967. A few months later Nagell's name was mentioned in a January 1968 edition of *Ramparts*, a new leftist magazine.[18] According to one of a series of articles on the Garrison investigation, Nagell's story from Leavenworth supported the theory that Oswald was the patsy in a conspiracy arranged by anti-Castro elements. Nagell had indeed sent a letter to the FBI warning of a plot to assassinate Kennedy in late September. He reminded the FBI agents of that letter while they interviewed him in the El Paso jail in December 1963. He accused the FBI of not doing enough to prevent the assassination. Also, Nagell now claimed that he was a CIA agent with an assigned task of killing Oswald after the assassination. He said he got cold feet and opted to arrange for his arrest in

El Paso. He claimed that the FBI seized his two notebooks with all sorts of information about the actors involved in the assassination plot. As a result, Nagell now claimed, the government threw the book at him.

While Nagell was at work on his disclosures, Calamia remained focused on his commitment to Nagell. Calamia hoped that the Fifth Circuit would see that the evidence of Nagell's insanity was overwhelming. The country's foremost authority on brain injury-related behavior had so testified. It was the government's burden to prove Nagell's sanity. How could reasonable persons consider Nagell to be sane beyond a reasonable doubt? There was also the issue of Nagell's intent on the day of the shooting. In his instructions to the jury, Judge Suttle considered it reasonable for the jury to infer that a defendant intends to commit an act if he understood "all the natural and probable consequences" of his conduct. In other words, if Nagell entered a bank with a gun, the jury could infer that he intended to rob it.

It took the Fifth Circuit more than eighteen months to review the appeal. A panel presided by Chief Judge Hutcheson had just ruled in a similar case (*Brock v. United States* 387 F.2d 254 [5th Cir. 1967]). Hutcheson observed:

> Appellate review of the sufficiency of the evidence is never an easy matter, and the difficulty is compounded when a jury in a criminal case has reached a verdict contrary to both medical testimony and visceral reaction. (*Id.* at 257.)

Many of the issues in *Brock* were similar to those in Nagell's appeal. On April 3, 1968, the Fifth Circuit reversed Nagell's conviction, remanding the case with directions to vacate the judgment and grant the defendant's motion for acquittal (*Nagell v. United States,* 392 F.2nd 934 [5th Cir. 1968]). It relied heavily on *Brock* in concluding that, "reasonable doubt must necessarily have existed in the minds of reasonable jurors." Although a trial judge has discretion to accept expert witness testimony, the defense evidence was overwhelming and the government's evidence too meager on the issue of insanity. In so holding, the court revisited Calamia's argument, which they had rejected without discussion in the first appeal, that the government did not prove Nagell's sanity beyond a reasonable doubt.[19]

Nagell had already served three years, but he was free at last. His only desire was to go to New York to be with his sister. He was still seeking greater disability compensation and custody of his children. Apparently, he made it to New York but only stayed a short time before moving to Europe. In October 1968, police in East Germany released Nagell from captivity that had lasted four months.[20]

Calamia did not hear about Nagel until 1975 when freelance writer Dick Russell asked to see Nagell's files in Calamia's office. "At my request, he obtained written permission from Nagell," Calamia recalled. "He spent considerable time reviewing the files. He asked a number of questions concerning my defense of Nagell and Nagell's assertions about Oswald. Several years later I declined another interview. Russell's book, *Hired to Kill Oswald and Prevent the Assassination of JFK,* came out. In the book, Richard Case Nagell is The Man Who Knew Too Much.

Russell had a different take on Nagell's arrests and convictions. According to Russell's investigation, and correspondence and interviews with Nagell and others, Nagell allowed himself to be arrested to avoid killing Oswald in a Kennedy assassination attempt. Russell believed that Nagell was railroaded in the courts through hospitalization and imprisonment because he knew too much. Like other Kennedy assassination conspiracy theorists, Russell outlined a government cover-up and urged the release of all government files on the Kennedy assassination.[21]

In 1992, Congress passed the President John F. Kennedy Assassination Records Collection Act, (Public Law 102-526, 106 Stat. 3443). The intent was to have all assassination-related materials housed in the National Archives and Records Administration (NARA). Nagell was not mentioned in any of the presidential and congressional investigations between 1963 and 1975: the Warren Commission on the Kennedy Assassination (1963–1964); the Rockefeller Commission on the Central Intelligence Agency Activities, including attempts to assassinate Castro (1975); the House Select-

Committee on Assassinations (1976–1979); reopening the Kennedy assassination investigation and investigating the death of Martin Luther King, Jr.; the Church Committee to investigate government intelligence activities (1975); or the Pike Committee to investigate intelligence activities. Information on Nagell appears only in the 1992 records collection in the context of Russell's book. The National Archives tried to contact Nagell at his Los Angeles apartment in 1995 and was informed that Nagell had died of complications from heart disease.[22]

In retrospect, when asked what his interest was in defending Nagell, at no fee, against all odds, Joe Calamia repeated what he told Russell in 1975. "The man was a real hero. He was wounded in combat defending our country. He nearly died in an airplane crash. I wanted justice for a veteran. He was not a hardened criminal and did not belong in prison."[23]

FEDERAL JUDGES: ATTITUDES
AND THE LAW OF CONTEMPT

The courts could not ignore the social changes and politics of the day. Opposition to the Vietnam War had spread within the Democratic Party led by Senator Eugene McCarthy. In March 1968, President Johnson chose not to run for a second full term. In April, civil rights leader Martin Luther King, Jr. was shot to death in Memphis. Immediately, riots and burning of ghetto buildings by African-Americans erupted in Washington and Detroit. A few days after Dr. King's funeral, President Johnson signed the Housing Rights Act. The legislation was in response to public pressure to end discrimination in the sale and rental of housing to African-Americans and other minorities. At the same time, Congress, fearful of increased violent antiwar demonstrations, added an antiriot provision to that law. *See* 18 U.S.C. § 231 (a)(1) and (3). One anti-war tactic used by many protestors was blocking entrances to the Selective Service Offices. Pressure on Congress to assure law and order resulted in the Omnibus Crime Control and Safe Streets Act of 1968, the Controlled Substances Act of 1970 and the Organized Crime Control Act of 1970.

In June 1968, presidential-hopeful New York Senator Robert Kennedy was assassinated following a California primary election victory in Los Angeles. The battle for the Democratic Party nomination was between Vice President Hubert Humphrey, now considered an "establishment" candidate, and Eugene McCarthy, who had support among liberal Democrats including many student activists. Humphrey won the nomination. On the Republican side,

Richard Nixon waged a tough law-and-order campaign. American Political Party candidate George Wallace was several points up on Nixon when it came to law and order. He decried crime in the street and liberal rulings of federal judges and the Supreme Court. If elected, Wallace was prepared to "throw those federal judges into the Po-to-mac." Nixon narrowly defeated Humphrey in the November 1968 elections. Earlier in August, some of the more radical groups camped near the Democratic Convention site in Chicago. Outside the convention, a riot erupted resulting in a number of arrests under the 1968 Housing Rights Act provision that prohibited riots (*United States v. Dellinger,* 472 F.2d 340 [7th Cir. 1972], *cert. denied,* 410 U.S. 970, 93 S.Ct. 1443 [Mem], 35 L.Ed.2d 706 [1973]).

The 1969 trials of the "Chicago 8" the year after enactment of the Anti-Riot Act brought before the courts the contentious issue of whether the law violated the defendants' First Amendment rights. Importantly, there came into question the extent to which judges could invoke powers of contempt.

Throughout the country, there were movements for free speech with expressions of explicit sex and profanity used by youthful protesters to make their point. These "make love, not war" tactics, often in furtherance of a cause, antagonized the more conservative citizenry. The entertainment industry had changed. Many words and actions on television and in the movies were no longer taboo. Mini-skirts were coming into vogue raising concerns about business attire. "Mini-skirts may be fine on stage, but they have no place in the office," an El Paso businessman warned the local secretaries' association.[1] Music lyrics were increasingly more explicit. The iconoclastic counterculture movement typified by psychedelic art, rock music with explicit lyrics, hippies with long hair and gaudy dress and drugs had spread from San Francisco's 1967 summer of love. There were no longer any sacred cows. There was rebellion against "the establishment" and its police, which protesters now referred to as "pigs." They targeted the courts. The courts were accused of fostering injustice, exemplified by the popular 1968 song, "Here Come Da Judge" in which a man is brought to court for doing the "boogaloo," a Harlem Puerto Rican dance. The decorum and formality in federal court proceedings was about to change. But this would not come easily.

As he demonstrated in the "commie" trials of the 1950s, Calamia was not a crusader for his clients' causes, only for his clients' rights. Whatever the clients' beliefs, it was about the law for Joe. America's changing social behavior was cause for concern. Calamia's concern was the erosion of the delicate balance between freedom of speech and the rule of law. Neither should be unbridled. On the one hand, there was contempt for the law as exhibited in the Chicago riots. On the other hand, one could also question law enforcement tactics used in the arrests under the 1968 Anti-Riot Act. The confrontation had moved to the courtroom. There, defendants, spectators and attorneys tested the long-established contempt powers[2] accorded to the courts. In 1968, the Warren Court was drawing to a close. Chief Justice Warren retired in June 1969. There was the expectation in many sectors that his successor would vote to reverse prior decisions. While some people had lauded the Warren Court for expanding rights and liberties, the conservative sector condemned its judicial "activist" decisions. Their hopes rested on the shoulders of Warren E. Burger (1907–1995), a jurist with a conservative approach in the Court of Appeals for the District of Columbia, nominated by a law-and-order-minded President Nixon.[3] It just didn't turn out that way.[4]

Calamia was no stranger in challenging a judge's contempt order, thanks to his successful appeal of Judge Thomason's contempt conviction of recanting witness Harvey Matusow. "I did not challenge the powers themselves," Calamia recalled. "These powers are innate to the court."[5] In *Matusow*, the Fifth Circuit recognized both the contempt power of a judge and the need for limitations on that power:

> The right to punish for contempt of court is a recognized exception which is as old as the Bill of Rights itself [. . .] courts of justice are universally acknowledged to be vested, by their very creation, with power to impose silence, respect and decorum in their presence and submission to their legal mandates.
> *Matusow v. United States*, 229 F.2d 335, 338 (5th Cir. 1956)

If Calamia had a crusade, it was not about testing the court's contempt powers. His crusade was seeking to assure that the court's ruling did not violate the defendant's rights. In his perspective, "the Bill of Rights can be used by some to sound like, 'yes, we have no bananas today.'" Comparing the vagueness in the use of a double negative to a broad provision of law, Calamia added, "The Bill of Rights must never cease to be a protection from potential rights' violations by the enforcer." Calamia's oft-stated concern was the risk that the "law-maker" (legislative branch) and the "law-interpreter" (judicial branch) may at times be in cahoots with the "enforcer."[6] Calamia had experienced a few years earlier that the object of a judge's contempt order could be the lawyer. In 1964, Calamia had been prevented from questioning potential jurors by Judge Hughes during the "la migra" Clanahan trial. Just in case, Calamia had in hand a copy of a 1962 U.S. Supreme Court opinion where an attorney sought to preserve arguments for appeal. The high court stated:

> The arguments of a lawyer in presenting his client's case strenuously and persistently cannot amount to a contempt of court so long as the lawyer does not in some way create an obstruction which blocks the judge in the performance of his judicial duty. The petitioner created no such obstacle here.
>
> While we appreciate the necessity for a judge to have the power to protect himself from actual obstruction in the courtroom, or even from conduct so near to the court as actually to obstruct justice, it is also essential to a fair administration of justice that lawyers be able to make honest good-faith efforts to present their clients' cases. An independent judiciary and a vigorous, independent bar are both indispensable parts of our system of justice. *In Re McConnell*, 370 U.S. 230, 236, 82 S.Ct. 1288, 8 L.Ed.2d 434 (1962).

Strict decorum was a must with El Paso's U.S. district judges Suttle and Guinn[7] and continuing with Judge John Wood (1916–1979)[8] who succeeded Suttle in 1970. Wood shared the El Paso federal court docket with Guinn but maintained residency in San Antonio. Both Wood and Guinn were known for an expedient handling of the docket. In one year, Wood disposed of some seven hundred El Paso cases, many of them drug trafficking charges. Wood soon came to be known in legal circles as "Maximum John" as he often handed out the maximum allowable sentence to drug traffickers. Wood's tenure was cut short in 1979 by a bullet from a "hit man" hired by an El Pasoan awaiting trial on drug trafficking charges. In 1968, however, an adversarial relationship had developed between the federal court and some of the local bar.

El Paso's fourth-floor courtroom was every bit as large and regal in appearance as visiting Judge Hughes once remarked when presiding in a case in El Paso. She was used to small facilities in the crowded Dallas federal courthouse. Evidence of this was that, much later, the blue drapes in her Dallas courtroom made a perfect fit in El Paso's small U.S. commissioner's hearing room. A second courtroom was constructed for Judge Guinn on the first floor. The rules were strict. All in the courtroom—officers, jurors and spectators (except defendants)—had to dress appropriately. Men were required to wear a coat and tie; women wore a dress or a skirt, blouse and coat). There would be no photography or tape recording. Silence was demanded, and disturbances were not tolerated. All had to rise when the judge entered the courtroom. Defendants and their attorneys were to be prompt. Judge Suttle went further. He ordered the press to remain behind the courtroom railing. He prohibited lawyers from making extrajudicial remarks to the press. Suttle's order came before the start of a fifteen-defendant bank robbery, bank burglary and prostitution conspiracy case were transferred to El Paso due to excessive publicity in central Texas. Suttle's publicity order became the standard for the Western District of Texas.[9] Similar rules applied in state court.

It was in this climate that a thirty-year-old El Paso man, called to jury duty in sixty-fifth District Court, refused to wear a coat in Judge Cunningham's courtroom. The news quickly spread in the El Paso county courthouse. Reporters in the *El Paso Times* and the *El Paso Herald Post* newsrooms almost dismissed the rumors as an April Fools' Day joke. Not so. In late March 1968, Bobby Spencer, owner of a gasoline station, told Judge Cunningham that he only wore a coat and tie at weddings and funerals. Judge Cunningham held him in contempt and sentenced him to three days in jail and a $100 fine. Spencer asked his attorney, Sam Paxson, to fight the contempt charge. However, Spencer's action was a direct disobedience of a judge's order and the state court rules, like those in federal court, allowed for summary judgment. Hence, an appeal to the Texas Supreme Court was the next step. Paxson asked Calamia to join him in developing and presenting the appeal. Spencer refused to pay the fine and remained behind bars after serving the three-day sentence. Wearing inmate coveralls, he was now in the company of accused bank robbers, rapists, narcotic addicts and burglars. An appeal would not have a chance in the higher courts.[10]

Tests of courtroom decorum were being repeated in other parts of the country. In one case involving the State of Washington's unlawful assembly law, the Ninth Circuit Court of Appeals upheld a contempt judgment against a defendant who refused to rise as the judge entered the courtroom. The defendant went limp and lay prostrate on the floor when ordered to approach the bench. The appellate court considered this behavior to be an obstruction of justice that occurred in the presence of the judge (*Comstock v. United States*, 419 F.2d 1128 [9th Cir. 1969]). The Seventh Circuit considered a similar issue (*United States ex rel. Robson v. Malone*, 412 F.2d 848 [7th Cir. 1969]). There, a teacher and a student had been taken into custody by the U.S. marshal when they refused to rise in open court. They were summarily sentenced later that day. The appellate court found that while the refusal to stand was an intentional disapproval of the administration of justice, there was no evidence of a disturbance. The court vacated their sentences because removing the defendants from the courtroom had been sufficient to maintain appropriate decorum.

In 1969, Calamia had a new partner, John Fashing, whom Calamia had met several years earlier while arguing a case before the Texas Court of Criminal Appeals in Austin. Fashing was a law clerk for Chief Justice Morrison. "I was impressed," Calamia recalls. "Justice Morrison highly recommended Fashing. Only problem was that he was in the Army. I told him I would hold a position open until he was discharged." It was a good choice for Calamia. Like Calamia, Fashing was a dedicated researcher and consummate brief writer. About one year after the coatless juror case, Calamia became involved in still another contempt case, this time involving El Paso attorney Richard T. Marshall. Marshall was a graduate of Cornell University with a law degree from Yale Law School, and a leading figure in El Paso's chapters of the American Trial Lawyers Association (ATLA) and the American Civil Liberties Union (ACLU). ATLA began in 1946 as an association of plaintiff's attorneys in workers' compensation cases and expanded to focus on justice and fairness for injured persons. The ACLU was founded in 1920 as an impartial defender of civil liberties. In 1969, the ACLU was not quite the darling of a law-and-order minded mainstream America. This was the organization that had defended John T. Scopes in the Tennessee monkey trial of 1925. It had defended against adverse government actions on behalf of unions, communists, Japanese Americans, African Americans and other marginalized segments of society. Many conservatives were troubled by the ACLU's involvement in landmark victories concerning a defendant's rights. The most controversial was the Supreme Court ruling in *Miranda v. Arizona* (384 U.S. 436, 86 S.Ct. 1602, 16 L.Ed.2d 694 [1966]) was still in the minds of many El Pasoans.

Marshall was defending Leopoldo Morales, an inhalation therapist at Hotel Dieu Hospital charged with quadruple murder. He had been convicted of the shooting death of an El Paso couple and the knifing death of their landlords. Morales also shot at a third person in the apartment building who escaped and testified as an eyewitness. Morales's death sentence was the first capital murder conviction in El Paso since the taxi driver torching case. The murders occurred while the nation was still in shock from the "born to raise hell" attitude of mass murderer Richard Speck, who in July 1996 had killed eight student nurses in a mad spree at a Chicago hospital.[11] In the Morales case, Marshall unsuccessfully worked at an insanity defense with the testimony of the same psychiatrist[12] who described Speck's "madonna-whore complex" in the Chicago trial. Marshall unsuccessfully appealed to the Texas

Court of Criminal Appeals. The Morales appeal moved through the federal courts and was eventually bundled with a number of death sentences cases, including Speck's, in two landmark Supreme Court decisions. The first established that capital punishment objectors could not be systematically excluded from a capital punishment case (*Witherspoon v. Illinois*, 391 U.S. 510, 88 S.Ct. 1770, 20 L.Ed.2d776 [1968]). The second declared the death penalty to be cruel and unusual punishment (*Furman v. Georgia*, 408 U.S. 238, 92 S.Ct. 2726, 33 L.Ed.2d 346 [1972]). As a result Morales's was resentenced to life in prison. Now for Marshall's contempt case before Judge Guinn.

On May 14, 1969, Marshall's client, Virginia Silva Palacios, was scheduled to appear before Judge Guinn at 12:30 p.m. for a habeas corpus hearing. Marshall was representing the sixteen-year-old defendant on immigration charges following an adverse administrative deportation hearing. For Marshall, this case had the potential for setting precedent. The case was referred to Marshall by Jack Wasserman, a prominent Washington immigration attorney and a former judge of the Board of Immigration Appeals. Wasserman believed that a favorable outcome would support a pending case in which he was representing important Washington figures. Marshall thought that testimony by a novice midwife who delivered the defendant in the United States would support a claim of unlawful detention of a U.S. citizen. Palacios was born to the wife of a Mexican "bracero" in Fabens, Texas, southeast of El Paso. She was then baptized in a Catholic church in Fabens.

On the day of the hearing, the defendant and her mother told Marshall that the midwife witness, who lived in Mexico, was ill and could not testify. Marshall hesitated to seek a continuance until he could verify that the witness really was ill. He called Guinn's secretary to request a delay until 2 p.m., on the assumption he could locate the witness some forty miles away in a Mexican rural town across from Fabens. He took the chore upon himself, as he could not find another Spanish-speaking attorney on short notice. Faced with this dilemma, Marshall again called the judge's secretary with a request that he be allowed to send another attorney, John Fashing, while he completed his search for the witness in Mexico. Marshall assumed that his request had been granted. He had success in verifying that the witness was too ill to testify. He was not so successful with Judge Guinn.

Back in El Paso, Fashing showed up before Judge Guinn as Marshall's associate counsel. Following government testimony and cross-examination, Fashing moved to delay the trial until 2 p.m., the time Marshall was expected to return. Observing that Marshall was not present, Judge Guinn found him guilty of contempt and assessed a $50 fine. Guinn then withdrew the summary contempt judgment and gave Marshall an opportunity for a show-cause hearing. This was not the first time that Guinn had held Marshall in contempt for being a few seconds late. In this case, Marshall considered that he had done the right thing for his client and retained Calamia to defend him. Judge Guinn affirmed his ruling but did not specify the nature of his action,[13] other than to stay payment of the fine while Marshall appealed.

It was déjà vu for Calamia. As in the contempt conviction of Harvey Matusow, a federal judge had again summarily convicted a person for contempt without regard to due process. A finding of summary contempt required (1) the action to occur in or near the presence of the judge; and (2) the judge to certify findings of facts and conclusions of law. Contemptuous conduct occurring outside the presence of the judge required due process. Calamia thought there was no contempt at all. "The judge can only punish for misbehavior in the court's presence, misbehavior of a court officer and disobedience of a court order. None of these applied."[14]

Marshall strongly believed that his appeal had merit when viewed through the prism of social unrest and a culture bent on challenging the rules of decorum. In early 1970 at an ATLA meeting, Marshall got a glimpse of a lawyer who, like Marshall, had a contempt case pending. William Kunstler and the Chicago 8 defendants he represented in the Chicago riot trials had been convicted of contempt and had to be chained and gagged by order of U.S. district judge Julius Hoffman.[15] Kunstler openly accused the trial judge of carrying out an injustice. Marshall was astonished to see Kunstler's followers, dressed in torn and colorful clothing, sitting on the floor in back of the conference room puffing marijuana cigarettes while their leader spoke. Kunstler finished his talk, and his followers left with him. When the smoke had cleared, Marshall spoke on his contempt case, expressing confidence that both his and Kunstler's contempt judgments would be reversed.[16]

On February 26, 1970, the Fifth Circuit ruled that Marshall's "conduct fell far short of contempt" (*In the Matter of Marshall*, 423 F.2d 1130 [5th Cir. 1970]). The panel reversed and ordered the proceedings against Marshall be dismissed. "[I]n contempt cases against lawyers the evidence must be carefully scrutinized in order to ensure that there is no undue interference with the attorney-client relationship" (*Id*). Citing *Parmelee Transportation Co. v. Keeshin* (294 F.2d 310, 313 [7th Cir. 1961]), the court warned that contempt powers should be used "sparingly and only when it is clearly demonstrated that the respondent's conduct is contumacious and tends to bring the administration of justice into disrepute." Here, the facts failed to support Judge Guinn's finding that Marshall's absence was prompted by disrespect for the court. On the contrary, Marshall "acted from concern for the rights of his client and with due respect for the court." There would be more contempt cases in Calamia's legal career, but he did not expect to be the one in Marshall's position before Judge Guinn.

At a typical Friday afternoon docket call, Judge Guinn required lawyers subject to appointment to represent indigent defendants to appear promptly at 1:30 p.m. The proceedings would continue until the list of indigent defendants ran out. Appointed lawyers and their new clients were then to meet to work out a defense strategy, when necessary, in a holding area secured by U.S. marshals adjacent to the courtroom. Some defendants were docile, but others looked at the attorneys wearing coats and ties with distrust. Calamia recalled a defendant's remark when he was in the holding area surrounded by several baddies, "Cuidado. El abogado es un espía." Alerted that he was seen as a spy, Calamia conversed with them in "caló," a variation of Spanish spoken in south El Paso, and eventually gained the trust of his indigent client.

One Friday afternoon, Judge Guinn was ready to begin promptly at 1:30 p.m. Calamia had arrived five minutes early. When Calamia's case was called, Judge Guinn announced, "You're not here on time. You are in contempt." For the record, Calamia asked the bailiff to verify the time by calling the telephone company's time and temperature number. The bailiff replied, "1:30." "You're cutting me too close," the judge stated. "I'm fining you $500." Calamia asked for a hearing, but that would be unnecessary. Judge Guinn had changed his mind. One week later, the clock was no longer on the courtroom wall.

FERNÁNDEZ AND THE FIFTH: NO SILVER PLATTER FOR THE FEDERAL TAXMAN

Too often in Calamia's early career, he had fought against practices in which expediency in prosecution trumped the rights of a defendant, particularly in state courts. Much had changed. The courts now avoided using evidence obtained by law enforcement officials in Juárez, where confessions induced by torture were a common practice. The federal rules of evidence and Justice Department guidance were quite specific when it came to protecting the rights of an accused. The state courts lagged somewhat behind, as it was still unsettled whether the entire Bill of Rights extended to the states by virtue of the Fourteenth Amendment's due process clause. It was not unusual for federal jurisdictions to accept evidence obtained by the state under less strict practices. One might say the more easily obtained evidence was handed to the federal government on a "silver platter." Supreme Court rulings would eventually bring some degree of parity in obtaining and using evidence in the dual court system; but the year was 1968 and in one of Calamia's cases, the evidence was disclosed nearly six years before.

The big question in Calamia's mind was the constitutionality of the federal government's evidence. The federal taxman was convinced that an El Paso doctor understated his income over a two-year period. The Internal Revenue Service (IRS) would not likely have had this suspicion had it not been for the cooperation of the doctor's wife six years earlier. The issue arose during the couple's contentious divorce proceedings in state court. Calamia knew all too well how many criminal cases began with accusations between a feuding couple. In his view, the government's evidence against his client was illegally obtained by collusion with his angry spouse. He decided that the information was compelled and was thus inadmissible. In Calamia's vernacular, the Fifth Amendment protects a person from being compelled to give incriminatory information to the "enforcer." The right against self-incrimination was one that continued to be difficult for lawmen and the public to fully embrace.[1]

A few years before, the IRS might have gotten away with using incriminating evidence compelled in a state jurisdiction. In 1962, the Fifth Amendment did not necessarily apply to state criminal jurisprudence. James Madison, the Father of the Constitution, would very much have wanted a specific application for both civil and criminal cases, but it was not to be when the Bill of Rights was ratified.[2] The authors of the Fourteenth Amendment may have wanted to extend the Bill of Rights to the states, but this intent was not clear when the Amendment was ratified in 1868. Nearly forty years later the Supreme Court refused to apply the Fifth Amendment's protection against self-incrimination where a defendant refused to answer questions in state court for fear of possible incrimination under federal law *Jack v. Kansas* (199 U.S. 372 26 S.Ct. 73, 50 L.Ed. 234 [1905]). In 1958, the Supreme Court affirmed a conviction using compelled evidence and again clarified that the Fifth Amendment protection limited only the powers of the federal government and not those of the states (*Knapp v. Schweitzer*, 357 U.S. 371, 78 S.Ct. 1302, 2 L.Ed.2d 1393 [1958]).[3] Clearly in 1962, Calamia's client, caught in the all the ugliness of a divorce proceeding, had little choice but to turn over professional business records that would surely incriminate him in federal court.

It was a different story in 1968. Calamia was now armed with two 1964 Supreme Court decisions that looked at the application of the Fifth Amendment differently. In *Malloy v. Hogan* (378 U.S. 1, 84 S.Ct. 1489, 12 L.Ed.2d 653 [1964]), the court held that the due process of law provision of the Fourteenth Amendment extended the privilege against self-incrimination to the states. In a case decided the same day, the Supreme Court went further, holding that "there is no continuing legal vitality to, or historical justification for, the rule that one jurisdiction within our federal structure may compel a witness to give testimony which could be used to convict him of a crime in another jurisdiction" (*Murphy v. Waterfront Com. of New York Harbor*, 378 U.S. 52, 77, 84 S.Ct. 1594, 12 L.Ed.2d 678 [1964]), *overruling United States v. Murdock*, 284 U.S. 141, 52 S.Ct. 63, 76 L.Ed. 210 [1931]).

To America's law-and-order movement in the late 1960s, this was just one more example of judicial activism by the Warren Court. Many Americans feared that such decisions were giving unreasonable defensive tools to the criminal element while hampering police and prosecutors. They saw the rise in crime and violent demonstrations as a product of a soft judiciary and slick defense attorneys. They had read about many a defendant taking the Fifth when questioned throughout the 1950s crusade against communism and the 1960s crusade against organized crime. Indeed Congress had been pressed to pass anticrime legislation to battle crime on the streets, organized crime and the growing drug problem.[4] To Calamia, however, it was about a long overdue evenhanded application of the Bill of Rights to all Americans. "These are protections against actions by the enforcer based on the presumption that an accused is innocent until otherwise proven guilty," Calamia stressed some forty years later. He warned, "Erosion of these rights can lead to tyranny. Tyranny abides with guile and deceit." On the other hand there is freedom, "which abides with truth and honor."

Now that the Fifth Amendment applied in state court, Calamia was prepared to assert that the evidence compelled from his client should be excluded under the Fourth Amendment protection against unreasonable searches and seizures. Even before his defendant's 1962 divorce proceedings had started the ball rolling in this tax evasion case, the Supreme Court had ruled that "all evidence obtained by seizures in violation of the Federal Constitution is inadmissible in a criminal trial in a state court" (*Mapp v. Ohio*, 367 U.S. 643, 81 S.Ct. 1684, 6 L.Ed.2d 1081 [1961]). That ruling had overturned what had been known as the Silver Platter Doctrine. In Justice Frankfurter's words: "The crux of that doctrine is that a search is a search by a federal official if he had a hand in it; it is not a search by a federal official if evidence secured by state authorities is turned over to the federal authorities on a silver platter" (*Lustig v. United States,* 338 U.S. 74, 69 S.Ct. 1372, 93 L.Ed. 1819 [1949]). With these recent Supreme Court decisions in hand, Calamia and Fashing were now at work in defense of El Paso physician Carlos A. Fernández.

Dr. Fernández was indicted by a federal grand jury in March 1968 on charges[5] that the income he reported for the 1961 and 1962 tax years was substantially less than what he earned in those years. At that time, Dr. Fernández approached Calamia with hesitancy considering his discussions with Calamia over his Fifth Amendment rights on a couple of occasions during his divorce proceedings six years before. Mary Guinn, the attorney representing Mrs. Fernández, obtained a subpoena ordering production of the doctor's professional business receipts for 1961. Dr. Fernández considered asserting the Fifth Amendment, but Calamia told him that he could not refuse to give evidence in state court even though it might incriminate him in a federal prosecution. Dr. Fernández complied but soon he dismissed the lawsuit and the books were returned to him, apparently without examination.

Later in 1962, Dr. Fernández again filed for divorce and he received another subpoena for the production of professional records. Once again, Calamia thought about the bigger picture and poured over the Supreme Court cases concerning a person's Fifth Amendment protections against "the enforcer's" actions. He saw the direction that the Warren Court was headed in interpreting the Fourteenth Amendment's "due process" and "equal protection" clauses. In this changing judicial thinking, Calamia's credo continued to be "make a record" even if the trial judge denies an objection or motion. In his experience, Calamia had learned to raise constitutional theory at all phases of a criminal case. During the adversarial divorce proceedings before Judge Cunningham, Calamia objected to the release of incriminating information. In his duty to defend his client, Calamia asserted that Dr. Fernández was invoking his right to protect his private papers. He insisted that if the books were to be shown to the government, the government should first have a federal warrant. It appeared that the doctor kept two sets of business records in what Calamia, Ms. Guinn and Judge Cunningham recognized as a potential tax evasion case.

Calamia recalled that Ms. Guinn advanced a theory that in a divorce proceeding, the community needed a receiver to whom Dr. Fernández should provide all information, including the books. Calamia protested that this was tantamount to the State of Texas obtaining information for use by the government without a federal search warrant. "Give me some tools," Judge Cunningham told Ms. Guinn. Calamia had made the point that Dr. Fernández was not waiving his Fifth Amendment protection. While not forcing Dr. Fernández to testify concerning the business receipts, Judge Cunningham required him to turn over the books and allow Ms. Guinn to make copies of the information. The record showed that Dr. Fernández did not voluntarily turn over the books. Calamia argued that the books were seized contrary to his client's Fourth Amendment protection against illegal search and seizure.

It was not long before the incriminating information got into the taxman's hands. An agent for the IRS testified that he went through state district court records and discovered the information. Apparently, a state court stenographer provided him the records. In July 1968, the government was ready to bring the case to trial before U.S. district judge Suttle. Calamia immediately sought to suppress the evidence. In a brief to the court, Calamia and Fashing argued that Mrs. Fernández violated the marital confidence between husband and wife in violation of the 4th and Fifth Amendments. The Supreme Court's decision in Murphy adopted an exclusionary rule:

> a state witness may not be compelled to give testimony which may be incriminating under federal law unless the compelled testimony and its fruits cannot be used in any manner by federal officials in connection with a criminal prosecution against him." (*Murphy v. Waterfront Com. of New York Harbor*, 378 U.S. 52, 79, 84 S.Ct. 1594, 12 L.Ed.2d 678 [1964]).

The government, represented by assistant U.S. attorney Caballero, recognized that *Murphy* was now the law, but argued (1) that *Murphy* did not apply retroactively, and (2) even if it did, that Dr. Fernández had waived his Fifth Amendment rights when he produced the information in the state divorce proceedings.

Judge Suttle listened intently at a November 1968 suppression hearing. Suttle had just completed his second year as El Paso's federal judge. He had established a reputation of being a studious jurist with an abiding respect for higher court precedents concerning defendants' rights regardless of the dislike by certain segments of El Paso, including in some law enforcement. At the close of arguments, Suttle took the matter under advisement.[6] Several months later, in April 1969, he granted the motion to suppress, concluding that Dr. Fernández had been compelled by state law to divulge the business records. Suttle concluded that because Dr. Fernández would not have produced the records if he could have invoked the Fifth Amendment, he did not intentionally abandon his right against self-incrimination. In his judgment, the *Murphy* decision established an exclusionary rule in those cases where testimony is compelled in a state court, which made the question of retroactivity moot.

With the principal evidence excluded, a team of Justice Department attorneys joined Caballero in the appeal under the Omnibus Crime and Safe Streets Act of 1968. This law was one of several passed by Congress in response to public outcry for law and order in view of increasing crime and civil disturbances. President Johnson's War on Crime Act provided funding and technical assistance to state jurisdictions and allowed the federal government to form partnerships with state and local governments to combat crime. It also allowed the use of court-ordered electronic surveillance for certain investigations. Finally, it allowed the government to appeal when a judge suppressed evidence considered to be substantial proof for an indictment.[7]

Judges Wisdom, Thornberry and Simpson heard the oral arguments in the Fifth Circuit's headquarters in New Orleans. Jimmy L. Tallant, of the Justice Department Criminal Section's Tax Division, recited the government's claim that Dr. Fernández had waived his Fifth Amendment privilege. Calamia countered that his client was compelled to turn over private documents to the government. At one point, the sound system's volume went up and with it Calamia's voice. Judge Wisdom stopped him and said, "Mr. Calamia. I want you to know that no one in this panel is hard of hearing." Calamia apologized, "I hope the Court will not hold this against my client." At the end of the day, the panel had narrowed the issues to one—whether Dr. Fernández's conduct in 1962 precluded him from asserting his Fifth Amendment privilege in the 1968 tax case.

The date was April 15, 1970, coincidentally the day when federal income tax returns are due to be filed. On this day, the Fifth Circuit ruled that Judge Suttle correctly decided that Dr. Fernández had been compelled to produce his income records without a waiver of his Fifth Amendment privilege. In short, the government could not use that information in its income tax prosecution. It did not appeal the case to the U.S. Supreme Court (*United States v. Fernández*, 424 F.2d 1291 [5th Cir. 1970]).

MUÑIZ AND HABEAS CORPUS: NO MEXICAN AMERICANS IN A GRAND JURY

The year was 1942. Samuel E. Muñiz, a Colorado native and an American citizen "of Mexican extraction,"[1] was described by some as small in stature and unassuming in mannerism. To others, he was a soldier with a bad reputation, but to a twenty-year-old El Paso woman and a Thirty-fourth District Court jury, Muñiz was a rapist. To Calamia, who met him twenty-five years later, Muñiz was a victim of discrimination, given the manner in which the jurors who convicted him were selected.

Muñiz found himself in El Paso courtesy of the U.S. Army. He was with the 691st Tank Destroyer Battalion. The United States had been at war in the Pacific and European theaters for seven months after the Japanese attack on Pearl Harbor. Things were not going too well for the Allies. The German Nazi forces had completed their occupation of France, pushed British forces out of Egypt and opened an eastern attack against the Soviet Union. The Japanese Imperialist forces had seized a number of islands in the Pacific Ocean and in Southeast Asia. It had been three months since the Japanese had captured Bataan in the Philippines after a three-month long valiant defense by American forces. The U.S. Navy had engaged the Japanese navy in the Coral Sea and the Midway Islands. Fear of Japanese attacks on the Pacific West Coast was heightened when a Japanese submarine shelled an oil refinery near Santa Barbara, California. Japanese forces occupied the outermost Aleutian Islands of Alaska. In this atmosphere, the United States began a mass evacuation of all people of Japanese ancestry from the Pacific Coast. Cooperation with Mexico and other Latin American republics was essential. The United States, under the Bracero Program,[2] would contract Mexican workers to alleviate the labor shortage in wartime America. The United States and Mexico would arrive at settlements on contentious issues and conclude defense agreements.[3]

In El Paso, the Fort Bliss military facility was a major training and deployment center for Army soldiers from all walks of life. In their time off, these young men would venture off post to the various entertainment venues at their disposal. There was also the lure of Juárez, Mexico, with its less restrictive bars, girly shows and legal prostitution. In El Paso there was the skating rink in Washington Park, the cafes, movie houses and bars in the downtown area. On their return to the post, the streetcars, taxis or private cars dropped off the soldiers at the main gate named after World War I hero and chaser of Mexico's Pancho Villa, General John J. Pershing. That main gate was located on high ground in an area known as Government Hill.

It was at this gate that a petite twenty-year-old widow dropped off an Army lieutenant from her car. The two were returning from a dinner party. When she was alone, the woman had trouble starting the car. It was not long before several G.I.'s offered to help by pushing her car downhill. It was during this downhill coast that Muñiz jumped on the running board and offered to help clutch-start the car. The woman refused at first. But when Muñiz persisted, she allowed him in the car. Muñiz drove the car away from the post and eventually headed for McKelligon Canyon, a canyon boxed in on the eastern side of the Franklin Mountains that transect El Paso. It was a popular place for daytime family picnics and a nighttime refuge for dating couples. The woman said that, once in the canyon, Muñiz beat her and threatened to kill her unless she had sex with him. Muñiz claimed the sex was consensual.

The woman was light of skin with blue eyes and dark hair. Muñiz was dark of skin and of Mexican extraction. He was promptly arrested and booked into the El Paso jail. Five days later, District Attorney Roy Jackson (1891–1955) presented the case to the grand jury. Muñiz was charged with rape. Jackson had been in office nine years. He moved to El Paso from his native Chillicothe, Texas, via Pecos, Texas after he earned his law degree from the University of Texas in 1922. Judge Howe of the Thirty-fourth District Court appointed El Paso attorney Joseph Roybal to defend Muñiz.

In less than ninety days, Muñiz went to trial. The trial was front-page news in El Paso's evening paper and inside page news in the morning paper. Other news stories told of Congressman Thomason's support for a bill that would outlaw the poll-tax. There was a front-page story about a mob that lynched two young black men after storming the Meridian, Mississippi jailhouse. The youths had been convicted of attempting to rape a white woman. In Europe, the Soviet army was repelling Nazi forces and in the Pacific the Japanese Navy laid siege to Guadalcanal. Gas was being rationed and El Paso was undergoing a milk shortage. Downtown movie theaters a short distance from El Paso's county courthouse advertised "The New York Adventures of Tarzan" and John Wayne's "Flying Tigers."[4]

At the trial, the alleged rape victim identified Muñiz as her attacker and retold the story of her drive to McKelligon Canyon and the attack. She insisted that Muñiz hit her and that she resisted until she was exhausted. Muñiz took the stand and testified that the woman "was a willing partner in love-making in the canyon and at a second time near Fort Bliss." Muñiz wore his military uniform and told of his family life, that of being the only boy in a family of sixteen girls. On cross-examination, Muñiz admitted he had a petty theft conviction and that he had been investigated by military police about an attempted attack on another woman. Military police testified that the defendant had a reputation of bad conduct toward women. Jackson told the jury, composed of middle-aged non-Hispanic-surnamed men, "to inflict severe punishment" on Muñiz. It took less than fifteen minutes for the jury to find Muñiz guilty and to assess a twenty-year sentence.[5]

Now behind bars, Muñiz felt he had been railroaded. His attorney sought a new trial. Judge Howe overruled the motion. Roybal gave notice of appeal. Under the law at the time, a defendant was allowed sixty days to file bills of exception. However, in Muñiz's case, these bills were not filed until eighty days later, on January 1943. The State contested the bills of exception before the Texas Court of Criminal Appeals. Roybal had construed, as allowable extensions, the time needed to prepare the statement of facts and the transcript. In its April 1943 ruling, the court held that deadlines were mandates. The judges narrowed the question to sufficiency of the evidence and observed that a dispute over the facts was a matter for the jury to determine. The court affirmed the judgment, concluding that the facts "abundantly supported not only the jury's finding of guilt but also the punishment assessed" (*Muñiz v. State*, 170 S.W.2d 767 [Tex.Cr.App. 1943]).[6]

Muñiz's lawyers did not raise a question of discrimination, although in other cases in El Paso and Hudspeth Counties, Roybal had filed motions to quash grand jury indictments based on systematic exclusion of American citizens of Mexican extraction. It would take another twenty-five years before that very issue would be raised by Joe Calamia. In his mind, the lawmen, prosecutors and the courts too often favored expediency over the rights of the accused, particularly when the accused was an American of Mexican extraction.

Americans of Mexican extraction living in Texas in 1942 were generally in friendly confines in the selected urban areas and in small farming communities near the Mexican border. As these individuals traveled further inland, some of them were subjected to discrimination in a racially segregated Texas. There were American citizens who were either born in the United States or naturalized former Mexican citizens. There were Mexican immigrants with legal permanent resident status. Others were here under guest workers programs, such as the U.S.-Mexico Bracero Program. In 1943, the level of discrimination was so high that the Mexican government refused to allow Braceros to work in Texas. This problem was so embarrassingly prevalent that the Roosevelt administration was forced into coaxing the State of Texas to establish a good neighbor policy to improve Anglo-Hispanic relations. Even more embarrassing was the fact that it took wartime fascist literature distributed in Latin America revealing photographs of signs in Texas restaurant windows proclaiming "No Mexicans" to bring this reality to Washington.[7]

In El Paso, Americans of Mexican extraction found the neighborhoods south of the railroad tracks to be a friendlier place to live. In large part, the residents there were unskilled and semiskilled workers. There, they talked in Spanish and developed a culture that was neither totally Mexican nor totally American. Still, there were several Hispanic families that made their homes north of the railroad tracks. These were small business owners, professionals and others who were more acculturated into mainstream America. The Spanish-surnamed represented about 46 percent of El Paso county's 131,000 residents in 1940. Their economic and political clout was far less proportional. Texas required that its resident citizens pay a poll-tax that resulted in a voting population that was not reflective of the city's total population. Accordingly, Americans of Mexican extraction were disenfranchised from the voting process.

Hispanics were also underrepresented among officers in El Paso's halls of justice. There were three Spanish-surnamed attorneys: one generally represented the Mexican consulate, another dealt with real estate and the third did not speak Spanish. None of the judges or prosecutors was Hispanic. Hispanics were also underrepresented in the jury selection system. Jurors were selected from a list of registered voters who had paid their poll-tax. In 1940, this resulted in structural discrimination given that of the 12,749 poll-tax holders, only 1,873 had Spanish surnames. This lack of representation in El Paso's criminal justice system may have been apparent to individuals like Muñiz. But his court-appointed lawyer in the appeal to the Texas Court of Criminal Appeals overlooked this, relying only on the question of disputed testimony, an argument that the appellate court rejected.

Muñiz served part of his twenty-year term in the state penitentiary in Huntsville. He was released on parole several times. Before long, he violated the terms of his parole. Soon, twenty-five years had passed since his conviction, and he was again behind bars. Muñiz continued to insist that he was innocent. He sought release time and again, but each time his written petitions were denied. Finally in 1967, his petition came before Thirty-fourth District Judge Ward. The times, the law and the courtroom actors had changed. Muñiz had been convicted two generations ago. Ward had replaced Judge Jackson, who as district attorney had prosecuted Muñiz in 1942. In 1968, the district attorney was University of Texas law school graduate Barton Boling. Then, there was Joe Calamia, who by that time had become well known among the Hispanics in jailhouse circles as "*el rit abogado.*" Calamia did not mind the recognition by those in the slammer as a lawyer who had met with success in habeas corpus cases. More importantly, Calamia took this recognition as a challenge to seek justice for the underdog even if it meant working for free as a court-appointed lawyer.

At the same time, a number of landmark rulings had extended civil rights to minority populations. A comprehensive civil rights law had been passed.[8] While the Sixth Amendment did not address representation for indigents, the U.S. Supreme Court had required the appointment of counsel for indigents accused of a federal crime since 1942 (*Johnson v. Zerbst*, 304 U.S. 458, 58 S.Ct. 1019, 82 L.Ed. 1461 [1942]). But the courts had not required the states to adhere to the rule. That matter was left to the legislature of each individual state (*Betts v. Brady*, 316 U.S. 455, 62 S.Ct. 1252, 86 L.Ed. 1595 [1942]). By 1963, much had changed. That year, the Warren Court mandated court appointed counsel for those who could not afford one (*Gideon v. Wainwright*, 372 U.S. 335, 83 S.Ct. 792, 9 L.Ed.2d 799 [1963]). In deciding *Gideon*, the court overruled *Betts* and its progeny.

The *Gideon* ruling, much to the dislike of strict constructionists and law-and-order conservatives, prompted Congress to pass the Criminal Justice Act of 1964[9] which required the federal courts to establish a plan for adequate representation of indigent defendants. On the surface, the *Gideon* ruling should not have been a problem in Texas. Since its inception as a republic in 1936, the Texas Constitution had guaranteed the right to counsel. As early as 1857, the Texas Code of Criminal Procedure required appointed counsel for indigents. The issue that evolved over the years involved the manner in which this right was applied in Texas. A principal question touched on a defendant's ignorance of this right, a matter that the Warren Court dealt with in *Escobedo v. Illinois* (378 U.S. 478, 84 S.Ct. 1758, 12 L.Ed.2d 977 [1964]) and in *Miranda v. Arizona* (384 U.S. 436, 86 S.Ct. 1602, 16 L.Ed.2d 694 [1966]).

To ensure that Muñiz had effective assistance of counsel, Judge Ward appointed Calamia to review Muñiz's habeas petition. To Calamia, the question over effective assistance of appointed counsel was still unsettled because of a residual concern that had yet to be addressed. He had long awaited a case that would provide an opportunity for overturning some inequities he had seen in the criminal justice system. Calamia suspected that Judge Ward also understood that there was a problem in the jury selection system, but this would not be a matter that would be resolved in the state courts. Calamia recalled Muñiz's appearance when meeting his new client in 1967. "He was a broken man. He was bitter that the 1942 jury did not believe his testimony that the sex was consensual. He complained about the treatment of prisoners in the Huntsville penitentiary and his assignment to shave the legs of death row inmates before they were executed in the electric chair."[10]

The fact that Muñiz was a Mexican-American soldier at the time of his conviction compelled Calamia to delve into the 1942 criminal justice system in as much depth as possible. Calamia recalled his own experiences when he returned from the Navy to continue his college education. There were arrests that he witnessed while working as a taxi driver, often in the heavy Hispanic areas south of the railroad tracks. He saw arrests that appeared to be based on physical appearances, perceived reputations, intuition and just plain being at the wrong place at the wrong time. He had a near-police beating, an experience that afforded him the opportunity to mingle with the poor and undereducated Hispanics who had little or no knowledge of the constitutional rights of the accused. He saw lawmen, prosecutors and judges that appeared to be answerable, not to their oath to protect and defend the Constitution of the United States, but only to the cultural and social norms of a non-Hispanic majority that wielded the political and economic power in El Paso. More than twenty years later, Muñiz presented

Calamia with an opportunity to investigate the El Paso criminal justice system that may have caused this man undue suffering.

Calamia examined Muñiz's petition. Muñiz continued to contend that the sexual encounter was consensual. Apparently, Muñiz thought that the more recent court decisions in this new era of tolerance would result in a reversal of his conviction. On the other hand, "*el rit abogado*" Calamia had seen many a petition denied on procedural grounds. He needed something of more substance. A new approach was necessary. But the first question to resolve was whether Judge Ward would allow a modification of Muñiz's petition.[11]

Calamia considered that a judge had a number of inherent powers. "There is a minimum authority and there are limits," Calamia recalled some forty years later. "Then there is an area between these in which a judge can exercise those inherent powers." With this in mind, Calamia approached Judge Ward for permission to amend the habeas corpus petition. To Calamia's surprise Judge Ward allowed it. This was a period in which state judges were closely following *Gideon* and were aware of the looming question of effective assistance of counsel.

In his review of the twenty-five-year-old trial records, Calamia studied the prosecutor's arguments and presentation of evidence. The arguments seemed to be intent on inflaming the emotions of jurors and thus were improper. This would be one ground for amending the petition. At the same time, Calamia observed that there was an absence of Spanish-surnamed persons serving on the jury that convicted Muñiz. He recalled, "In my early years in trials, I would see very few Mexican Americans in the petit juries, even though they accounted for nearly half of the population. I had serious concerns about the manner in which Texas selected its grand juries. The system allowed for the people in power to assure that these jurors were handpicked. It was a system open to discrimination against Mexican Americans." The same problem existed with the petit jury system. In 1942, jurors were selected from panels made up of poll-tax holders selected by lottery. Inherently, the jury that convicted Muñiz did not have any Hispanic-surnamed members.

In 1942, the Texas grand jury selection system, charged with presenting the formal charges, was a carefully crafted selection process. The importance of a grand jury cannot be overstated. The Constitution guarantees that no person can be held answerable to a serious criminal charge unless the charge is made by a grand jury. This guarantee is rooted in English law as a safeguard against unwarranted criminal prosecution and as a means for citizens to investigate a number of matters, including conditions in the county and the misconduct of an individual. The selection process began with the appointment by the Thirty-fourth District Judge of at least three, and not more than five, qualified El Paso county residents to form a grand jury commission. The judge then instructed the commissioners to select sixteen qualified county residents for consideration as grand jurors. In turn, the judge tested the qualifications of the persons on the list and empanelled twelve of them as a grand jury. To qualify, the juror had to be a resident and freeholder of the county on the county's poll-tax holder's list. The juror could not have a criminal record. And the juror had to be able to read and write the English language, be of sound mind and of good moral character. That jury would serve for a specific term. In 1942, there were four grand jury terms.

Calamia examined the makeup of the grand jury that indicted Muñiz less than ninety days before his conviction. He found that there were no persons with Spanish surnames on that grand jury or on the grand jury commission that named that grand jury. There seemed to be a similar pattern over a ten-year period. Calamia also entertained the hunch that this practice was widespread throughout Texas. It was certainly material if the system had lent itself to exclusion of certain segments of society.

Calamia's next step was to compile a ten-year jury composition record along with statistics of several populations broken down by Spanish surnames. The population statistics would include overall population, poll-tax holders, property owners and public school enrollment. These data were to be presented in a manner that would show a pattern of systematic exclusion of Mexican Americans as jury commissioners, grand jurors and petit jurors in El Paso county.

This would be consistent with the principle of proportionate distribution, a principle established by the courts in numerous cases of systematic exclusion of blacks. As a sign of the changing times, District Attorney Boling agreed to stipulate to the statistical comparisons presented by Calamia and Fashing.

Next, Calamia and Fashing researched the law to ensure that Mexican Americans constituted a separately identifiable ethnic group in the county. They found a solid case in a 1954 Supreme Court decision holding that the systematic exclusion of persons of Mexican descent from serving as jurors in Jackson County, Texas, violated a defendant's equal protection of the laws guaranteed in the Fourteenth Amendment (*Hernández v. Texas*, 347 U.S. 475, 74 S.Ct. 667, 98 L.Ed. 866 [1954]). Still, Calamia recognized that this was not always the case. Even though the Supreme Court, more than one-half century before, had made a similar ruling in *Carter v. Texas* (177 U.S. 442, 20 S.Ct. 687, 44 L.Ed. 839, [1900]) concerning the "exclusion of Negros," Texas courts had a different view. They held that the Fourteenth Amendment contemplated only two classes, white and Negro and observed that:

> Mexicans are white people, and are entitled at the hands of the state to all the rights, privileges and immunities guaranteed under the Fourteenth Amendment. So long as they are so treated, the guarantee of equal protection has been accorded to them (*Hernández v. State*, 251 S.W.2d 531, 536 [Tex.Cr.App. 1952]).

The U.S. Supreme Court reversed (*Hernández v. Texas* 347 U.S. 475, 74 S.Ct. 667, 98 L.Ed. 866 [1954]). Chief Justice Warren observed that community norms from time to time might define other groups that need the aid of the courts to secure equal treatment under the laws. In support of identifying those citizens of Mexican descent as a separate class, the justices considered testimony by responsible citizens that distinguished between "white" and "Mexican." They heard instances of segregation of children of Mexican descent. They heard of instances of "No Mexicans Served" signs in that community's restaurant and courthouse toilets marked: "Colored Men" and "Hombres Aquí."

Times had indeed changed in El Paso in 1967. District Attorney Boling was quick to stipulate that Muñiz "was and is a member of an ethnic group known as American Citizens of Mexican Extraction." Judge Ward convened a plenary hearing. The statistical information presented by Calamia and Fashing was accepted but the prosecutor and Calamia had different interpretations. The State argued that Muñiz's lawyers in 1942 knew and understood criminal procedure concerning jury selection and did not raise a discrimination issue. Calamia argued that Muñiz only had a seventh-grade education and was not aware that he had any right to contest "the grand jury, the special venire jury panel, or the petit jury that tried him." The State observed that Muñiz's attorney had on other occasions filed motions to quash indictments and petit jury panels on claims of systematic exclusion of American citizens of Mexican extraction. The State claimed that Muñiz was informed of these options but possibly chose to decline. Calamia argued that the record did not document that this ever took place.

The State contended that the grand jury commissioners had been instructed by Judge Howe to not exclude persons from grand jury service based on race, creed or color. Calamia contested this point by referring to the Texas grand jury selection procedure. He noted that under the law, it was only up to the trial court to pass on the qualifications and excuses of persons who appear on grand jury lists and on petit jury service lists. The State defended the practice of using a jury wheel with names of individuals from a list of poll-tax holders as a means to form petit jury panels. The State defended the grand jury selection process as one intended not to exclude anyone on the basis of race, creed or color.

The State observed that in various years, a Spanish surname appeared among grand commissioners and grand jury panels in the ten years of statistical information gathered by Calamia and Fashing. Calamia countered that during this statistical period (sixty-two grand jury terms and 186 jury commissioners), it was always the same Spanish-surnamed South El Paso businessmen that served as a jury commissioner. Calamia further contended this same businessman had served six times as a grand juror in the sixty-two grand jury terms. Other Spanish-surnamed grand jurors also served multiple times. These included businessmen, educators and, interestingly, the banker who had denied Calamia a loan when starting out his law practice. The total grand jury list had 1,007 surnames, of which thirty-two were Spanish surnames. However, Calamia pointed out that the Spanish surnames represented seventeen persons. He added that of the names on the grand jury list, 744 names actually appeared as grand jurors. Of this number, twenty-one grand jurors were Spanish-surnamed. Again, Calamia contended that this number actually represented fourteen "safe" handpicked Spanish-surnamed grand jurors. In summary, there were several occasions when there were no Spanish-surnamed grand jurors. One of these included the grand jury that indicted Muñiz.

The State justified the exclusion of Spanish-surnamed persons under the auspices that many of them did not qualify because of their inability to read and write English. Calamia argued that during the ten-year statistical period under review, 25 percent of property owners in El Paso county were of Mexican descent, as were half of the school's enrollment.

The State denied that District Attorney Jackson in 1942 had improperly elicited testimony that Muñiz had a history of prior assaults. It also denied that Jackson had made improper statements to the jury with the intent to inflame the jury.

After the hearing, Judge Ward denied the petition and prepared forty-six findings of fact to support his conclusions of law. Calamia agreed to these as to form only. Later, a supplemental set of twenty-one facts was prepared at Calamia's insistence. The supplement did not change Judge Ward's conclusions. He overruled the systematic exclusion argument, concluding that the Texas jury selection system of 1942 and the current system did not violate the federal or state constitutions. He also concluded that Muñiz had not been denied any of his constitutional protections. Finally, Judge Ward concluded that Muñiz had waived his complaint of systematic exclusion in 1942, such that the issue could not be properly raised twenty-five years later.

Calamia had not expected a favorable state court decision. His intent was to exhaust state remedies so that he could move the case to the federal courts. Judge Ward directed a submission of the record to the Texas Court of Criminal Appeals. In less than three weeks, that court denied relief without a written order. The next step was the U.S. Supreme Court.

Calamia first considered whether the case met jurisdictional standards. He had exhausted his state remedies, and there seemed to be a significant federal question in that the Texas grand jury selection system lent itself to discrimination against an identifiable minority group in violation of the due process of law provision of the Fourteenth Amendment. Finally, there were the two points of error that were denied by the highest court of criminal jurisdiction in Texas. Calamia chose to frame the issues to the U.S. Supreme Court as both an appeal of the Texas decision and a petition for writ of certiorari. The State responded with a motion to dismiss for want of jurisdiction. The Supreme Court granted the motion to dismiss, accepted the pleadings as a petition for writ of certiorari, and then denied relief (*Muñiz v. Beto*, 393 U.S. 988, 89 S.Ct. 467 [Mem], 21 L.Ed.2d 450 [1968]). "The Supreme Court can deny certiorari at its own discretion," Calamia recalled some four decades later. "The appeal was a long shot hope that the Supreme Court would accept jurisdiction directly," he added, reflecting his strategic vision of covering all possible bases. In January 1969, Calamia deferred to his back-up plan, an appeal of the Texas appellate court decision before U.S. district judge Ernest Guinn.

The first federal step did not go well for Calamia. He reasserted his arguments from the unsuccessful state proceedings. Four months later, Judge Guinn held a hearing to entertain arguments from both sides. Another month later, Judge Guinn adopted Judge Ward's initial and supplemental findings and conclusions and denied the petition for writ of habeas corpus. A week later, Judge Guinn supplemented those findings with a reiteration of the facts of the 1942 conviction and its unsuccessful appeal in 1943, along with the more recent unsuccessful state appeals. The judge also included Muñiz's detention status and the record of the federal court proceedings. Judge Guinn cited *Townsend v. Sain* (372 U.S. 293, 318, 83 S.Ct. 745, 9 L.Ed.2d 770 [1963]), observing that the federal courts should not "be used to subvert the integrity of state criminal justice or waste the time of the federal courts in the trial of a frivolous claim." Calamia's response was an appeal to the Fifth Circuit raising some twenty-eight issues.

The Fifth Circuit issued its opinion in 1970 (*Muñiz v. Beto,* 434 F.2d 697, 1970, 5th Cir.). The court skipped over the first contention, that of the constitutionality of the Texas jury election system, observing that it had been deemed constitutional in several instances. The panel focused on the second issue, concerning application of the jury selection system in a manner that resulted in total or substantial underrepresentation of Mexican Americans in the juries that indicted and convicted Muñiz. The opinion recounted the laborious process Calamia followed "with commendable diligence" in representing Muñiz (*Id.* at 698). The panel accepted at face value that Mexican Americans were a separately identifiable ethnic group in El Paso county, a matter that the State did not contest. The court reviewed at length Calamia's interpretation of the statistical information that the state courts and Judge Guinn had rejected. It concluded: "These figures do more than speak for themselves—they cry out "discrimination" with unmistakable clarity" (*Id.* at 702). In so holding, the court rejected the State's argument that exclusion may have been justified because many Mexican Americans were not able to read, write, speak, or understand English.

The court also rejected the theory that Muñiz had waived his right to raise the jury composition argument because his attorney did not raise the issue in the original appeal. A waiver is the intentional relinquishment of a known right. Moreover, Muñiz could not have waived his constitutional right when the state courts had not recognized the right of Mexican-American defendants to protest the exclusion or underrepresentation of Mexican Americans in a grand or petit jury. Citing (*Sánchez v. State,* 243 S.W.2d 700

[Tex.Cr.App. 1951]), the court reiterated that Texas did not consider Mexican Americans to be a separate race, "but white people of Spanish descent." It was not until the U.S. Supreme Court's ruling in *Hernández v. Texas* (347 U.S. 475, 74 S.Ct. 667, 98 L.Ed. 866 [1954]) that Texas allowed Mexican Americans to make such a protest (*Muñiz*, 434 F.2d at 704).

Turning to the State's argument that modern-day concepts of jury composition should not be given retroactive application, the court noted that it was neither announcing nor following a new doctrine. It was simply applying Supreme Court rulings in *Strauder v. West Virginia* (100 U.S. 303 [1879]) and *Norris v. Alabama* (294 U.S. 587, 55 S.Ct. 579, 79 L.Ed. 1074 [1935]) in which racial discrimination in jury selection was deemed to be a violation of the Fourteenth Amendment's due process clause. Judge Gewin agreed with most of the opinion, but he dissented on the question of retroactivity because the majority opinion relied on cases involving a racially identifiable group and not specifically Mexican Americans.

Finally, the court chose not to consider Calamia's argument that the prosecutor's actions in the 1942 trial denied Muñiz a fair trial. It reasoned that the grand jury composition alone was sufficient to set aside the conviction. It also assumed that Texas would not allow such demeanor in a new trial, if Texas chose to go that route. Texas chose not to go that route.

Change and Reflection

1970s AND BEYOND: TURMOIL AND CHANGE

"We were behind the national trends, but we are quickly catching up." This was a comment often heard in the halls of El Paso's county and federal courthouses in the 1970s. El Paso county now had nearly 360,000 residents, of which about 340,000 lived in the city limits. More than 60 percent of that population was now of Spanish surnames. The city was more cosmopolitan in character as social and economic interaction with national and international urban centers increased. The business district was no longer concentrated in the downtown area. El Paso's economy was changing with the benefits of industrial growth in Juárez. Of great impact were the federal government's Great Society programs. These included War on Poverty and civil rights regulatory programs that grew out of the social upheavals in 1960s urban America.[1] There were also federally funded programs addressing nutrition, job training, educational advancement, public housing and legal assistance.

El Pasoans had plenty of economic concerns. Inflation raged. Some blamed it on Great Society spending coupled with the Vietnam War effort. Foreign oil producers had capitalized on America's dependence on imported oil. Gasoline prices went up. There were shortages. The dollar floated against foreign currencies as the United States went off the gold standard. America pulled out of the Vietnam War. The Watergate scandal led to President Nixon's resignation.

El Paso's criminal justice system was adjusting to these rapid changes. Colleagues that little resembled those in 1949 now surrounded Calamia. The legal community had grown six-fold. Of

183

the six hundred lawyers, twenty-five of them were women and nearly half had Spanish surnames.[2] El Paso county had three times as many district courts and county courts at law than in 1950. More were to be added. In the 1970s, faces had changed. Thirty-fourth district judge Jerry Woodard had replaced Judge Ward, who had moved on to the Eighth Court of Civil Appeals. Forty-first district judge Robert Schulte had replaced Judge Mulcahy. Sixty-fifth district court was now presided by Edward Márquez. He succeeded Judge Fant. It was during Fant's illness that the El Paso Bar had called upon Calamia to temporarily serve as Sixty-fifth district judge.[3] District judge Hans Brockmoller was now the senior district judge having presided over the 120th District Court since its creation in 1957. Five more district courts had been added, including one specializing in domestic relations presided by district judge Henry Peña. Former county court at law Judge George Rodríguez, Sr. was now the 168th district court Judge. District Attorney Edwin Berliner was now the 171st district court judge. Former municipal court Judge Sam Callan was now the 205th District Court judge and El Paso attorney Sam Paxson was now the 210th District Court judge. Calamia's pre-*Gideon* challenges of the 1950s and 1960s over effective assistance of counsel were no longer as critical. El Paso's federal and state courts would have publicly funded public defender offices in 1976 and 1987.[4] The poor also had legal services made available to them through federally funded legal aid organizations.

New laws and a growing population made for a more litigious El Paso county. The number of civil suits in state court, about one-half of them being divorce cases, had nearly tripled since the upstart Calamia practiced in 1950. Similarly, the number of felony indictments in state court had tripled since 1950.[5] More attorneys were challenging the status quo, influenced by civil rights laws and more liberal court rulings. The banks, the jail system, the juvenile justice system, a clothing manufacturer, the public schools, the university, the elections system and even judges faced legal challenges.[6]

The governance of the city's political and economic development agenda was no longer in the hands of a few.[7] The impact of the voting and other civil rights decisions of the Warren Court[8] was being felt throughout Texas, including the far west. The Twenty-sixth Amendment to the U.S. Constitution no longer allowed literacy tests or poll-taxes to qualify voters. The National Voting Rights Act of 1965[9] gave the Justice Department considerable oversight of elections. Texas was now forced to conform to a "one person, one vote" standard (*Kilgarlin v. Martin*, 252 F. Supp. 404 [S.D.Tex. 1965]).[10] Under the Voting Rights Act, the courts imposed single-member districts for the largest metropolitan counties but soon the Texas legislature adopted single-member representation for all of the state. The Voting Rights Act was amended in 1975 to require the Department of Justice to approve reapportionments in legislative representation before they took effect to ensure adequate minority representation. The court decisions and the voting rights laws had given more political clout to urban and suburban dwellers, of which minority groups accounted for large numbers in Texas.

In 1968, the one-person, one-vote principle extended to Texas counties (*Avery v. Midland County*, 390 U.S. 474, 88 S.Ct. 1114, 20 L.Ed.2d 45 [1968]). El Paso's four commissioner's court precincts were well out of proportion.[11] County officials agreed that distribution must be more proportionate, but there was ongoing discussion on whether the distribution should be based upon registered voters or population. It took a 1970s citizen's suit in U.S. District Court to settle the matter (*Pate v. El Paso County*, 337 F.Supp. 95 [W.D.Tex. 1970]) *aff'd*. 400 U.S. 806, 91 S.Ct. 55, 27 L.Ed.2d 38 [1970]).

Calamia's partner, John Fashing, represented the plaintiffs. The suit claimed that staggered election terms might deny the right to vote to some residents. The panel, consisting of El Paso Federal District judges Suttle and Guinn and Fifth Circuit judge Joseph Ingraham, agreed with the plaintiffs plan calling for just under 24,000 registered voters in each of the four precincts. The panel saw no problem with the Texas Constitution's provision that commissioners were to be elected in staggered terms.

The social fabric in El Paso was also affected by national trends. The sexual revolution that started in the 1960s was now focused on premarital sex, birth control, single-parent households and gay rights. Topless bars, adult movie houses and pornographic literature had made their way into El Paso, supported by the constitutional guarantee of free speech. In the county courthouse, divorce filings now outnumbered the issuance of marriage licenses. The feminist movement had arrived. At one point, feminist leader Gloria Steinem drew a full house at the University of Texas at El Paso (UTEP).

A civil rights movement by sectors of the Mexican-American population had also gained strength, manifested by new Hispanic organizations, mostly led by young Mexican Americans calling themselves "Chicanos." Often they challenged the standards and behavior of the older Hispanic community leaders. Inspired by these events, El Paso's newer generations of Hispanics voiced their concerns over inadequate housing, water and sewage services, educational programs, political representation and facilities. There were marches and other protests, including a student takeover of the UTEP administration building followed by an unsuccessful lawsuit alleging discrimination against Mexican Americans. On September 16, 1970, mainstream El Paso was shocked when throngs of young Mexican Americans took to the streets downtown in protest over inadequate housing, education and political power. Police prepared for the worst as they donned antiriot gear and positioned themselves at key intersections along the protest parade route. The Mexican characteristic of the protest march, starting with the September 16 date that commemorates the start of Mexico's fight for independence from Spain in 1810, upset many El Pasoans, including Hispanics. The protestors' use of the Mexican flag and banners of the Virgin of Guadalupe, along with the black-thunderbird-over-red flag symbolic of the César Chávez-led United Farm Workers Union, added to that anger. The September 16 marches were repeated in subsequent years.

In 1972, there was even an unsuccessful push by Chicanos to elect their gubernatorial candidate under the La Raza Unida Party platform. El Paso hosted the national convention for this splinter party. Three of the "big four" in southwestern Hispanic politics,

Rodolfo "Corky" Gonzales of Denver, José Angel Gutiérrez of south Texas and Reies López Tijerina of northern New Mexico, led the controversial convention proceedings and its equally controversial platform. César Chávez, the leader of the United Farm Workers Union, stayed in his native California. His support was for the Democratic Party platform that endorsed his boycotts of some California grape and lettuce growers.[12]

As it turned out, one of the La Raza Unida delegates was tried and convicted of assaulting a U.S. border inspector on his return from Juárez. Federal Judge John Wood had handed him a five-year sentence. Calamia was retained by the Mexican American Legal and Defense Education Fund (MALDEF) to appeal the conviction of the twenty-nine-year-old University of Colorado student. Calamia successfully argued that Judge Wood had erred in allowing the Spanish-surnamed federal prosecutor to cross-examine the defendant about a prior arrest and to make prejudicial remarks in his closing arguments (*United States v. Sánchez*, 482 F.2d 5 [5th Cir. 1973]). On remand, a more cautious prosecutor's argument ended in a conviction.[13]

The education scene was changing too, but few expected that El Paso's largest school district would be brought into federal court for violations of the 1964 Civil Rights Act. Judge Suttle, El Paso's more "activist" federal judge according to some, was called to rule on a civil rights case involving the propriety of a school dress code that prohibited long hair on male students. Judge Guinn, El Paso's pro-community and law-and-order judge, was called to rule on a civil rights case on the quality of facilities and education in largely Mexican-American schools. Their initial rulings were predictable.

Judge Suttle considered the long-hair case in a period when longer hairstyles on men were making their way to El Paso. Some saw the trend as part of the hippie culture. Others saw it as a way to attract attention, and still others said it was an attempt to defy authority. The school district defended the prohibition as necessary for discipline and sanitary conditions. Following several days of testimony, Judge Suttle concluded in a lengthy order that "one's choice of hair style is constitutionally protected" (*Karr v. Schmidt*, 320 F. Supp. 728, 731 [W.D.Tex. 1971]). The ruling was appealed and reversed by the Fifth Circuit sitting *en banc*, meaning that all fifteen judges participated. In a split decision, the appellate court ruled "neither the Constitution nor the federal judiciary it created were conceived to be keepers of the national conscience in every matter great and small" (*Karr v. Schmidt*, 460 F.2d 609, 618 [5th Cir.1972]), *cert. denied* 409 U.S. 989, 93 S.Ct. 307, 34 L.Ed.2d 256 [1972]).

About the time that Judge Suttle was presiding over the case, Congress created a fifth federal court for the Western District of Texas and President Nixon nominated San Antonio attorney John Wood to fill that position. "Maximum John" Wood, a strict constructionist, took over Judge Suttle's El Paso docket. Judge Suttle returned to San Antonio.

In contrast to Judge Suttle's liberal ruling, Judge Guinn curtly dismissed the Mexican-American discrimination suit. After a short hearing, he ruled that discrimination in the schools was a matter for the U.S. commissioner of education and not private individuals (*Alvarado v. El Paso Independent School District*, 326 F.Supp. 674 [W.D.Tex. 1971]). The Fifth Circuit reversed (*Alvarado v. El Paso Independent School District*, 445 F.2d 1011 [5th Cir. 1971]). The three-judge panel remanded with direction that the district court conduct a full and complete hearing to determine if the desegregation policies of the school district—especially as they related to student assignment, desegregation of faculty and other staff, majority to minority transfer policy, transportation, school construction and site selection, and attendance outside system of residence—complied with federal principles.

Judge Guinn would continue to share the El Paso docket with Judge Wood until his death in 1974. Guinn was succeeded by William S. Sessions, a forty-four-year-old graduate of the Baylor University School of Law. Sessions was in private practice in Waco, Texas, through 1969 and later served as U.S. attorney for the Western District of Texas. He would handle part of the El Paso docket through 1980 when he returned to San Antonio as chief judge for the Western District. He left the judiciary to head the Federal Bureau of Investigation through 1993.

These were years in which Calamia would preside over the El Paso Bar Association. One of his initiatives during this era was to join U.S. District Judge Guinn in hosting a conference for the judges of the Fifth Circuit. Supreme Court Justice William Powell, to whom the Fifth Circuit reported, was a special guest. The judges addressed a number of issues, including press coverage and abuses in civil rights petitions over moral issues such as pornography. During the conference, some of the judges took time to visit an ailing Judge Thomason, who died later that year. In Thomason's death, Calamia had lost a good friend and mentor, recalling the jurist's words in a number of cases: "You're making some unusual points, but I'll give your defendant a fair trial"; and on other occasions: "Your points are beyond those for this court, but I'll give your defendant a chance to appeal."

Government, together with its criminal justice system, had grown enormously. The city and the county had shared the same building for several decades, but it was during this time that city hall moved to another part of downtown. Facing crowded conditions and inmate complaints, the city went out of the jailhouse business, contracting with the El Paso sheriff's department. County jail inmates sued in federal court, charging that overcrowded conditions and treatment constituted cruel and unusual punishment. This time it was Judge Sessions who found for the plaintiffs in a decision that riled many El Pasoans. They had to pony up some $17 million to build a new jail separate from the county courthouse. In later years, a jail annex would be built near the eastern city limits. These improvements did not come easily. Nearly one year after his order to limit jail population to five hundred inmates, Judge Sessions held the commissioner's court in contempt and gave them five months to comply. For a while, they considered rebuilding the old jail as a temporary solution. Instead, commissioner's court opted to rent part of the ninth floor of a downtown hotel that for decades had been a Hilton Hotel.[14] In the middle of this controversy, the local sheriff was charged with misuse of county resources and was eventually removed from office. During his career, Calamia, had at times sought legal remedies against the sheriff's department; he was now asked by the sheriff to defend him.[15]

Calamia did not consider himself to be a cop-hater. Yet, he understood that from time to time he had upset police in criminal cases through his vigorous cross-examinations, his precision in explaining the law and preserving trial error, and in his defense strategies that often included pleas of insanity and sudden passion. Even if unpopular, these strategies had led to acquittals, the lesser of possible penalties and new trials or dismissals ordered by the appellate courts. "It was a matter of ensuring that the enforcer did not violate the defendant's Bill of Rights protections," Calamia recalled. "It was also a matter of my duty to do my best to represent my client's interest in accordance with the law." This honor and tenacity was reason enough for the sheriff, police and public officials to seek out Calamia when they got into trouble with the law. Through his efforts, several police officers were reinstated or received lesser penalties. El Paso police used his counsel to press for salary increases. Calamia successfully defended the mayor and city aldermen on charges of violating one of the state's recent sunshine laws requiring open public meetings.[16]

In the 1970s and beyond, Calamia would not let success get in the way of his integrity, honesty, or his mission to ensure the protection of the Bill of Rights. More than half a century after Calamia's beginnings in what is now the boarded-up Caples Building, retired district judge and appeals court justice Jerry Woodard recalls:

> The changes brought by the U.S. Supreme Court under Chief Justice Earl Warren had finally worked their way into the laws of the State of Texas, causing the pain of change, confusion and the newly decided error of our old ways. Few local lawyers were equipped to apply the new concepts to their customary way of litigating. The exception was Joe Calamia. Preservation of error became an overriding trial strategy in our system. To be able to exercise this strategy, one had to have a vast knowledge of federal law, a nimble mind to recall it and the courage to recite it. Mr. Calamia took the lead in this field.[17]

PATE AND FILING FEES: NOW CHUY DE LA O CAN RUN FOR MAYOR

Jesús de la O was a resident of El Paso's south side. Known to many as Chuy de la O, he was blind in one eye and received a disability pension. In the late 1940s, de la O wrote songs and poetry in Braille hoping to supplement his income by selling these compositions. In his words, he was a common man for the common people. The man was the very stereotype of a less-than-wealthy Mexican-American activist in El Paso's world of ward politics. He passed out leaflets. He knocked on doors. He extolled the benefits of re-electing that one or two Mexican-American office holders whose Democratic Party voting bloc of El Paso's largely Mexican-American precincts would surely ensure a continued hold in office. In those days, the certain winners in Texas's general elections were the winners of the state's Democratic Party primary elections. Chuy de la O had no money to spare. He was not one to seek public office. He considered that such privilege was for those who had the support of business leaders and the means to pay a filing fee. The Texas Election Code in effect for the 1970 Texas primary elections (Vernon's Ann.Civ.Stat. Election Code arts. 13.07-13.16) established a filing fee of $50, which could be considerably greater when the county's Democratic Party assessed the costs of running the primary election.

Calamia had honed his legal skills in criminal law, often at no fee, to protect the constitutional rights of the accused. In his crusades, Calamia often invoked the Fourteenth Amendment's "due process of law" protection against certain state government actions. In the case of voting rights, Calamia's focus shifted to the "equal protection" clause of the Fourteenth Amendment.

In a few short years, the U.S. Supreme Court had extended the one-person, one-vote principle in lawmaking representation to the counties (*Avery v. Midland County,* 390 U.S. 474, 88 S.Ct. 1114, 20 L.Ed.2d 45 [1968]). In early 1970, Calamia was assisting his partner Fashing in litigating a citizen's complaint that would force El Paso county commissioner's court to achieve proportional redistricting. However, there was more to do. Calamia believed the primary elections' filing fee system discriminated against potential candidates who could not afford to pay. Texas was one of a few states with such a law and the only one in which candidates covered all of the costs associated with a primary election. Calamia saw discrimination in favor of the wealthy. But he needed a case. He found it in William Pate, an aspiring lawyer and one of the plaintiffs in the redistricting case that was pending in federal court.

A Democrat, Pate sought to unseat a two-term Democratic incumbent. Pate's decorated war veteran status also attracted Calamia's sense of concern for war heroes. Pate refused to pay the filing fee required to run as a Democratic Party candidate for county commissioner in the May 1970 primary election. It would take a U.S. Supreme Court decision, begun by Calamia and Fashing in El Paso, to wipe out this form of discrimination and eventually overcome the resistance of politicos throughout Texas. It would also open the door to political office for Chuy de la O and others with similar backgrounds. They could now run for office without having to meet the test of wealth.

The State of Texas saw no harm in requiring potential candidates to pay several thousand dollars in filing fees. This was a time when the annual household income in El Paso county averaged $7,900. The fee, intended to cover the cost of the primary election every two years, had been in practice for seventy-five years. In 1896, legislators considered that this practice would result in one less financial burden to taxpayers. This was a Texas whose constitutional government was under the tight reins of the electorate. Texas sought the least amount of power possible in its executive branch and only trusted its legislature to convene every two years; and only in the first three months. The land commissioner, the treasurer, the agricultural commissioner and others were elected by voters. The electorate also voted the judiciary into office, from the lowest to the highest courts. Significant changes in law required voters to approve proposed amendments to the state constitution. Clearly, this was a principle of the least amount of intrusion by a government accountable to the Texas electorate. The principle was laid after the Civil War Reconstruction and at a time when the state's population and its centers of political power were predominately rural in lifestyle and philosophy. The population and its lifestyles were increasingly shifting to an urban setting and the empowerment of women, Americans of Mexican descent and Americans of African descent. Somehow, this form of state government had to adjust to federal civil rights legislation and the Great Society programs. There were federal revenue sharing and federal grants programs covering issues that ranged from the arts and education to water quality and transportation, all of which came with strings attached. The states had to follow the laws and rules set out by Uncle Sam.

Texas government leaders saw the voter registration fee as being no different from that required of businesses and professionals. To them, fee requirements assured Texas voters that there was order and clarity in the nomination of candidates. To Calamia, the arguments for a filing fee smacked of those arguments used in Texas and other solidly Democratic Party southern states to defend the poll-tax and Jim Crow legislation that sustained separate public facilities for blacks and other disenfranchised minorities. A state surely had the power to levy taxes, charge fees to get revenue to cover expenditures and ensure their collection. There was also the argument that if a state can demand an equal fee for a driver's license from all Texans, it can surely demand an equal poll-tax for voting from all U.S. citizens living in Texas. The Supreme Court actually bought these arguments in a 1937 ruling that affirmed the Georgia poll-tax and set the standard for the next twenty years. "The payment of poll-taxes as a prerequisite to voting is a familiar and reasonable regulation long enforced in many states and for more than a century in Georgia" (*Breedlove v. Suttles,* 302 U.S. 277, 283-84, 58 S.Ct. 205, 82 L.Ed. 252 [1937]). The high court rationalized that good ol' boys in power did no wrong, when it stated, "It is fanciful to suggest that the Georgia law is a mere disguise under which to deny or abridge the right of men to vote on account of their tax" (*Id.* at 283).

The Texas filing fees also went back to the 1890s Jim Crow era, but there was little legal precedence that would put a challenge of that law in the same category of the post-Reconstruction Era laws that were specifically designed to disenfranchise blacks and eventually other minorities. To Calamia, the effect was the same, but one could not litigate a constitutional challenge based only on instinct or the signs of the time. He needed solid case law in a legal arena where there was limited precedent. To be sure, the U.S. Constitution explicitly gave the states the right to run general elections. At the same time, by interpretation, the constitution established the right to vote in federal elections. Importantly, the constitution gave Congress the power to ensure that right.

Calamia was aware that Texas had used the Democratic Party's primary elections as a private club restricted only to white citizens. This practice of white-only primaries became law in 1923. The Supreme Court outlawed the white-primaries practice in 1944 (*Smith v. Allwright,* 321 U.S. 649, 64 S.Ct. 757, 88 L.Ed. 987 [1944]). The court, in that case and others before it, ruled that the right to vote in state elections and eventually the primary elections, while not explicitly mentioned in the constitution, is implicit by reason of the First Amendment. *See also United States v. Classic* (313 U.S. 299, 61 S.Ct. 1031, 85 L.Ed. 1368 [1941]); *cf., Murdock v. Pennsylvania* (319 U.S. 105, 63 S.Ct. 870, 87 L.Ed. 1292 [1943]). Calamia, like Texas politicians and their financial backers, clearly understood the importance of the Texas biannual primary elections.

Like most southern states in the 1970s, Texas was still essentially a one-party state. The Democratic Party candidate faced little or no opposition in the November general election. A conservative agenda ruled the Democratic Party, a backlash against that Republican Party-led Congress that imposed post-Civil War

Reconstruction. Change was in the making. Somehow Texas managed to elect a liberal Democratic senator and a conservative Republican senator in the space of four years, but this was under unusual special election circumstances. In both cases, the Texas governor had appointed a seemingly unelectable person to fill vacant Senate seats.[1] In 1957, the liberal Democrat Ralph W. Yarborough (1903–1996) won against that unelectable person in a special election to fill the Senate post vacated by Price Daniel (1910–1988) upon his election as governor of Texas. In 1961, Texans elected Republican John G. Tower (1925–1991) in a special election beating that same unelectable person who had been appointed by Texas Governor Price Daniel to fill the post vacated by then-Vice President Lyndon B. Johnson.

Calamia looked for a way to challenge the constitutionality of the filing fee system despite the lack of specific precedents. "My only refuge was to look at the similarity of the Supreme Court's rulings concerning the poll-tax," Calamia recalled more than a quarter of a century later. The Twenty-fourth Amendment that banned the poll-tax and literacy tests in federal elections was now the law.[2] The voting tax, like other Jim Crow laws, was a subterfuge to counteract the Fifteenth Amendment's extension of the right to vote to all citizens regardless of race. To Calamia, the Texas filing fee law ran deeper. It had the effect of ensuring that the wealthy candidates, or candidates supported by wealthy backers, stayed in power. It kept many qualified candidates from running for office. It deprived the less wealthy from the opportunity to run for office. In short, it selectively limited a voter's right to chose from among qualified candidates.

"Such a law would have kept a poor struggling young lawyer from running for office in the mid-1800s Illinois," Calamia would remind the courts later. In his passionate remarks, Calamia stressed the immortal words of that young Illinois lawyer. He remembered that Illinois lawyer in struggles testing the very existence of a nation dedicated to "the proposition that all men are created equal." That lawyer was determined to win a bloody struggle to ensure that "government of the people, by the people, for the people shall not perish from the earth."[3] The U.S. Supreme Court had just cited that portion of President Lincoln's Gettysburg address in its landmark one-person, one-vote ruling (*Reynolds v. Sims,* 377 U.S. 533, 84 S.Ct. 1362 [1964]). "A citizen, a qualified voter, is no more or no less so because he lives in the city or in the farm" (*Id.* At 568). That decision asserted, "since the right to exercise the franchise in a free and unimpaired manner is preservative of other basic civil and political rights, any alleged infringement of the right of citizens to vote must be carefully and meticulously scrutinized" (*Id.* at 562).

Calamia continued to search for substantive points of law to assure that the courts would carefully and meticulously scrutinize the Texas filing fee system. He was intrigued with the Warren Court's bold actions concerning the poll-tax. The constitutional amendment outlawing poll-taxes affected only the election of federal officials. Texas came around two years later. That was the year in which the U.S. Supreme Court overturned *Breedlove v. Suttles* (302 U.S. 277, 283-84, 58 S.Ct. 205, 82 L.Ed. 252 [1937]). In *Harper v. Virginia Board of Elections* (383 U.S. 663, 86 S.Ct.1079, 16 L.Ed.2d 169 [1966]), the court held state poll-taxes unconstitutional.

There were important points of law in this decision that Calamia felt he could apply to filing fees. The constitutional power of Congress to oversee freedom of voting rights extended to the primaries. There was the question of discrimination by wealth and its impact on voters' rights. In *Harper,* the Supreme Court concluded "that a state violates the equal protection clause of the Fourteenth Amendment whenever it makes the affluence of the voter or payment of any fee an electoral standard. Voter qualifications have no relation to wealth nor paying or not paying the voter tax" (*Harper,* 383 U.S. 666). Calamia reasoned that this principle should govern filing fees. "Wealth, like race, creed or color is not germane to one's ability to participate intelligently in the electoral process" (*Id.* at 668). Finally, the Supreme Court talked about the signs of the times that had required the court to repudiate the separate but equal doctrine. Regarding the poll-tax, the court restated, "In approaching this problem, we cannot turn the clock to 1868 when the Amendment was adopted, or even 1896 when *Plessey v. Fergu-*

son was written, [. . .] wealth or fee paying has, in our view, no relation to voting qualifications; the right to vote is too precious, too fundamental to be so burdened or conditioned" (*Id.* at 669, 670).

In early 1970, Calamia filed suit in El Paso's federal district court asking that a three-judge court be convened to declare the Texas filing fees statute unconstitutional.[4] The practice of having a three-judge federal court rule on the constitutionality of a state statute was established by Congress following a Supreme Court decision that upheld authority of a federal court to enjoin enforcement of a state law that violated federal constitutional rights (*Ex parte Young*, 209 U.S. 123, 28 S.Ct. 441, 52 L.Ed. 714 [1908]). Congress feared that one judge could "precipitously" enjoin a state and passed the three-judge law in 1910. The practice was later limited to apportionment cases under Public Law 94-381 in August 12, 1976. The suit was filed on behalf of William Pate and directed at the El Paso County Democratic Executive Committee. Under Texas law, that committee had the legal power to assess fees to cover the cost of the election. The committee based the fees on the percentage of the annual salary of the office sought. Refunds were possible after the actual election expenses were covered. Pate would have had to have his name on the ballot.

Calamia was focused on an effective and lasting outcome. "The filing fees law should be overturned completely, and all Texans who seek office should be allowed to be on the ballot without payment of fees," Calamia thought. He remembered his partial successes in fighting discriminatory practices at local, state and federal government levels. Few cases resulted in 100 percent relief. Legislative bodies could quickly change some practices or laws that would partially satisfy his claim and thus reduce the effectiveness if not eliminate the court remedy that he sought.

Only a few months earlier, he and Fashing had been before El Paso's county commissioner's court urging them, to no avail, to redistrict their precincts to comply with what he considered a very clear one-person, one-vote principle mandate one year earlier by the Supreme Court. The county commissioners questioned the City of El Paso's population estimates, preferring to wait until the 1970 census figures were in. They questioned the inclusive nature of the Citizens for One Man, One Vote and Better Government, preferring to include the advice of several local groups, ranging from the National Association for the Advancement of Colored People and the Mexican American Political Association to the John Birch Society and George Wallace's American Political Party.[5] Running out of patience, Calamia and Fashing filed a lawsuit in September 1969, only to be reproached by the county judge. A Democrat, the county judge charged that the lawsuit was a political maneuver of El Paso's fledging Republican Party. Holding nothing back, Calamia lashed out, "Commissioner's court members fear that if they voluntarily complied with our request to redistrict, their political positions would be jeopardized in some future election."[6]

In the case of the filing fees law, those in control of El Paso's Democratic Party in 1970 seemed to welcome the challenge. After all, this was a leadership that was on the side of liberal Senator Ralph Yarborough. In 1970, Yarborough was waging a defensive campaign against onslaughts of his conservative opponent Lloyd Bentsen. El Paso County's Democratic Chairman George McAlmon had a reputation of being a liberal and friend of the Mexican Americans. He spoke fluent Spanish. He, along with County Judge Colbert Coldwell, was instrumental in the election of Alicia Chacon as the first Mexican American named as state Democratic Party committee-woman. McAlmon, along with former county judge and political activist Woodrow Bean, supported Chacon in her campaign for a seat on the all-white Ysleta Independent School District Board. They also led legal and political activities against the incumbent board that refused to accept her victory.[7] In the case of the filing fees issue, the law was the law and this liberal Democratic Party leadership had to join the conservative Democratic Party leadership elsewhere in Texas to defend the Texas filing fees law.

More immediately, Calamia focused on a strategy. "Let's stop the committee from assessing fees for the May primary and allow Pate and others to be placed on the ballot without fees." It would take a while for the lawsuit to get past El Paso's district judge and into a three-judge court. A three-judge court convened in Dallas a month before the May primary election. The panel was headed by Fifth Circuit Judge Homer Thornberry. Thornberry, prior to his appointment as a federal judge in El Paso, had paid the filing fee many times as a congressman from the Austin area. Judge Thornberry ordered the El Paso county Democratic Party to waive Pate's fees.[8] Pate's name was put on the party ballot. The incumbent trounced Pate. Wise to the ways that lawsuits can quickly lose standing, Calamia had made the point to the judges that Pate also intended to run in future party elections. He also assured intervention status for a citizen eligible to vote in El Paso county and who intended to vote for Pate in a future party election.

The case that began in El Paso had now opened up a can of worms in other Texas counties. Prospective candidates from other counties joined Pate. The three-judge court combined three pending cases. Van Phillip Carter sought to get his name on the ballot in a statewide Democratic Party race for General Land Office and did not pay his fee. Another, Theodore H. Wischkaemper, sought to get his name on the ballot for the Tarrant County Democratic Party race for county judge. Wischkaemper, like Pate, was ordered on the ballot without payment of the assessment. Like Pate, he also lost to the incumbent. On the other hand, the three-judge court did not order Carter placed on the ballot since his application was not notarized, but at the same time they did not rule on the filing fee claim. The three judges also allowed one voter from El Paso county and one from Tarrant county to intervene.

The three-judge court arrived at a decision eight months later (*Carter v. Dies*, 321 F. Supp. 1358 [N.D.Tex. 1970]). It was a few days before Christmas. The primary elections had come and gone. The general elections had also come and gone. The majority opinion, written by Judge Taylor, cited the Texas white-primary abolition case for the proposition that the primary elections, while state actions, were subject to the Fourteenth Amendment's equal protection clause. The majority traced the rights of voters, beginning with an 1886 Supreme Court decision that established the right to vote as a fundamental political right (*Id.* at 1360, *citing Yick Wo v. Hopkins*, 118 U.S. 356, 370, 6 S.Ct. 1064, 30 L.Ed. 220 [1886]). The ruling then zoomed to the 1964 one-person, one-vote ruling in *Reynolds*, citing the Supreme Court's call for the right to vote "in a free and unimpaired manner" (*Carter*, 321 F.Supp. at 1361, *citing Reynolds v. Sims*, 377 U.S. 533, 561-62, 84 S.Ct. 1362, 12 L.Ed.2d 506 [196M4]). Next, the court turned to *Williams v. Rhodes* (393 U.S. 23, 30, 89 S.Ct. 5, 21 L.Ed.2d 24 [1968]), noting that the effectiveness of the vote in that case was qualitative in nature in that the voters were desirous of voting for a specific candidate who espoused their political beliefs (*Carter*, 321 F.Supp. at 1361). The court recognized that Williams established that states must demonstrate a compelling state interest before infringing on the First Amendment freedoms applied to the states by the Fourteenth Amendment.

This court considered that the Texas practice of collecting revenue to cover the cost of the primaries did not rise to the level of a compelling state interest. In its view, the assessment was a tax in the form of filing fees that imposed not only a wealth requirement directly on the candidates but also on the voters they sought to represent. Accordingly, the filing fees were unconstitutional because "they infringe upon the exercise of voting and associated rights without any compelling justification" (*Id.* at 1363).

Judge Thornberry, in a concurring opinion, focused on the right of an American citizen to associate in order to advance political beliefs and to be able to vote effectively. Thornberry noted that the only way to be nominated by the Democratic Party was to pay a fee, without there being an alternative, such as nominating petitions. He observed that a Democratic Party nomination was tantamount to a general election victory in November. For this reason he gave greater importance to having Texas adhere to a principle of an effective vote in the primaries. Thornberry rejected the State's argument that the high fees serve to limit candidacy to serious candidates. "The seriousness and legitimacy of a political effort is not to be measured by the bullion with which it is bulwarked" (*Id.* at 1364 [Thornberry, J., concurring]). Thornberry also rejected the State's argument that the high fees served to regulate the ballot to avoid confusion among voters since this purpose could be served by imposing reasonable fees (*Id*). He concluded, "I would emphasize, however, that two of our most precious freedoms are at stake, and thus the dimensions of reasonableness within which the State may safely impose a fee are indeed low and narrow" (*Id.* at 1365).

The reaction in Austin was one of disbelief. Governor Preston Smith predicted the decision would "bring about a tremendously chaotic situation." He continued, "If there is no filing fee, there will be no limit to the number of candidates in any particular race. This means we are going to have to find the revenue from tax sources, a further imposition on tax payers." Calamia retorted that governors always predict the collapse of state government because of a court decision. "This decision will strengthen our government, not weaken it, although it may weaken the position of those now in office whom the public may decide are less qualified than those who now run against them. If the people decide at the outset, what complaint can anyone have against the winner, that he never should have been allowed to run?"

"The point is that the people will now have the right to make the choice from all candidates, rich and poor alike, and if we believe in the system dependent upon the will of the people, we cannot but help believe their decision, based on a broader scope of choice will be better than it was under the former procedure. It prevented qualified men from being included in the group from which the choice was to be made solely because of their lack of funds or their unwillingness to compromise their principles by being required to accept or seek campaign funds in order to run."[9]

The decision went to the Supreme Court under the automatic appeal provision of the three-judge court law. The Supreme Court was in transition. It was now some two years since a law-and-order-minded President Nixon had named Warren E. Burger as chief justice in the hope that there would be some undoing of the "liberal" Warren Court decisions. Sitting with Burger was William Douglas, a Franklin Roosevelt appointee. There were Eisenhower appointees William Brennan and Potter Stewart, Kennedy appointee Byron White and Johnson appointee Thurgood Marshall. Then there was Harry A. Blackmun, the only other Nixon appointee. There were two vacancies. The two Nixon nominees, William H. Rehnquist and Lewis Powell, were not to take office until early 1972.

Texas moved quickly in 1971 in the hope of getting a favorable Supreme Court decision. The governor called a special legislative session to change the filing fee law. The legislature responded with changes that would go into effect for the 1972 primary elections contingent on a Supreme Court decision, in the event the Court ruled before May 1972. Under the contingent legislation, the assessments were capped at 8 percent of an annual salary for a two-year term and 16 percent of the annual salary of a four-year term. Texas would waive the fee if the applicant presented a notarized petition signed by 10 percent of the entire vote cast for governor in the county's last general election. Calamia, in a supplemental brief, accused the State of devising "an invidious scheme of discrimination against those without funds to pay unconstitutionally high filing fees [. . .] for the purpose of circumventing the three-judge decision." He questioned the strict conditions of the petition process.[10]

It was the first Monday of October 1971. The Supreme Court, with two empty associate justices' chairs, had the Pate filing fee appeal on its calendar along with others that affected Texas and El Paso. One case involved the University of Texas Board of Regents' action to block the sale of "The Rag," an underground newspaper, at UTEP, the University of Texas at Arlington, and the University of Texas at Austin. There was the appeal of a $2.5 million libel judgment against Newsweek by UTEP's track coach over an article entitled "The Angry Black Athlete." There was an appeal over the Immigration and Naturalization Service's requirement for aliens to show their registration cards to the INS. Calamia and Fashing joined the team of plaintiffs' lawyers. Calamia had brought his mother Laura, wife Hortencia, son Mark and daughter Virginia to Washington. Calamia was allowed twenty minutes more than the usual thirty minutes to present his arguments.

The Fort Worth lawyers and Calamia argued that the filing fees were "exorbitant, arbitrary, capricious, irrelevant, unreasonable and outrageously high without any reasonable relation to any legislative purpose." Calamia argued that the fees and the petition conditions in the contingent Texas law were discriminatory. As Calamia spoke, a large man suddenly jumped to his feet and screamed remarks at the court. "Just a moment, Mr. Calamia. We have a problem here," uttered Chief Justice Burger as the courtroom bailiffs quickly surrounded the unruly individual who shook the visitors' bench as if to lift it out of place. The spectator was eventually subdued by several men, handcuffed and removed from the courtroom. Calamia continued with his arguments. At one point, one of the justices interrupted him, expressing concern that Calamia had not cited a precedent specific to discriminatory filing fees. "Mr. Calamia this practice has been the law for two hundred years. Are you telling us that two hundred years of this practice is wrong?" Calamia, remembering the parallel he had drawn between the filing fees issue and the now-discredited poll-tax, responded: "Your Honor, two hundred years of practice does not make it a right law!" Calamia vented his frustration at Texas. He mentioned the Jim Crow laws enacted to hinder the right to vote. He urged the court "to close every door" to ensure that Texas eliminated a discriminatory filing fees practice. The court reporter paused his note-taking as if questioning if the remarks should go on the record. Calamia would later receive a scolding from his mother for his response to the justice "You should be more polite!" On the other hand, Laura Calamia said nothing about his remarks on Texas's practices.[11]

A team of lawyers joined John F. Morehead, a special assistant attorney general, who argued the case for Texas. Morehead, a big fellow attired in a western-cut suit and boots, introduced himself as the representative of the "sovereign State of Texas." Quickly, Justice Black quipped, "What are you doing here?" The big Texan ignored the comment and proceeded to argue the State's case. He defended the filing fees scheme, reiterating three principal arguments. The fees allowed the state to have orderly elections without the confusion of multiple candidates. To eliminate the fees could create splinter parties and cause a breakdown of the state's two-party system. Texas had modified its law contingent on a Supreme Court decision. Morehead argued that there was a stigma attached to a pauper's oath as a condition for a ballot by petition. He further argued that the filing fees were no more discriminatory than the required license fees from business or professional men or the payment by workers of union dues. Texas considered that wealth had little to do with qualifications. A person did not have to run in a party primary, as that person could have his name in the general election if he did not want to pay a filing fee. "No voter is fenced out of the voting booth by the filing fee requirement. The filing fee simply limits the persons for whom the voter may cast his ballot."

On February 24, 1972, the Supreme Court rendered a unanimous decision. The high court affirmed the decision that the Texas primary election filing fee system contravened the equal protection clause of the Fourteenth Amendment (*Bullock v. Carter,* 405 U.S. 134, 92 S.Ct. 849, 31 L.Ed.2d 92 [1972]). Justices Powell and Rehnquist had just joined the court but had not taken part in the decision. Chief Justice Burger delivered the opinion, concluding that Texas had failed to establish the requisite justification for the filing fee system. While the court recognized the validity of a filing fee, it criticized the requirement for candidates to shoulder the cost of the primary election without a reasonable alternative means to get on the ballot. In this manner, "the State of Texas has erected a system that utilized the criterion of ability to pay as a condition to being on the ballot, thus excluding some candidates otherwise qualified and denying an undetermined number of voters the opportunity to vote for candidates of their choice" (*Bullock,* 405 U.S. at 149).

The Supreme Court first narrowed the threshold question to "whether the filing-fee system should be sustained if it can be shown to have some rational basis or whether it must withstand a more rigid standard of review" (*Id.* at 142). The justices focused not on the rights of candidates, but on the extent and nature of the impact on the rights of the voters. The Texas law had an exclusionary mechanism that limited the voter's choice of candidates. The court reasoned that the fee system "tends to deny some voters the opportunity to vote for a candidate of their choosing; at the same time it gives the affluent the power to place on the ballot their own names or the names of persons they favor" (*Id.* at 144). While Texas has a need to regulate the ballot in primary elections and provide a means for financing the elections, the solutions should not be arbitrary. The justices rejected the argument that a candidate could avoid the fees by running in the general election or by a petition that required them to abandon their party affiliation. "We are not persuaded that Texas would be faced with an impossible task in distinguishing between political parties for the purpose of financing primaries" (*Id.* at 147).

Texas sought a stay of the order, arguing that the primary election process may be "severely hampered if not utterly destroyed in certain instances by the lack of availability of funds from filing fees." Texas said it needed a constitutional amendment to allow for the use of public funds to cover the primary election costs. As the Texas legislature only met every two years in regular session, it would be 1973 before it could consider passing a proposed constitutional amendment with a public vote thereafter. The State argued, "Voting and the election process is the very life blood of constitutional government in this state and of this nation. It should not be threatened, hampered, disrupted or brought to a stop upon an issue as to how it is to be financed without affording adequate time for unhurried decisions as to how to resolve the complicated issue required." The Supreme Court did not buy the argument.

Back in El Paso, Democratic Party Chairman George McAlmon welcomed the Supreme Court's decision. McAlmon said the legislature could have worked out an effective solution, but instead chose patchwork legislation. In the meantime, McAlmon took a $50 donation from Democratic Party candidates in lieu of a fee. Something good had come out of the voters' challenges. Texas had now liberalized its voter registration laws. Voters could now register throughout the year up to thirty days before an election as opposed to a January-only period.[12] The Texas governor, although unhappy with the decision, made preparations to find the funds to finance the primary elections. A 1916 Texas Supreme Court decision had ruled that the use of tax money to finance the primaries violated the Texas Constitution. Texas would, therefore, have to modify its election laws to allow for reasonable fees. Texas would also allow candidates to be placed on the ballot by a petition of voters in lieu of a filing fee.

Calamia and Fashing were out some $2,500, not including the hundreds of hours spent with no fees charged. Calamia said after the decision: "We acted for the benefit of the public in the belief that we were not living in a true democracy, the type of government that Lincoln described. Texas should get in line with the great majority of other states in making it easier for any would-be candidate to offer himself for office." Likewise, Fashing saw the decision with optimism at a time when some were looking at this new Supreme Court to undo some of the civil rights decisions of the Warren Court. He observed, "The Burger court has shown it will protect basic human and political rights of those who are not wealthy [. . .]. The Court is interpreting the Fourteenth Amendment as a living thing that must be interpreted in light of the current needs of the nation in respect to equal protection of the law for all citizens."[13]

Texas would adopt a more uniform filing fee system and allow for petitions by voters in lieu of the filing fees. Soon this mechanism, like that of single-member districts following the one-person, one-vote principle, would apply to city elections and school district elections. By 1981, Chuy de la O was still a constant visitor in City Hall. He complained about closed meetings. He detested a litter problem in El Paso. He asked for higher wages for police and firemen. "I try to help everybody," he clamored. "I stand up for people's rights and help senior citizens." Now in anger that the incumbent mayor was running for Texas governor, de la O declared his candidacy for mayor. He announced, "I want to save El Paso from going to the dogs!" Before long, he obtained a sufficient number of signatures from qualified voters to allow him to run. Like Pate, de la O lost the election. But thanks to Pate's cause, Chuy de la O, even with no money to spare, could now run for office.

JUDGE V. JUDGE: INVESTIGATIVE GRAND JURIES

Calamia, the criminal and constitutional law expert that other lawyers would go to in difficult moments, was also the one to go to in those moments of difficulty involving judges. Calamia had had the honor in 1966 of being unanimously selected by the El Paso Bar to fill the Sixty-fifth District Court judgeship for some twenty-seven days while the incumbent was ill. Calamia had also known the honor of being appointed a federal district attorney in the defense of a federal agent. Now Calamia was being asked to seek justice for a state judge against what he considered an unconstitutional grand jury report. That report of the "conscience of a community," as grand juries are often called, reflected the community's frustration over the growing drug epidemic in El Paso and conflicts in the federal and state courthouses over enforcement of drug laws and the bashing of law enforcement. The manner in which the report was handled reflected a frustration by some community leaders over significant political changes that were occurring in El Paso, in part from the liberal court decisions and a nontraditional mayor and city council.

The federal government's get-tough approach to drug offenders had mixed results in El Paso. Operation Intercept, President Nixon's 1969 assault on drug smuggling from Mexico, was intended to get the Mexican government's cooperation. However, it was the interdependent El Paso and Juárez economies that felt the brunt of the law enforcement siege on the border. A few drugs were seized, and the illegal drug market dried up temporarily. When the siege was lifted, it was the beginning of the end of the traditional way of doing trans-border business. For nineteen days, every vehicle entering El Paso from Juárez across the international bridges was checked for drugs. Trunks were opened and searched. Hoods were opened, and the engine compartments were searched. Occupants were often told to get out to allow for a more thorough vehicle search. Nixon had sent his war on drugs emissaries Assistant Attorney General Richard Kleindienst and G. Gordon Liddy to gain the support of the El Paso business community before the action began.

It was on a hot August afternoon in a dimly-lit, makeshift conference room hidden on the fifth floor of the federal courthouse that Liddy told El Paso's movers and shakers of the Administration's frustration with the drug epidemic and Mexico's lack of cooperation in the drug war. Mexico was to be taught a lesson. The United States would put the squeeze on Mexico by blocking the border from illegal drug trafficking. As it turned out, the squeeze was more on business. On both sides of the border, this new policy served to severely disrupt business. From that day on, no longer would federal inspectors wave drivers through from Mexico. Long waits at the international bridges were now to be expected. The impersonal culture characteristic of a large metropolis had found its way into the El Paso metropolitan area. The customs and immigration directors that had close ties to El Paso and Juárez power brokers were soon gone. Operation Intercept saw only four arrests and less than fifty pounds of marijuana seized at the bridges. Perhaps a more lasting impact was that Operation Intercept had also exposed the porous nature of the border in the wide-open areas away from the ports of entry. One year later a federal official said, "Dope seizures have been getting bigger since Intercept. Let's hope that means we are now nabbing the big-timers and not that weed smuggling has increased." The underground culture of drug traffickers and users underwent an even more radical change. A more sophisticated illegal drug business supplanted the traditional Juárez drug empire started by La Nacha in the 1930s. Organized crime began exploiting the lucrative drug business along the border. Large international cartels saw the opportunity to operate with air and inland routes to the drug market in the interior of the United States. One cartel even bragged of having its own air force.[1]

Drug use by youth was no longer a problem confined to El Paso's less affluent south side. Once upon a time, the bulk of drug defendants were Hispanic-surnamed. Now the Smiths and Jones outnumbered the Garcias and Gonzalezes seven to one. El Paso had one tough district attorney in Jaime Boyd, the one time assistant U.S. attorney who replaced District Attorney Boling. Boling had been named to head the Texas attorney general's office that opened in El Paso. Drug raids were now taking place throughout the city. In one year, drug raids netted some eight hundred persons, many of them youth. Pot was selling for $1,000 a pound. Those aged twelve to twenty-five outnumbered their older counterparts nine to one. Roll-your-own cigarette paper was selling in amounts far greater than the demand for Prince Albert and Bull Durham among the traditional tobaccos. Youth, some of them from the more affluent families, were being brought before judges facing stiff penalties for possession of marijuana, even in small amounts. Several lawyers now specialized in defending both local and out-of-town residents against charges stemming from vigorous law enforcement.[2]

The growing drug culture among youth created pressure for more lenient treatment of young defendants. Federal drug smuggling convictions carried five- to twenty-year federal mandatory prison sentences. A lighter sentence of two to ten years, with probation possible, could be assessed if the defendant pleaded guilty to the federal offense of not paying a tax on marijuana smuggled from Mexico. The government had suffered a setback when the Supreme Court ruled the marijuana tax law unconstitutional (*Leary v. United States*, 395 U.S. 6, 89 S.Ct. 1532, 23L.Ed.2d 57 [1969]). This law had allowed convictions on possession of marijuana on the presumption that it was smuggled from Mexico and thus subject to taxation. In El Paso, the U.S. attorney's office had used this law to deal with the less serious marijuana cases. The get-tough drug laws of the 1970s provided enforcement tools like wire taps, mandatory prison sentences, use of paid informants, undercover tactics, no-knock property entry and conspiracy criminal charges potential. These tools were intended to deal with drug trafficking organizations and big quantities of illegal drugs. At the same time, these laws, while not admitting to social reasons for the growth of a drug culture and refusing to succumb to pressure to legalize marijuana, recognized the large number of youth that were being placed in the slammer for possessing small amounts of marijuana. Funds and facilities for rehabilitation, treatment and drug abuse prevention were authorized. The government eventually reduced the first-time drug possession sentences. At least half of the states had moved to soften drug law violation penalties. Neighboring New Mexico now considered possession of marijuana to be a misdemeanor offense but drug pushers faced a $5,000 mandatory fine even for a first offense.[3]

Incentives for local enforcement were included in the tough drug laws of the 1970s. They envisioned a coordinated approach against drugs through a task force consisting of state, local and federal officers. Undercover agents now had better-quality intelligence from various sources. The U.S. Drug Enforcement Agency (DEA) was created in 1973 to put an end to the interagency jurisdictional conflicts that many believed undermined enforcement of drug laws.[4] In El Paso, this meant the end of the U.S. Bureau of Narcotics and Dangerous Drugs one-person office and the transfer of a large number of U.S. Customs agents to DEA. The DEA created the El Paso Intelligence Center (EPIC) that combined the intelligence gathering efforts of U.S. Customs and the U.S. Border Patrol. The center monitored the air, land and sea for suspected drug smuggling operations. The DEA had the primary authority to investigate federal drug offenses. However, this did not necessarily mean that the government would prosecute all these cases in federal court. The government would focus on the biggies. There were the large seizures of marijuana, heroin and cocaine intercepted at the international bridges and by the Border Patrol at its inland checkpoints on the highways leading out of El Paso. There were also the conspiracy cases involving plots to smuggle illegal drugs supported by a variety of overt acts.

One would think that the coordination tools in the war against drugs would result in fewer battles over jurisdiction by law enforcement authorities. El Paso's federal court had a couple of tough federal judges. Judge Guinn was tough on drug pushers. "Maximum John" Judge Wood was even tougher. Local police, sheriff deputies and Jamie Boyd, the county's tough-on-drugs district attorney, were working closely with DEA and the U.S. attorney. District Attorney Boyd, a former assistant U.S. attorney, soon moved back to El Paso's federal courthouse when Judge Guinn appointed him as U.S. magistrate. There was also a change in the Thirty-fourth District Court where almost all criminal cases were prosecuted. A crack soon developed in the drug war cooperation between the government and the state.[5]

William S. Sessions, a Nixon appointee, had succeeded Morgan as U.S. attorney for the Western District of Texas, headquartered in San Antonio. Ralph Harris was the assistant U.S. attorney in charge of the office in El Paso. The federal prosecutors recognized that a large number of individuals were being arrested by U.S. Customs and Immigration inspectors at the international bridges for smuggling small amounts of drugs. They also recognized that federal undercover agents, working with local police, were also making arrests involving small amounts of drugs. However, the federal government's focus was supposed to be the "big stuff," that is the big pushers, organized drug cartels. As a result, some drug cases arising from these circumstances were turned over to the State for prosecution.

Steven Willis Simmons was El Paso's district attorney given that Boyd had returned to the federal courthouse as U.S. magistrate. Simmons was now expected to prosecute the small cases in which, for the most part, the primary government witness was a federal border inspector or a federal undercover agent. Thirty-Fourth District Court Judge Jerry Woodard was now expected to rule on these drug cases. Simmons and Woodard were certainly younger than their predecessors. An El Pasoan since 1952 and a former assistant county attorney, Simmons took office in 1971 at the age of thirty-six. He was a graduate of Texas Western College and the University of Texas and had his law degree from South Texas College of Law. In administering the oath of office to Simmons, Woodard emphasized a district attorney's special duty to protect the innocent and the rights of all, including those who may be guilty.[6] Woodard, age thirty-eight when taking office in 1969, was an El Paso native with family roots in El Paso's lower valley. He received his law degree in 1959 from Baylor University School of Law. Observers at Woodard's investiture ceremony considered Woodard to represent "strong and new ideas brought into political and judiciary circles by 'a new breed'." They viewed the "new breed" as progressive persons in a number of professions with a "metropolitan outlook and contemporary feeling for young America."[7] Both Simmons and Woodard understood their roles in applying the law in this period.

The Warren Court's rulings on the rights of the accused were making their way to El Paso. Case preparation for Simmons involved a legal check of the lawmen's arrest information by his staff of assistant district attorneys. Not all the cases presented by police for prosecution passed muster. For Woodard, the judge's role in presiding over a case was one of being neutral. The burden was on the government to prove its case in application of the principle that the accused is presumed to be innocent until proven guilty. This contrast in the manner of prosecuting cases in the state and federal courts led to complaints by some federal officers. It was only a matter of time before there would be a clash between the federal and state courts. Little did Calamia suspect that he would be called upon to defend Judge Woodard against a federal judge in a case that tested the extent of federal judicial involvement in the decision of a state judge that was not to the satisfaction of the federal government.

The case of federal judge v. state judge began in April 1971 with an apparent conflict over the testimony of a U.S. customs agent concerning the status of a Texas undercover officer. The undercover officer, identified as an informant, had arranged to buy marijuana from two individuals. A year later, in the trial of the defendant, the customs agent identified the Texas lawman as an officer. Clarence Moyers, a young attorney with well-coiffured long hair, represented the defendant. It had been one year since he had scored a short-lived victory against the El Paso Independent School District's prohibition against long hair on boys. Moyers spotted the DEA agent's apparent contradiction and charged that the federal agent had committed perjury. In turn Simmons asked Judge Woodard to declare a mistrial. Judge Woodard granted the request.[8]

News of Judge Woodard's ruling quickly rippled across the street to El Paso's federal courthouse. A few days later, Judge Woodard's court reporter was ordered by Judge Guinn to bring all the trial records before a U.S. district court grand jury. Woodard and Simmons were invited, but declined to appear. The two state assistant district attorneys who handled the case were subpoenaed by the federal grand jury.[9] As the grand jury met on the fourth floor of the federal courthouse, the rumor mill was in full swing on the other floors and across the street in the multistory building shared by El Paso's city and county officials. Rumor had it that the government was investigating state officials. Finally these rumors came to rest on June 15.

That day, the federal court was called into session. The session was short. "Deliver the indictments to the clerk," Judge Guinn said. After thanking jurors for their service, the federal judge said, "The court notes the special report of the grand jury. It will be filed with the clerk and released at the proper time." A surprised assistant U.S. attorney Harris replied, "Yes, Your Honor."[10] A report of federal grand jury proceedings had been made public. There were no indictments resulting from the two-day grand jury session—only a report. Sixteen of the twenty-three grand jurors concurred with the report. The federal prosecutor did not sign the report. Yet, the two-page report was made public. Excerpts were printed in El Paso's two daily newspapers.

The report criticized the manner in which Woodard and Simmons handled the drug case during the April trial.[11] Simmons told the press that the federal grand jury may have found differently if it had had all the facts. He said, of the grand jury's recommendations, that his office required government witnesses to review case histories before trial and to properly prepare those witnesses before and during the trial. Judge Woodard was silent for a while. The report had questioned why he would grant the motion to dismiss before the trial jury had a change to consider the case.[12]

Ironically, not too long before, across the street in Judge Woodard's court, a state grand jury had met to deal with questions concerning an exchange of land between the city council and a local land developer. Mayor Bert Williams and a slate of four aldermen were elected in 1971 over the slate supported by the traditional group of organized businessmen. That council changed the leadership of the city's principal advisory commissions and single-purpose districts dealing with planning and zoning, housing and water utilities. The new leadership allowed some business interests, many from outside El Paso, to purchase some of the city's public lands. The Williams administration's revamped El Paso Housing Authority, led by former county judge Woodrow Bean, directed construction of public housing units throughout the city, even in places near more affluent neighborhoods.

The grand jury dealt with one of the controversial Williams administration matters; at least that's what some outside of the William's administration circle thought. What that state grand jury thought, what it discussed and what it might have concluded, was all kept secret. As in the federal grand jury case, there were no indictments. As in the federal case, rumor had it, the grand jury had issued a report. Unlike the federal grand jury report, Judge Woodard did not make the report public. Pressure had mounted to release the report, but Judge Woodard did not budge. El Paso's afternoon paper quickly drew a contrast between Judge Guinn and Judge Woodard. The editorial stated: "Weeks ago, an El Paso County Grand Jury completed a study of land swaps made by the City of El Paso in which the city failed to follow proper procedures and gave away more than it got. The jury's critical report is still kept secret, and there seems no ready explanation why two jury reports (an Otero County Grand Jury report on drugs in schools) can be made public, while a third must be kept under wraps." Woodard asked the Texas attorney general for a written opinion:

Can a grand jury's report or recommendation, given to a district court, not involving criminal matters, but of probable public interest, be disclosed, particularly when less than nine (9) Grand jurors sign the report or recommendation?

One thing was obvious from the federal grand jury report released by Judge Guinn. At least some of the grand jurors echoed the sentiment in various sectors of El Paso that some criminals were being let loose on technicalities and that cops were being treated unfairly. After all, a grand jury, whether state or federal, had long been considered to be the conscience of a community. English noblemen had extracted from King John a guarantee of a grand jury as a protection against unjust charges by the king's men. The U.S. Constitution recognized the British grand jury tradition in the Bill of Rights, which provides that no "person shall be held to answer for a capital, or otherwise infamous crime, unless on a presentment or indictment of a Grand Jury." The federal and state grand jury systems differed in the selection process, but otherwise had similar functions.

A federal grand jury was constituted differently than a state grand jury. The Texas grand jury selection system was the one that Calamia had successfully challenged as discriminatory against Mexican Americans going back to selection practices in the 1940s. The way the system worked in the 1970s, Judge Woodard would appoint three to five "intelligent," property-owning citizens with no felony convictions as a grand jury commission. That commission then selected fifteen to twenty prospective grand jurors from the last tax roll and gave the names to Judge Woodard in a sealed envelope. The judge would then come up with twelve qualified grand jurors. Under the federal system, prospective grand jurors were drawn at random from lists of registered voters in El Paso county and summoned to appear before Judge Guinn. Judge Guinn would then select twenty-three qualified persons as the federal grand jury. Like the state system, the jurors would hear testimony and review documentary evidence in cases brought to its attention by an assistant U.S. attorney. As in the state system, an indictment could be returned based only on probable cause. Finally, as in the state system, a federal grand jury could investigate other matters, if these matters were addressed through the U.S. attorney.

So it was with this federal grand jury. The carefully crafted report of its secret deliberations focused on the serious drug problem in El Paso and the atmosphere that surrounded the state trials. It vented its criticism at the conduct of the defense attorney, the district attorney and the district judge. Yet it defended the conduct of the federal agent. One was not certain what to call the grand jury product. It was not an indictment presented by the assistant U.S. attorney. It was not a presentment or a charge brought by the grand jury without the U.S. attorney's help. Still, it was just a matter of time before Judge Woodard broke his silence. Prudently, Woodard prepared himself by having that all-important consultation with Calamia, the lawyer who saw a real demon in the manner in which the federal government went after what he considered to be strictly a state matter.

An *El Paso Times* editorial later echoed Calamia's thoughts. The *Times*, El Paso's morning paper, had changed in its ownership. As in the case of El Paso's locally owned banks and major retail stores, the change in ownership resulted in a loss of local control. For a while, the Times wrote stuff that was not quite the thinking of old guard El Paso. Among others, the Times had questioned the practices of the Texas Youth Commission and practices concerning the arrest and detention of juveniles. In the federal grand jury report case, the Times editorialized: "How would a federal judge feel if an El Paso county grand jury reviewed one of the cases before him and came up with a criticism of his handling of the case? Why should the federal courts interfere with state courts and their powers?" In Calamia's view, the grand jury investigation amounted to a review of the discretionary powers inherent in a state court system. "The action was unconstitutional as it was outside the powers granted to the federal government," Calamia recalled more than thirty years later. Through Calamia's prior actions, both state and federal judges' decisions had been reversed based on trial error over a specific Bill of Rights question. In this case, the issue at hand was, in a sense, a broader one, that of an intrusion by the federal government on the rights reserved to the people and the states. A number of critical questions arose. Could a federal grand jury investigate state matters and issue a report critical of state officials? Did the federal government interfere, contrary to the constitution, with those discretionary powers given to state judges? How can one seek corrective action against the mighty power of a federal judge? Unlike Texas, where judges were and still are elected, a federal judge was and still is appointed for life.[13]

About three weeks after the report was released, Woodard broke his silence. He filed an application to expunge the grand jury report. He asked Guinn to rescind the order and strike the report from the official record. He termed Judge Guinn's decision to release the report as an extraordinary action that "intruded and trenched upon and into matters clearly within the exclusive jurisdiction, authority and purview of the State of Texas." Woodard questioned the constitutionality of the investigation and release of the report. He warned these actions opened the door to future grand jury reports on the conduct of state-federal relations. In asking for the report to be removed from official records, Woodard wanted Judge Guinn "to make it known that the dignity of a state court cannot be impinged upon by the actions of a federal grand jury under the circumstances of this case."[14]

A few weeks transpired. In mid August, Judge Guinn requested assistant U.S. attorney Ralph Harris to file a brief as a friend of the court to look at Judge Woodard's claim.[15] In the brief, Harris observed that any reference to Woodard was general and that the report was only a recommendation and opinion of a grand jury that were of general interest to the community. He did not consider the constitutional authorities mentioned by Woodard to be convincing. Harris, focusing on the public's right to know, concluded that there was sufficient authority to release the report to the public. He cited authorities in support of his conclusion that grand jurors were not bound to follow orders of the judge or prosecutor, calling jurors "instruments of the community," that "reflect the sentiment of the particular locale, the *fam publica*." Among other authorities, Harris referred to an appellate court decision in a New Jersey grand jury report case, "What cannot be investigated in a republic is likely to be feared. The maintenance of the popular confidence required that there be some body of layman which may investigate any instance of public wrong doing."[16]

Calamia and Fashing filed a response a week later questioning Harris's refusal to comment on the contents of the report. They accused the U.S. attorney's office and other federal agents of triggering, if not directing, the grand jury investigation. They claimed that federal prosecutors proposed evidence that led to the report. They argued that the purpose of the report was to "whitewash" the federal agent by maligning a district judge and the district attorney. They questioned the political timing of the report, in that both Simmons and Woodard were up for reelection. They contended that "The government surely would not support a report that criticized a federal judge or a federal district attorney concerning their exercise of their discretionary powers." Calamia cited the federal grand juror's handbook and various cases in furtherance of the argument that there were limits to grand jury power; in particular, they were subject to a federal judge's supervision. They should address themselves to the issue of whether crimes are committed and to who committed those crimes.

To Calamia, the issue was not one of the public's right to know, but rather that of judicial interference. He noted that the law governing special grand juries with investigative powers provided a number of safeguards because of the touchy nature of an investigation. He noted that the grand jury report was not one issued by a special grand jury under that statute. "Here, not a single step was taken to protect the due process rights of the state district court and the district attorney. The U.S. attorney simply ignored this injustice in his brief." Calamia concluded: "the Federal Government has interfered with states' rights too often in modern American history, and it is time that the door is closed to such abuses of power." He warned that to permit the report to stand would establish a precedent that would do great harm to state-federal relations. He asked that the report be expunged "to protect the dignity and due administration of justice in all state courts."[17]

Harris and Calamia submitted their legal briefs to Guinn, who seemed predisposed to accept Calamia's earlier suggestion for a hearing to clarify what motivated the report. Calamia, however, was having second thoughts. Instead, he opted for the appellate route. He asked the federal appellate court to order Guinn to expunge the grand jury report.[18] A few weeks later, a Fifth Circuit Court of Appeals panel, responding to the petition for writ of mandamus, ordered Guinn to rule within ten days.

Guinn responded that he had nothing to do with the grand jury investigation. He added that a federal judge does not have the power to censor, control or suppress actions by a federal grand jury. He likened the independence of a grand jury to the freedom of the press. He emphasized the point by citing a Seventh Circuit case. "Its authority is derived from none of the three basic divisions of our government, but rather directly from the people themselves." *See In re April 1956 Term Grand Jury*, 239 F.2d 263, 269 (7th Cir. 1956). Guinn then referred to the issue of jurisdiction and observed that he never believed he had the jurisdiction to pass on matters before they were submitted to a grand jury. He assumed that Woodard wanted a hearing on the nature of the matters before the grand jury and a determination of whether the substance of the report was proper. In this manner, Guinn reasoned, Woodard's case would go on to the Fifth Circuit for review.

Judge Guinn went a step further before ruling on the matter. He observed that after the grand jury proceeding, he learned that the issue before the grand jury involved District Attorney Simmons, district judge Woodard and a U.S. customs agent. Guinn added, "The agent had made numerous narcotic cases which were pending in the state court and some of which were connected with the case that was dismissed. Likewise, he had made numerous federal narcotic cases in which a federal grand jury had returned indictments." Guinn then made another observation, "The U.S. attorney had reason to believe that there was a possible conspiracy to discredit this officer in order to prevent the prosecution of these state and federal cases in which he was involved." Judge Guinn considered this circumstance to be one of "proper inquiry." He commented that the agent had "been accused, tried and convicted of perjury by statements made to the newspapers, but without an opportunity to defend himself." Guinn then referred to a recent state grand jury investigation of perjury charges against the agent. He observed that as with the federal grand jury report, the state grand jury "found the so-called perjury charges wholly unfounded." Guinn denied the application to expunge the grand jury report with a closing comment. "It is the opinion of this court that it has no discretion and power to pass upon the propriety of a report by a federal grand jury. If it did have such power, it would find that the conduct of this report was proper."[20]

The federal judge's reasoning infuriated Calamia. He appealed to the Fifth Circuit, asking it to expunge the report or order Judge Guinn to do so. The appellate brief was filed on December 20, 1972. Calamia and Fashing pointed out that it was Guinn who ordered the state court reporter to provide information to the federal grand jury. They cited a case in which the courts had ruled that powers of a grand jury are not unlimited and are subject to a judge's supervision (*Branzburg v. Hayes*, 408 U.S. 665, 687, 92 S.Ct. 2646, 33 L. Ed.2d 626 [1972]). They sought to establish that a grand jury was part of the judiciary and that in this case it abused its "proper functions" by issuing a report that had no relation to federal matters. They charged that the federal judge abused his "proper functions" by filing the report. The brief referred to the powers and functions described in the federal grand jury handbook and observed that this was not a case of an investigative special grand jury. Under the law governing such special grand juries, investigation procedures established a number of procedures to assure that the constitutional rights of the persons named be protected. Calamia agreed with Harris that the harm was already done, but disagreed that the issue should be dropped. "The public has a right to know if the government was wrong," he stated. "On its face, it is a clear abuse of power by the executive and judicial branches." He warned that to affirm Guinn's decision would set an undesirable precedent allowing grand juries to fight political and public issues in the news media by use of a grand jury report.

Calamia turned to the contents of the report: "It is apparent that the government used the grand jury in an effort to bolster and whitewash an apparent government witness in the eyes of the public." Less than ten years before, Calamia had been temporarily named assistant U.S. attorney to defend a federal officer against what the federal government considered were unfounded state murder charges. An angry State of Texas and its influential west Texas residents wanted that officer tried in the state courts. Ironically, now Calamia was defending the right of the State of Texas to keep the federal government from usurping those discretionary powers of Texas state judges. No jurisdiction, plain and simple, Calamia thought, citing the Tenth Amendment. "The powers not delegated to the United States by the Constitution, nor prohibited by it to the States, are reserved to the States respectively, or to the people." Filing the report was an abuse of power, Calamia thought, this time citing the Ninth Amendment. "The enumeration in the Constitution of certain rights shall not be construed to deny or disparage others retained by the people." Calamia concluded, "Where is there found in the Constitution or laws of the United States a delegation to federal grand juries or federal courts to take reports on state court proceedings in cases like the one at bar? The federal government may not act upon matters otherwise within the control of the states." U.S. District Court Western District of Texas, El Paso Division, In Re: Report of Grand Jury Proceedings Filed on June 15, 1972, RP 72-CA 175, Notice of Appeal, October 20, [1972]).

The Fifth Circuit ruled in July 1973 that Judge Guinn had erred in rejecting the request for expungement of the report. *In re Grand Jury Proceedings*, 479 F.2d 458 (5th Cir. 1973). The court was cautious. A three-judge panel held that the substance of the grand jury report concerned mostly local and state affairs and required Judge Guinn to expunge the part of the report that dealt with such matters. But the panel did not order expunction of that part having a federal purpose. Moreover, it chose not to settle the larger issue of whether a federal grand jury has authority to make reports.

Calamia asked the Fifth Circuit to reconsider this larger issue, this time *en banc*, with all the judges participating. He argued that to allow the part of the report concerning the credibility of the federal witness was tantamount to permitting declarations that federal government witnesses are excellent witnesses. Calamia sought to get attention. He likened this to accusations of perjury against President Nixon's staff under investigation by a congressional committee for their role in the Watergate affair. He warned that with the current ruling, a federal judge in the Watergate investigation could issue and make public a report, like the one on Woodard, this time assuming President Nixon to be guilty and recommending impeachment. Calamia cited numerous cases that seemed to indicate that the courts were moving in the direction of limiting grand juries to only issuing indictments or declaring a "no bill" in cases where there was not probable cause for a criminal charge. [21] The Fifth Circuit denied the request.

JONES: CRIMES OF SUDDEN PASSION AND REFLECTION

The year was 1986. Joe Calamia and his new partner Charles Mallin scored an appeals court victory in the reversal of a murder conviction, the sort of thing that stirs anger in the public and often translates into harsh criticism of criminal defense lawyers. A homosexual male prostitute had escaped both a death sentence and a life sentence for the bludgeoning death of another homosexual. The murder occurred in 1980, and the defendant was found guilty more than a year later. Calamia was convinced that the defendant's state of mind was such that he acted out of sudden passion. However, the argument seemed so unbelievable that neither the prosecutors nor the judge, and certainly not the jury, took it seriously. In contrast, the Texas Court of Criminal Appeals took the constitutional basis for Calamia's arguments very seriously. Eventually, the defendant pled guilty to a charge of murder and was sentenced to twenty years in prison. This and other cases involving a defense of sudden passion led the Texas legislature to rethink this part of the penal code a few years later. In the fourth year of the twenty-first century, a much older and retired Joe Calamia seemed to have awakened from nearly a decade of depression induced by a debilitating illness. It was as if he had been jolted by the legislature's action in eliminating sudden passion as a defense for taking the life of a person.

More than a decade earlier, Calamia was finishing his thirty-third year of law practice with Mallin, the last of his partners. Mallin joined Calamia's practice in 1979 following the election of

Calamia's former partner, John Fashing, as a county court at law judge. Calamia's criminal law practice, and a healthy civil practice, had been going well in a legal community that had grown in number and diversity. Lawyers could now advertise and the legal industry, like that of business, government and lifestyles, had become more impersonal than in the "good old days" when Calamia began his practice. A vision of what was to come in the 1970s and beyond came from the words of a young lawyer, who was the first to advertise in El Paso after the U.S. Supreme Court ruling (*Bates v. State Bar of Arizona*, 433 U.S. 350, 97 S.Ct. 2691, 53 L.Ed.2d 810 [1977]). "People in the legal business are racing to put together a paper mill for routine services."[1]

In the 1970s and the 1980s, Calamia's legal skills had been called upon in defense of a number of controversial cases involving some high-profile persons. The city's public inspector faced a firing over negligence charges. There were the acquittals of the mayor and mayor pro-tem on charges of violating the recent Texas open meetings laws. The sheriff's troubles over misuse of public funds resulted in a lesser penalty by virtue of a guilty plea. Calamia fought the lawman's ouster from office on the grounds of a little-known Texas statute. Having lost at the intermediate appellate court, Calamia was prepared to go to the top, but his client had had enough. In a few years, Calamia would again be called by the El Paso Bar to do special duty before a state district court in a case involving a runaway jury's charges against a state judge. Once again, Calamia faced the question of the constitutionality of a grand jury's report. He understood the degree to which judges enjoy immunity. Calamia played the role of a special district attorney in advising the grand jury on the law. The jurors did not like his advice and indicted the judge anyway. Now Calamia was in a position where he must defend the judge. He succeeded in vacating the indictment, much to the dislike of the grand jury foreman.[2] In another case, Calamia was called to defend El Paso's police chief over the seizure of material from one of the several adult entertainment stores that now called El Paso home.[3] Other cases Calamia successfully challenged included a contempt charge over a wiretap order that the telephone company ignored, police undercover tactics and the constitutionality of searches and seizures in drug, immigration and other cases.[4]

In 1981, however, Calamia and Mallin were called to defend a male prostitute, accused of murdering another homosexual in a tryst at a local motel. This case would extend for the next seven years. The saga began in 1980, when Steven Blaine Jones, a twenty-four-year-old male prostitute from Hollywood, killed the other homosexual in a hotel room with a socket wrench and strangled him to death with a rope. The two had arranged the tryst at a motel after the soon-to-be victim had offered a ride and some drinks to Jones. Jones had hitchhiked his way to El Paso from California. He was used to being the dominant partner in his homosexual encounters, but the other fellow wanted Jones to play the submissive role. Jones would have none of it. He would not have his hands tied to a television set with a rope that the other man held. The other man blocked his attempted escape. Out of anger, Jones reached for an opened toolbox and hit the victim repeatedly on the head. Jones then grabbed the rope that the partner dropped and strangled him until he stopped breathing. Jones fled, leaving his identification card in the hotel room. He was arrested a year later in California.

Jones went on trial a year later in 171st District Court with Calamia and Mallin at his side. The State's evidence, presented to a jury with eleven female members, was generally undisputed. Evidence showed that Jones had killed the victim in the west El Paso motel room. However, the State and the defense differed over Jones's intent. District Attorney Simmons and his assistant Gary Weiser argued that Jones killed the man with intent to rob him. The prosecution charged that Jones stole a diamond ring from the victim and fled in the victim's leased company car. To Simmons, Jones was a "street-wise male prostitute" who killed the victim because he needed money. In contrast, Calamia placed Jones on the witness stand where he could tell jurors about how the victim, a bigger person than Jones, wanted to force himself on Jones in a dominant role.

District Judge Edwin Berliner's instructions to the jury included both murder and voluntary manslaughter. The jury found him guilty of murder after some five hours of deliberation. With a guilty verdict, Calamia now argued for a more lenient sentence before a jury in the sentencing phase. Calamia argued that Jones had been provoked and that the victim tried, "to take his last bit of dignity" from Jones.[5] Weiser would have none of that. He argued that the testimony of what occurred in the motel room was uncorroborated. "He took a life, no matter what the circumstances," Weiser told jurors, as he emphasized that this was not a time to show compassion or mercy.[6] It took the same jury less than three hours to recommend a ninety-nine-year prison sentence.

The verdict and sentence were not what Calamia expected. He had hoped that the sudden passion argument would result in a conviction for voluntary manslaughter, a lesser offense than murder and a sentence of no more than twenty years. He thought, "Maybe the jury didn't consider the lesser offense that involved sudden passion." In his view, Judge Berliner's instructions to the jury left little chance for jurors to consider Jones's state of mind. He was certain that he and Mallin had recommended instructions to the judge for the jury to test the guilt of a crime committed out of sudden passion. In criminal cases, the judge's instructions to the jury about the applicable laws come both at the beginning of the trial and at the close of the trial. The instructions outline the cornerstones of the elements of a crime charged in the indictment and the all-important principles of the defendant's presumption of innocence and the State's burden of proof. In the Jones case, Calamia also thought the testimony was sufficient to prove that Jones acted out of sudden passion. He was convinced that Jones felt very strongly that he could not play a submissive role, and when the victim tried to force him to go against these convictions, his state of mind was no longer one capable of cool reflection but rather was transformed into one of uncontrolled rage.[7]

The appeal was before the Eighth Court of Appeals in El Paso. Although notice of appeal was filed in 1982, the appeal was not submitted until October 1983.[8] Until a few years before, this court heard only civil appeals. Before 1981, criminal appeals from the district courts went directly to the Texas Court of Criminal Appeals, the last recourse for criminal cases in Texas. The restructuring added criminal appeals jurisdiction to the intermediate courts of appeals. In their appeal, Calamia and Mallin alleged error in the terms of the indictment, the manner in which the jury was selected in a capital crime case, introduction of "gruesome photographs," and omissions in the jury instructions. Their principal point was that the trial court erred in failing to instruct the jury on the issue of sudden passion. The instructions should have specifically stated that it was the State's burden "to prove beyond a reasonable doubt that Jones did not act under the immediate influence of sudden passion arising from an adequate cause."

The Eighth Court of Appeals overruled all of Calamia and Mallin's points of error (*Jones v. State*, 689 S.W.2d 510 [Tex.App.— El Paso 1985]). However, the panel analyzed the sudden passion instruction issue in more detail in view of the case law that had been developing in the highest courts. Under the Texas penal code in effect at the time of the trial, sudden passion covered a direct cause of death that arose from provocation at the time of the killing. However, it had taken a Texas Court of Criminal Appeals decision in late 1978 to establish that sudden passion was an element of the offense of voluntary manslaughter (*Braudrick v. State*, 572 S.W.2d 709 [Tex.Cr.App. 1978]), *cert. denied*, 440 U.S. 923, 99 S.Ct. 1252, 59 L.Ed.2d 477 [1979]). In *Braudrick*, the court closely examined the relationship between murder and voluntary manslaughter, and concluded that the penal code "creates [an] illusion that voluntary manslaughter has one additional element not found in murder." That element was sudden passion; accordingly sudden passion must also pass the "beyond reasonable doubt" test.

Additional law on sudden passion had developed after the jury verdict but before the Eighth Court of Appeals considered the case. The Texas Court of Criminal Appeals ruled in January 1983, that if the issue was raised, a sudden passion instruction must be submitted to the jury:

> The distinguishing feature between murder and voluntary manslaughter is not a fact that must be proven beyond a reasonable doubt to establish voluntary manslaughter, nor is it a

fact that must be disproven by the State to establish murder in the absence of some evidence raising an issue as to that fact. If the issue is raised, then it must be disproven to establish murder. (*Cobarrubio v. State*, 675 S.W.2d 749, 751 [Tex.Cr.App. 1983])

In short, the jury charge must include an instruction that the prosecution must prove, beyond a reasonable doubt, that a defendant "did not act under the immediate influence of sudden passion arising from an adequate cause."

The justices understood the implications of *Cobarrubio*, but their focus was on the State's argument, that even if not stated in a precise manner, the trial judge must include a *Cobarrubio*-like instruction on voluntary manslaughter. The State argued that the defense neither requested the instruction nor objected to its omission. Calamia and Mallin countered with an aggravated rape decision in 1983 by the Fort Worth Court of Appeals in which lack of precision in a judge's instruction was found to be "fundamental error." The Texas Court of Criminal Appeals affirmed that decision in early 1985 (*Almanza v. State*, 686 S.W.2d 157 [Tex.Cr.App. 1984]). But the Court of Appeals in El Paso looked at *Almanza* differently, and held that by not objecting to the judge's instruction, the defendant in effect had waived error.

It was 1986 and the case was now before the Texas Court of Criminal Appeals.[9] Citing *Castillo-Fuentes v. State*, 707 S.W.2d 559 [Tex.Cr.App. 1986] and *Lawrence v. State*, 700 S.W.2d 208 [Tex.Cr.App. 1985], Calamia and Mallin now argued that sudden passion was Jones's only defense and thus the requirement of a precise instruction in *Cobarrubio* applied. Calamia contrasted the situations in the two cases. In one case, the primary argument was self-defense such that the absence of a sudden passion instruction was not reversible error. But in the second case, as in the *Jones*' case, the absence of the instruction was reversible error.

The Court of Criminal Appeals reversed and remanded for a new trial (*Jones v. State*, 720 S.W.2d 535 [Tex.Cr.App. 1986]). The majority agreed that under *Almanza*, "failure to object at trial preserves nothing for review," but such is not the case when charge error is raised in an appeal for the first time. The court held that the trial court erred by omitting "the issue of sudden passion in the paragraph of the charge applying the law of murder to the facts of the case" (*Id.* at 536). The court then conducted a harm analysis and concluded that since Jones's principal defense was that of voluntary manslaughter, the degree of harm was "egregious" or so openly and conspicuously bad that it denied the defendant a fair trial.

Presiding Judge Onion "vigorously" dissented (*Id.* at 538). He was not sold on Jones's defense. He considered that both sides had ample support for their respective positions, and he urged a quick decision, instead of remanding and giving the six-year-old case "another whirl in the appellate orbit" (*Id.* at 537). He concluded, "But then, who said that the name of the game was quickness" (*Id.* at 538).

By early 1987, the *Jones* ruling officially arrived in El Paso's 171st District Court. This was not one of those cases that El Paso District Attorney Simmons was willing to let go easily. A local man had been murdered, and the public expected justice. His better option was to retry the case. It would be another year before the case was ready for another whirl in the criminal justice system orbit. The grand jury reindicted Jones in early 1988 on a murder charge. This time Jones was provided an appointed lawyer from El Paso county's recently instituted public defender's office.[10] Jones also figured he had learned a few legal moves now that he had a few years' imprisonment under his belt. These petitions were to no avail in the 171st District Court, now presided by Peter Peca who had succeeded Berliner. In May 1988, Jones determined it was best to plead guilty to the murder charge. He was sentenced to twenty years in prison with credit for the more than six and one-half years he had already served. Jones's life had been spared, and he had avoided a ninety-nine-year prison sentence. The victory that Calamia had engineered in a defense of sudden passion likely was a factor in the bargaining for the lesser twenty-year sentence.

Calamia had turned sixty-seven in 1988. This was an age when many lawyers put away their law books and ventured into another field, if not retiring. Calamia might have been a state or federal district judge. He had excellent firsthand experience and knowledge of the inner workings of the state and federal court systems, including the appellate levels of those systems. He had scored victories in numerous civil and criminal cases. He had argued hundreds of cases before juries. He had taken more than fifty cases to the state and federal appeals court, with significant success. His reputation as a skillful criminal defense attorney was to be admired and respected. His criminal case victories were not necessarily only those that ended in acquittals, but also those cases that resulted in less time spent in prison or on probation. He continued to do anything to help his clients, except break the rules. He was still the meticulous Calamia, in an age when many legal services were dealt with routinely through forms. He continued to study the law and kept up with changes in the law and major court decisions. He was still the same Calamia in the courtroom, pursuing a point often and loudly. While some differed with his tactics, none could argue with his success and integrity. Some would still roll their eyes in disbelief as Calamia brought out a point of law that few would have considered as valid. Still, many of them some years later would shake their heads in disbelief when the appeals court had validated his argument.

Some twenty years after the Warren Court's ruling in *Gideon*, federal and state public defender offices were now acceptable. Several government and private foundation-funded legal aid clinics served the poor. Prosecutors and police had the Warren Court's *Miranda* warning language down pat.[11] In a newspaper pro and con account twenty years after *Miranda*, District Attorney Simmons reflected a strong public sentiment that the warning was obsolete and predicted the *Miranda* warning practice would eventually be eliminated. He believed that an exact phraseology was necessary in the decade following *Miranda* "when police were not as well-educated or trained and investigative techniques were less sophisticated." He complained that many criminals had escaped justice because the warning was not given in a certain manner. He concluded, "Now courts are holding that you don't have to use the exact language." Calamia countered that denial of the *Miranda* warning tips the scales of justice toward the State's side, "It's minority groups and the uneducated that don't know their rights, and before they can waive their rights, they have to know (what rights they have)." Even with *Miranda*, it was estimated that about half of criminal defendants confessed to charges.[12]

Calamia was still the feisty hard-hitting lawyer, ready to take on a legal battle, no matter how big or small. In 1983, one incident brought back memories of a fight with City Hall in 1952. On Veterans Day, Calamia would show the criminal justice system that he was still around. He would fight City Hall in the lower courts, once again as he did at the start of his career forty years earlier in defense of a taxi driver who had received a traffic ticket. This time, it was over parking tickets on November 11, a weekday. Calamia paid homage to veterans. He had served in World War II and admired those who served in that and other wars. He had defended decorated war heroes. November 11 was a day for paying homage to American veterans. It was also a holiday when presumably public offices were closed. Surely, it was safe to park one's car in downtown El Paso without feeding the parking meter. Not so for city government! El Paso city council did not celebrate the holiday on that day. Calamia returned from the courthouse and found seven parking tickets on his car's windshield. It just didn't seem right. Armed with photographs, Calamia contested the ticket in county court at law arguing that the city failed to provide adequate notice on the parking meters. His ticket was dismissed, and the city changed the notification on the meters.[13]

Many years later, a conversation with Calamia was no different from one in previous decades. The conversation was, in one form or another, about the law and the Bill of Rights. He would still flail his hands, stand up on occasion and raise his voice as if making an argument before the jury. But suddenly, strange things began to happen.

Calamia began to lose his enthusiasm. Calamia appeared to be forgetful in court. His voice was weakening. The excitement of correcting an injustice was not there. He kept more and more to himself. The early morning racquetball game was no longer a lure. At home, his boxing and weightlifting equipment was no longer in use. The Arabian horses that roamed his large estate no longer strode with Calamia in the saddle. Calamia's law practice stopped abruptly. His law practice suffered. Soon, he was back to where he started, at the low-occupancy, low-rent Caples Building. He had moved to a much smaller home than the extensive multi-acre home in El Paso's gentrified Upper Valley. His horses were gone. His gun collection was gone. His extensive collection of law books dwindled. Only a few remained, stacked and unused in his home. Day by day, his depression grew in deeper as his wife, Hortencia, and other family members sought to understand the problem and its roots. After all, this was a man who, in defending many of his clients, had taken the precaution of having them examined for neurological disorders or other ailments. For about a year, his doctors were certain that Calamia was suffering from severe depression. It was another year or so before there was an answer to the mystery.

Calamia's depression, according to a neurologist, was a symptom of something else, a physical disorder that was creeping into his neural system. It was a progressive deterioration of the nerve cells that control muscle movement. It would lead to shaking of one's hands and legs. There would be difficulty in walking, movement and coordination. The disorder was known as Parkinson's disease. There was no cure, only medication to control some of the symptoms. But to Calamia, this would be another fight. There would be difficult days. There would be so-so days. And on occasion, there was a good day. He gradually returned to his exercise equipment at home even if every step and every movement was a struggle. He began to converse with his relatives, friends and other acquaintances. Most importantly, Calamia removed the accumulated dust off his law books. However, it would be a while before he would recover his long engrained and intuitive personality to go after those real demons that tend to erode the constitutional rights guaranteed for all Americans.

Much had happened in America. The Cold War, which had pitted democracy against communism in an ever-present threat of nuclear holocaust throughout his career, suddenly was no more. The Soviet Union's communist empire began to crumble, epitomized by the dismantling of the Berlin Wall. However, global tensions of a different nature would remain with terrorist bombings of a U.S. Embassy in Somalia and a U.S. naval vessel in waters off the Arabian Peninsula. On September 11, 2001, the world-wide terrorist threat against America's way of life struck in the heart of Americans as hijacked commercial airplanes deliberately crashed into New York's World Trade Center's twin towers and the Department of Defense's seemingly impenetrable Pentagon building. A fourth hijacked airliner was forced to crash in a Pennsylvania field by passengers who resisted the armed hijackers. The United States responded with a coordinated occupation of Afghanistan, where the terrorist cells responsible for the terrorist attacks had been building up strength for several years. The United States even occupied Iraq, ousting a brutal dictator believed to be harboring weapons of mass destruction.

A new sense of alarm now gripped America over the global terrorist threat, as Congress passed a series of national security measures to guard against future attacks, which, as one might expect, would be controversial as questions would arise on just how far these measures would go before they impinged on the personal freedoms guaranteed in the Constitution. Calamia abhorred the attacks as much as he did the attack on Pearl Harbor in 1942, which had prompted him to join the Navy and fight to defend America's way of life. Accordingly, he wholeheartedly supported America's response. One might think that the potential constitutional issues—arising from America's domestic response—would be matters that would awaken Calamia's intuitive reaction to go after perceived demons. On the other hand, perhaps this lack of reaction was predictable when one considered his experiences in defending leftists and communists during the McCarthy era.

Calamia reacted only when a specific issue that, like a real demon, would raise its ugly head and he was not one to challenge a national security effort, albeit when a specific defendant's rights issue came his way. Moreover, Parkinson's disease was wearing him down. As time went on, Calamia's intuitive reaction would awaken to something he did not like about the changes in the Texas penal code.

In 2004, Calamia was still about the law. He was no longer able to practice law. He was no longer able to look into the law with the tireless intensity and methodical precision that he displayed in the past. However, he would find a renewed passion to again delve into the law, its current applications and prospects for its application in the future. Importantly, he would share his observations with whomever in El Paso's legal community would lend him an ear. He looked at court decisions that touched on the ever-changing standards of the American people; because of his training and experience, he understood the extreme caution that was necessary to uphold the protections guaranteed by the Bill of Rights and the Constitution. These documents must remain of the people and for the people.

Calamia soon found a demon which he considered to be real, in Texas's revision of its penal code, in particular that portion he understood so well and adroitly used in his criminal defense practice, a murder defense of sudden passion. The penal code had undergone a major change. In 1993, the Texas legislature looked at those intricate and seemingly precise provisions covering the crime of murder with a new set of eyes.[14] It had been influenced by a defendants' rights counterrevolution associated with the President Ronald Reagan era. The public demanded that murderers be locked up for good or executed. The public was fed up with criminals being let loose through technicalities. The consensus was that it was time for a "good cleanup" of these criminal statutes. The legislature changed its penal code effective January 1, 1994.[15]

The Texas penal code and Texas code of criminal procedure that had been in force for twenty years. These codes had set up various degrees of felonies and misdemeanors, meaning that offenses against a person were categorized differently.[16] Calamia understood in his defense of the murder case involving Jones, the male prostitute, that an issue of "sudden passion arising from an adequate cause" was an element of voluntary manslaughter, a lesser-included offense of murder. He clearly remembered from the appeals court victory that a precise jury instruction must place the burden on the prosecution to prove beyond a reasonable doubt that sudden passion did not exist. It did not matter that lack of an unanimous verdict could result from disagreement about the sudden passion issue (*Ruiz v. State*, 753 S.W.2d 681 [Tex.Cr.App. 1988]). To Calamia's clients this often meant a sentence less than death or life in prison. To some sectors of the public, however, a defense of sudden passion was an outrage, and the legislative changes sought to placate an angry public.

The legislature was clear on its mandate to "deal with conduct that unjustifiably and inexcusably causes or threatens harm to those individual or public interests for which state protection is appropriate." In furtherance of this, the new law sought to ensure public safety using the deterrent value of punishment as necessary to keep the criminal from again doing harm. In Title 5, Offenses Against the Person, the legislature took out "voluntary and involuntary manslaughter" from the definition of criminal homicide. From now on, this definition covered only murder, capital murder and manslaughter with varying degrees of punishment. Murder remained a felony of the first degree. Manslaughter, referred to as criminally negligent homicide, was now a state jail felony and no longer a Class A misdemeanor. The definitions for "adequate cause" and "sudden passion" remained for the crime of murder. However, a new subsection was added:

> At the punishment state of a trial, the defendant may raise the issue as to whether he caused the death under the immediate influence of sudden passion arising from an adequate cause. If the defendant proves the issue in the affirmative by a preponderance of the evidence, the offense is a felony of the second degree.

Clearly, the Seventy-third Legislature tossed out the issue of sudden passion as a defense to a murder charge. Should it arise, an issue of sudden passion would now be dealt with in the penalty phase.

By 2004, Steven Blaine Jones, the defendant in Calamia's 1986 appellate court victory, was now in his second year as a free man, having served a twenty-year sentence. Calamia was fighting his battles at home against that insidious and debilitating Parkinson's disease. El Paso county counted some 720,000 inhabitants and bore little resemblance to Calamia's El Paso of 1949. It was also a more prosperous and dynamic community than the one that Calamia lived in when his declining health forced him to leave his law practice. Another generation was now in charge of the criminal justice system. More than 1,200 lawyers now practiced in El Paso. Four federal district judges [17] handled El Paso's portion of the Western District of Texas. The other nine judges, not including three in senior status, covered cases in the San Antonio, Austin, Del Rio and Midland-Odessa. The Western District now had fourteen U.S. magistrates, three of them in El Paso.[18] Only the judiciary now occupied the 1935 vintage federal courthouse that once housed most of the federal agencies. A new federal courthouse would soon be built on an adjacent city block, covering all of it but the historic Catholic church that so often served as a nearby spiritual refuge for federal and state government officials.

The communications system in Calamia's heyday of legal practice—waiting for publication and mail delivery of slip opinions—had given way to the world wide web information superhighway. Federal court dockets were now on the Internet.[19] Supreme Court and appellate court decisions were now posted on government web pages soon after opinions were delivered.

The Texas judicial system had changed as well from the system that Calamia left some twenty years before. Seventeen district courts occupied the El Paso county courthouse. Seven county courts at law, with various specialties, handled misdemeanors.[20] The world of electronics had invaded the state court system too. Computer keyboards and laptop computers now rested on judges' benches. Lawyers routinely surfed the Internet in their legal research, as specialized websites led to less and less use of the old-fashioned procedures of pouring over tomes and tomes of law books. Computer-generated forms for legal documents, ranging from wills to jury instructions, became the norm. Surrounded by these marvelous inventions of the electronic age in a world of rapid change in criminal law, Calamia continued to call on his colleagues, many of them considerably younger.

The local Bar had not forgotten the "old guys." "Lawyers are heroes!" the El Paso Bar Association had proclaimed in 2001, in recognition of the various lawyers in El Paso who had been in practice for at least fifty years. Among them was Joe Calamia, "A Champion of Early Civil Rights." Near the end of 2004, Calamia's involvement in one of those early cases, involving the defense of a Communist Party supporter, was summarized at an El Paso Bar Association luncheon.[21] Times had indeed changed. Nearly fifty years after Calamia's involvement in the "commie" trials, the crowd of lawyers was shown excerpts from *Salt of the Earth*, the union organizer's movie produced by blacklisted pro-communist Hollywood directors and writers. The forbidden movie, whose star, the Mexican Bette Davis, a Mexican actress Calamia sought to keep in the United States, was now accepted as good cinema. More important to Calamia, the fundamental liberties he sought to protect in the appeals court victories of that dark age of McCarthyism were now inscribed into the law.

Edward Sherman, Tulane University law professor and Calamia's one-time assistant in a bank robbery case that tested Calamia's tenacity, continued to communicate with Calamia. "Joe is always telling me about some recent case, developing trends in the law and interesting cases he was working on." Sherman went on:

> For many years he carried the load for the El Paso Bar in representing persons who had few resources to pay a lawyer or whose case was clearly meritorious despite the odds against them. We lawyers, as well as the community at large, owe Joe a great debt of gratitude for upholding and living by the ideals of our profession.[22]

His colleagues also honored Calamia by presenting him with the "Magnum War Horse" award. His fellow lawyers remembered his feisty behavior, his twenty-seven-day stint as Sixty-fifth District judge and his record as "a defender of justice for lifetime."[23] Former district judge and court of appeals justice Jerry Woodard recalled Calamia's defense in his own case against a federal judge:

> Another thing I immediately recall about Mr. Calamia was his deep respect for the courts and our judicial process. Although he was always firm and insistent in his representation of his clients, he also was dutifully courteous to the presiding officer and ever-faithful to the rules of procedure.[24]

When asked about the most important qualities of a good lawyer, Calamia replied, "Integrity, honesty, tenacity." "We still discuss legal issues, new developments in the law and the state of the law in the United States and Texas," former district judge Robert Dinsmoor remarked. "He maintains himself current on legal developments in criminal law." Eighth District Court of Appeals Chief Justice David Wellington Chew, son of Calamia's first law partner, continues to be astonished by Calamia's mental capacity. "He regularly provides me with suggestions, commentary and legal opinions on various criminal law issues," wrote Chew, who added, "I value greatly his sage advice and opinion."[25] Thirty-Fourth District Judge Bill Moody praised Calamia's courage, integrity and hard work. "Mr. Calamia and I have remained in contact even though he has not actively practiced law for the last several years. He remains, however, a great student of the law and continues to call me frequently to discuss new case law, particularly that on the federal side."[26]

Calamia's speed bag still hangs in his back yard. A quick left. Then a quick right sends the bag in motion as he works on his coordination. Sometimes the mental and physical signals hit just right. Not so at other times. Once on the fixed bicycle, the spinning movement on his weary legs he looks forward to. Walking is a problem, although at times the mind-body signals seem to hit just right. A walker helps. A wheelchair helps. Hand-finger coordination is not what it once was. Sometimes, laying flat on his back brings instant relief. The law books on the decorative wooden shelves that once adorned his law office are getting heavier and more difficult to handle. Reading can be a problem at times. The print seems to get smaller and smaller. The light needs to be brighter. Yet there is the lure of finding his way to the large Early American style dinner table and its wooden Chippendale chairs that dominate the family living room space. There, a large fluorescent lamp shines brightly. Its rays illuminate the opened pages of a five-inch-thick book with a maroon leather cover; a book containing some 2,000 pages that surely must weigh several pounds. Its inscription reads, *Constitution of the United States*. In that heavy tome is the principal case law on each of the articles of this charter of U.S. law and on the protections of all Americans contained in its Bill of Rights. Surrounding the supreme law of the land are other books on criminal law procedure and stacks of slip opinions on a variety of cases.

These documents are not unused. Their pages are turned, used so much that they are torn. Key sentences and paragraphs are underlined with thick black lines. Calamia sits. He rests his arms on the table. He shuffles the papers about and raises his head. A sudden glow fills his countenance that seemed pale a few minutes earlier. His eyes, sleepy only a few minutes ago, now shine with a certain sparkle of confidence and assurance. Calamia is ready to talk about the law. Dr. Albert C. Cuetter, his physician, once wrote to him after his checkup:

> Your Parkinson's disease has been well controlled. Due to your perseverance, determination and steadfast attitude you are winning the battle to Parkinson's disease. Also, you have maintained good reasoning and a high level of function. You have a neuronal reserve so high and abundant that you can lose half of it and you will still function at a high level with a robust cerebral cortical endowment.[27]

Amid such encouragement by his colleagues, his doctor and his wife Hortencia, son Mark and daughter Virginia, Calamia's thoughts went back to a review of the law, the way it was changing and wondering, "Were all the changes for the better? Perhaps to a large extent." However, the elimination of the sudden passion defense in the Texas penal code hit him right where it hurt; his intuitive reaction to an effort by, in his vernacular, "the lawmaker" and "the enforcer" may deny a defendant's constitutional right to a trial by a fair and impartial jury on all the facts of an accusation. Texas, however, had also seen action on the sudden passion defense as one that would minimize the effects of reversible error. In other words, if a trial court erred in refusing to admit evidence relevant to the sudden passion issue, the error would be limited to a new punishment stage hearing and not to the entire trial (*Sánchez v. State*, 23 S.W.3d 30,34 [Tex.Cr.App. 2000]). Unlike the federal courts and other jurisdictions, Texas does not have sentencing guidelines for jurors to follow, other than the ranges of punishment allowed for various types of offenses stated in the Texas penal code.

Calamia could not accept Texas's elimination of sudden passion, which in effect eliminated an accused person's *mens rea* or state of mind as a factor to consider as an element of murder. Now, the felony-murder rule did away with the need to inquire into *mens rea* in a homicide case since Texas now considered that the nature of a murder takes care of the mental state issue. In short, a person may be found guilty of murder without proof of a culpable mental state. Thus a sudden passion issue was no longer one to be brought up in the trial phase in support of a lesser-included offense of voluntary manslaughter. In fact, the offense of voluntary manslaughter was eliminated from the code. An issue of sudden passion can only be brought out as an ameliorative issue in the sentencing phase.

Calamia's immediate reaction was that in placing the issue of sudden passion in the sentencing phase, after a guilty verdict of murder, Texas is denying a defendant a constitutional right to have a jury consider all the elements of an alleged offense and decide guilt or innocence beyond a reasonable doubt. He opens that large 2000-plus page tome on the U.S. Constitution. His voice, although weakened by the strain of battling Parkinson's disease, suddenly picks up strength and booms into a loud roar, as if one had stepped on a lion's tail. "Look here!" Calamia exclaims with his face flushed and his hands uplifted, and he reads, "In all criminal prosecutions, the accused shall enjoy the right to speedy and public trial, by an impartial jury."

Calamia then went on to assert his view that a state of mind, such as an issue of sudden passion, is an innate characteristic in the conduct of a person and thus a factor to consider in a murder case. At the same time, Calamia reflected on the requirements of the "due process of the law" clause of the Fourteenth Amendment that, with certainty, extended Sixth Amendment rights to the Texas courts. Calamia recalled the Supreme Court's decisions in *In re Winship* (397 U.S. 358, 90 S.Ct. 1068, 25 L.Ed.2d 368 [1970]) that the prosecution must prove beyond a reasonable doubt every fact necessary to constitute the crime, and in *Mullaney v. Wilbur*, (421 U.S. 684, 95 S.Ct. 1881, 44 L.Ed.2d 508 [1975]) that the state "must prove beyond a reasonable doubt the absence of the heat of passion on sudden provocation when the issue is properly presented." In the past, Texas's highest Court of Criminal Appeals had applied these principles in *Cobarrubio v. State* (675 S.W.2d 749 [Tex.Cr.App. 1983]), which Calamia had argued in defense of Steven Blaine Jones's crime of passion.

Calamia, in his mid 80s, is at times confined to a wheelchair. Yet, he is still quite visible behind the pile of law books and advanced slip opinions scattered on the large wooden dining room table in the family living room. He shakes his head at listening to the analogy of the federal sentencing system to the change in Texas's homicide law concerning sudden passion. "True, but the courts continue to hold sacred the Sixth Amendment right to a jury trial," Calamia responds rhetorically, citing *Apprendi v. New Jersey* (530 U.S. 446, 120 S.Ct. 2348, 147 L.Ed.2d 435 [2000]) and *Blakely v. Washington* (542 U.S. 296, 124 S.Ct. 2531, 159 L.Ed.2d 403 [2004]). In those cases, the Supreme Court ruled that that Sixth Amendment right, applicable to the states by the Fourteenth Amendment, prohibits the enhancement of criminal sentences beyond statutory maximums that are based on facts other than those that a jury had determined beyond a reasonable doubt. In Calamia's view, it is only a matter of time before a sentencing jury will recommend what amounts to an enhanced sentence on elements of a sudden passion issue that were not considered in the trial phase. Then, that portion of the Texas penal code will be in for a test of Sixth Amendment constitutionality, perhaps in the Supreme Court.

And so Calamia continues to look at the law with the passion typical of his days in law practice, "The right case has to come up some time." Then, with a seemingly woeful countenance as if to be passing the torch to the next generation of idealistic defendants' rights fighters, Calamia sighs, "Someone has to find the right case."

ENDNOTES

THE QUEST BEGINS
A WHIRLWIND OF IDEALISM: YOUNG JOE

[1]D'Antonio, William V. and Forum, William H. *Influentials in Two Border Cities: A Study in Community Decision-Making.* (South Bend, Indiana: University of Notre Dame P. 1965) 57–100.

[2]*El Paso Herald Post*, "Who Runs El Paso," 16–19 Aug 1986.

[3]Calamia, Joseph A. Interview with author, 30 Sep 2005; Interview, Joe A. Calamia and Raymond Caballero, 21 Oct 2003; El Paso County Historical Society, Hudspeth City Directories, 1906–1923.

[4]Calamia, Joseph R. Calamia, historical notes on Calamia and Amity-Miller family, undated.

[5]C. L. Sonnichsen Special Collections, UT El Paso, Oral History No. 421, interview with Laura Calamia by Sarah E. John, 2 Sep 1976.

[6]Calamia interview with author, 10 Nov 2006.

[7]Calamia interview with author, 14 Feb 2006. Calamia recalled, "I am very grateful to the Veterans' Administration who supported us veterans during our law school studies at SMU." He also recalled support from El Paso lawyer Frank Galván, whose brother Robert Galván attended SMU with Calamia.

As of June 22, 1944, (Servicemen's Readjustment Act [G.I. Bill of Rights] PL78 [346]). The Servicemen's Readjustment Act of 1944 put higher education within the reach of millions of veterans of World War II and later military conflicts. Anon. *Education in the United States: A Historical Perspective* (New Jersey: Prentice Hall, 1976).

C. L. Sonnichsen Special Collections, UT at El Paso, Oral History No. 284 interview with El Paso lawyer Albert Armendáriz, 10 Jul 1976. Armendáriz recalled: "I'm very grateful to the Army because I wouldn't be a lawyer today if it weren't for the G.I. Bill, because when I got out of the Army I only had a high school education, so I had to go to UTEP. Luckily at that time they had a program that was available to veterans where if you had a B+ average in sixty hours of college work, they would accept you into an accredited law school. I came back to UTEP with high school only, took sixty hours after a ten-year absence and made a B+ average and got into the University of Southern California. I don't have a BA degree; my son does, but I don't. I just have the Juris Doctor because I am a product of the G.I. Bill."

[8]*El Paso Herald Post*, "The Chicano Movement," Bob Ybarra, a fifteen-part series on conditions and social inequities involving El Paso Hispanics, 7 Dec 1971–14 Jan 1972.

[9]Geraldine Campbell Michaelbust interview with author, 5 Jan 2007.

[10]C. L. Sonnichsen Special Collections, UT El Paso, Oral History No. 257, 17 Jul 1978. Wellington Y. Chew (1920–1977) was the first Asian American to be licensed to practice law in Texas in the late 1940s.

CALM BEFORE THE STORM: THE JUDICIARY IN THE 1950S

[1]El Paso County Historical Society, Archive of telephone and city directories, 1950–51.

[2]Broaddus, J. Morgan, Jr., *The Legal Heritage of El Paso* (El Paso: Texas Western P, 1963) 197–199.

[3]D'Antonio and Forum, 131.

[4]Broaddus, 141–142, 151–153. The U.S. Western Judicial District of Texas was established by Congress in 1884. Prior to that federal cases were taken to San Antonio for trial. Five federal judges preceded Judge Thomason, E. B. Turner (1885–1888), Thomas S. Masey (1888–1916), Du Val West (1916–1917), William R. Smith (1917–1924) and Charles A. Boyton (1924–1927). Thomason, Robert Ewing, *Thomason: The Autobiography of a Federal Judge*, edited and annotated by Joseph M. Ray, (El Paso: Texas Western P, 1971) 102–108.

[5]*El Paso Herald Post*, 10 Sep 1956.

[6]U.S. Congress, Biographical Directory. William Homer Thornberry (1909–1995) received his law degree from the University of Texas in 1936. He served in the Texas legislature as district attorney, and in seven congresses from 1949 through 1963. He was appointed U.S. District Judge for the Western District of Texas in 1963 until his resignation in 1965 to serve as circuit judge for the U.S. Court of Appeals for the Fifth Circuit through 1995. Thornberry was nominated to succeed Supreme Court Justice Abe Fortas when Fortas was nominated to replace Earl

Warren as chief justice. Fortas's withdrawal from consideration in 1968 made Thornberry's nomination moot.

[7]C. L. Sonnichsen Special Collections, UT El Paso, *El Paso Herald Post* Morgue, D. W. Suttle. U.S. Congress, Biographical Directory. John Nance "Cactus Jack" Garner (1868–1967) served as Uvalde county judge, Texas state representative and U.S. congressman until his election as vice president in 1932, a post he held until 1941.

[8]C. L. Sonnichsen Special Collections, UT El Paso, *El Paso Herald Post* Morgue, Ernest Guinn. The Western District of Texas, headquartered in San Antonio, Texas. By 1968 was subdivided in divisions for El Paso, Midland, Del Rio, San Antonio and Austin. Adrian Spears of San Antonio was the senior judge followed in seniority by Judge Jack Roberts of Austin, Judge Suttle and Judge Guinn.

[9]C. L. Sonnichsen Special Collections, UT El Paso, Oral History No. 284, Armendáriz, 10 Jul 1976. Armendáriz recalled, "I set up office in the Banner Building above Kress with $40 I borrowed from Dad to pay [the] first month's rent. It was a small one room office, but I was met by three persons on [my] first day."

[10]Bass, Jack, "The Fifth Circuit Four," *The Nation*, 3 May 2004, 30–32. This article and his book *Unlikely Heroes* (New York, Simon and Schuster, 1981) praise the courage of Chief Judge Elbert Tuttle and judges John Minor Wisdom, John Brown and Richard Rives in applying the judicial review principles of *Brown v. Board of Education* in crucial decisions in the segregated South that advanced the movement for equality for African Americans and other minorities.

[11]Alien Registration Act, 54 Stat. 671, passed by Congress on June 29, 1940 made it illegal for anyone in the United States to advocate, abet or teach the desirability of overthrowing the government. The law also required all alien residents in the United States over fourteen years of age to file a comprehensive statement of their personal and occupational status and a record of their political beliefs. The main objective of the act was to undermine the American Communist Party and other left-wing political groups in the United States. In *Dennis v. United States*, the court limited its review to that of whether § 2 or § 3 of the Smith Act, inherently or as construed and applied in this case, violated the First Amendment and other provisions of the Bill of Rights and whether either § 2 or § 3, facially or as applied in the instant case, violated the First and Fifth Amendments because of indefiniteness.

[12]Section 9(h) of the Taft-Hartley Act of 1947 required officers of labor unions to sign affidavits indicating that they were not members of the

Communist Party, supporters of that party or generally advocated the violent overthrow of the government. (*American Communications Ass'n. v. Douds*, 339 U.S. 382, 70 S.Ct. 674, 94 L.Ed. 925 [1950]) affirmed that the provision did not violate the First Amendment.

[13]Supreme Court Chief Justice Earl Warren (1891–1974) served from 1953 until 1969, a period of expanding civil liberties. A governor of California (1943–1953) with no judicial experience at the time, he was appointed to the high court by President Eisenhower. The Warren Court's rulings that expanded civil rights were praised by some and condemned by others who accused the court of overreaching its authority.

[14]Broaddus, 141–142, 253. The Thirty-fourth District Court was created by the Texas legislature on April 9, 1883 to cover El Paso, Presidio and Pecos counties. In November of that year, legislation required the election of a district judge and a district attorney in each judicial district in Texas. This coincided with a special election in El Paso county that resulted in the county seat being moved from Ysleta to El Paso in a case where the voting potential of El Paso was multiplied by seven. T. A. Falvey was elected in the 1884 general election, the first after the coming of the railroads, in one of the most colorful campaigns in El Paso history. He resigned in 1892 and was succeeded by A. M. Walthall. Biographical note on page 222.

[15]Broaddus, 153–155. The Forty-first District Court was created by the Texas legislature on April 19, 1899 with concurrent jurisdiction in El Paso county, with the exception of the power to empanel a grand jury, which was retained by the Thirty-fourth District Court. James M. Coggin of Eagle Pass, Texas, was appointed as judge. Mulcahy was born in El Paso county in 1890 and received his law degree from the University of Texas.

[16]Texas, State Senate, SR 251 Feb 18, 1999. Broaddus, 161. The Sixty-fifth District Court was created by the Texas legislature on March 15, 1915. The Act limited its jurisdiction to El Paso county and reorganized the Thirty-fourth judicial district to include El Paso and Culberson (Hudspeth not created then) counties. The Forty-first Judicial District was limited to El Paso county. Ballard Coldwell was the first judge of the Sixty-fifth Judicial District.

[17]Broaddus, 46, 162–164. The Texas legislature authorized El Paso county Court to administer Texas criminal and civil laws in 1851 after the county's creation in 1850.

[18]*El Paso Times*, 11 Nov 1961.

[19]*El Paso Times*, 15 Apr 1955.

[20]El Paso county Historical Society, *Password*, Vol. XXXV, 126, "El Paso's Court of Appeals; Eighty Years of Judicial Service, 1911–1991," Schulte, Robert R., and Osborn, Max N.

[21]Calamia interview with author, 24 Mar 2006.

A QUICK START: CORRUPTION AND CAVALIER ATTITUDES

[1]Calamia interview with author 3 Dec 2004; 8 Jul 2005.

[2]*El Paso Times*, 24 Sep 1959. Campbell was sheriff from 1949–1953; he died on September 23, 1959.

[3]U.S. Senate Resolution 231, Eighty-first Congress (1950) authorized the Subcommittee on Investigations of Loyalty of State Department Employees (Tydings Committee). Chairman Millard E. Tydings held hearings from February to July 1950.

[4]*El Paso Herald Post* and *El Paso Times*, 1 May–30 Jul 1950.

[5]*El Paso Herald Post*, 27 Jun 1950.

[6]Calamia interview with author, 18 Feb 2004.

[7]*El Paso Herald Post*, 28 Jun 1950.

[8]Calamia interview with author, 14 Feb 2006.

[9]*El Paso Times*, 10 Dec 1943. Report on *Harold A. Fairchild v. Marie Carter Fairchild*, Forty-first District Court, 1943. "Chihuahua divorce laws are applicable to its citizens, but cannot be imposed upon the citizens of any of the states of the United States." Mulcahy vacated the divorce granted to the Fairchilds by a Juárez judge in July 1941.

[10]*John S. Martin, d/b/a Martin Brokerage Co., et al v. Joe Campbell, Sheriff of El Paso*, County, Texas, Forty-first District Judicial District, Petition for Temporary Restraining Order, No. 68999, June 29, 1950. TRO signed by Forty-first District Judge Mulcahy on June 29, 1950. Permanent injunction signed by Judge Mulcahy on October 2, 1950.

[11]*El Paso Herald Post*, 28 Jun 1950.

[12]*El Paso Herald Post*, 29 Jun 1950.

[13]*El Paso Herald Post*, 6-7 Jul 1950.

[14]Calamia interview with author, 30 Sep 2005.

[15]City of El Paso, Corporation Court dockets, Books 62, 63 and 83–87, 1949–1955.

[16]Calamia interview with author, 21 Oct 2003.

[17]Calamia interview with author, 24 Nov 2005.

[18]Calamia interview with author, 24 Mar 2006.

[19]Calamia interview with author, 4 Mar 2006.

[20]*El Paso Times*, 4 Dec 1954.

[21]Calamia interview with author, 30 Sep 2005.

SETTING PRECEDENTS: THE EARLY CASES
THE EARLY CASES: SEEMINGLY INNOCUOUS, BUT . . .

[1]*El Paso Times*, 27 Apr 1955.

[2]In Escobedo, argued April 29, 1964, and decided June 22, 1964, the Supreme Court held: "Under the circumstances of this case, where a police investigation is no longer a general inquiry into an unsolved crime but has begun to focus on a particular suspect in police custody who has been refused an opportunity to consult with his counsel and who has not been warned of his constitutional right to keep silent, the accused has been denied the assistance of counsel in violation of the Sixth and Fourteenth Amendments; and no statement extracted by the police during the interrogation may be used against him at a trial" (*Escobedo v. Illinois*, 378 U.S. 478, 84 S.Ct. 1758, 12 L.Ed.2d 977[1964]). Escobedo was a twenty-two-year-old Hispanic arrested with his sister in connection with the fatal shooting of his brother-in-law. While Escobedo was in custody, his lawyer was denied access to Escobedo even though the latter requested so see him.

In its ruling, the Supreme Court observed that Escobedo was not advised of his right to remain silent and was interrogated such that he made a damaging statement that was used against him at his trial. Escobedo is seen as a sidewalk to the Supreme Court ruling in *Miranda v. Arizona*, (384 U.S. 436, 86 S.Ct. 1602, 16 L.Ed.2d 694 [1966]). In *Miranda*, the Supreme Court ruled in part that Escobedo stressed the need for protective devices to make the process of police interrogation conform to the dictates of the privilege.

[3]In *Miranda*, the Supreme Court held in part: "In the absence of other effective measures the following procedures to safeguard the Fifth Amendment privilege must be observed: The person in custody must, prior to interrogation, be clearly informed that he has the right to remain silent and that anything he says will be used against him in court; he must be clearly informed that he has the right to consult with a lawyer and to have the lawyer with him during interrogation, and that, if he is indigent, a lawyer will be appointed to represent him." Further, the Supreme Court held: "If the individual indicates, prior to or during questioning, that he wishes to remain silent, the interrogation must cease; if he states that he wants an attorney, the questioning must cease until an attorney is present."

DRUG LAWS: TOUGH BUT WITH RESERVATIONS

[1]Special Senate Committee to Investigate Organized Crime in Interstate Commerce, 82d Cong., 1st Sess., 1951 and Boggs Act of November 2, 1951, 65 Stat. 767.

[2]Opium Acts of 1909 (35 Stat. 614) and 1914 (38 Stat. 275).

[3]Marijuana is also spelled marihuana.

[4]Ignacia Jasso (La Nacha) and her husband Pablo Gonzales (El Pablote) took over the Juárez drug trade in the 1920s. Through the 1960s, La Nacha operated a "shooting gallery" with impunity just a few blocks from the Rio Grande. *Herald Post* reporter M. R. "Bob" Ybarra, interviews with Armando Chávez M., 1970, following Chávez' publication of "Historia de Ciudad Juárez."

[5]Calamia interview with author, 3 Dec 2004.

[6]*El Paso Times*, 8 Feb 1956.

[7]*El Paso Times*, circa 1956.

[8]El Paso county Historical Society, *Password*, Vol. XXXV, 130, "El Paso's Court of Appeals: Eighty Years of Judicial Service, 1911–1991," Schulte, Robert R. and Osborn, Max N.

[9]The first count alleged that "Juan Ávalos Guevara, Jr., being then and there a transferee required to pay the transfer tax imposed by law, acquired and obtained, by transfer, from some person to your Grand Jurors unknown, 50 Marihuana Cigarettes, without having paid such tax." The second count alleged that Ávalos Guevara "Transported and concealed, and facilitated the transportation and concealment of 50 Marihuana Cigarettes, knowing that said Marihuana had been acquired and obtained without the transfer tax, provided in Section 4741 (a) of Title 26, U.S. Code, having been paid."

[10]22 U.S.C. § 4744 (a)(2) provided that "proof that any person shall have in his possession any marihuana and shall have failed, after reasonable notice and demand by the Secretary or his delegate, to produce the order form required by 4742 to be retained by him shall be presumptive evidence of guilt under this subsection and of liability for the tax imposed by section 4741 (a)."

CONSTITUTIONALITY: THE FOURTEENTH AMENDMENT AND THE STATES

[1]C.L. Sonnichsen Special Collections, UT El Paso, Oral History No. 177, interview with 168th District Judge George Rodríguez, Sr., 29 Jul 1975. Rodríguez, a son of a Juárez attorney, judge and diplomat, was born in Washington, DC, in 1909, received his law degree from the University of Arizona in 1933. He was elected an El Paso county court at law judge and subsequently, a district court judge.

[2]Vernon's Ann. P. C. arts. 1257a, 1257b, 1257c further defined adequate cause as something that would commonly produce a degree of anger,

rage, resentment or terror in a person of ordinary temper sufficient to render the mind incapable of cool reflection.

[3]Calamia interview with author, 25 May 2006.

[4]The court followed two general principles laid down by the Supreme Court in 1935 and 1942. It reasoned that the withheld testimony, "taken as a whole, gave the jury the false impression that his relationship with petitioner's wife was nothing more than that of casual friendship [. . .]. This testimony was elicited by the prosecutor who knew of the illicit intercourse between Castilleja and petitioner's wife. Undoubtedly Castilleja's testimony was seriously prejudicial to petitioner. It tended squarely to refute his claim that he had adequate cause for a surge of 'sudden passion' in which he killed his wife. If Castilleja's relationship with petitioner's wife had been truthfully portrayed to the jury, it would have, apart from impeaching his credibility, tended to corroborate petitioner's contention that he had found his wife embracing Castilleja. If petitioner's defense had been accepted by the jury, as it might well have been if Castilleja had not been allowed to testify falsely, to the knowledge of the prosecutor, his offense would have been reduced to 'murder without malice' precluding the death penalty now imposed upon him" (*Alcorta*, 355 U.S. at 31–32).

[5]Calamia interview with author, 28 Jul 2006.

[6]Calamia interviews with author, 26 Jan 24 Mar and 9 May 2006.

[7]Calamia interview with author, 2 Sep 2004

[8]Smith, Oliver, letter to Calamia, 8 Oct 1975.

[9]Calamia interview with author, 28 Sep 2004.

LIGHT IN A DARK PERIOD
THE COMMIES ARE COMING: MINE-MILL AND HOLLYWOOD

[1]"Commies" is used here to emphasize the vernacular used by communism foes during the McCarthy era as reflected in the various print media of that period.

[2]*El Paso Times*, 9 Mar 1955.

[3]C. L. Sonnichsen Special Collections, UT El Paso, Oral History No. 284, Humberto Silex, 28 Apr 1978.

[4]Clinton Jencks (1918–2005) was born in Colorado Springs and served in the Army Air Corps during World War II. He was assigned by Mine-Mill to Local 890 in 1947. In the aftermath of his legal battles following the Empire Strike, Jencks went on to teach economics at San Diego State University until his retirement in 1988. (*The Guardian*, obituary, 31 Dec 2005).

[5]*Silver City Daily News,* 17 Oct 1950–15 Feb 1952. Western New Mexico University, Miller Library, Bibliography of *Silver City Daily News* Articles and Advertisements about the Empire Zinc Company Strike.

FIRST COMMIE TRIAL: *SALT OF THE EARTH*

[1]Section 212(a)(27) kept out aliens who would participate in activities that would be prejudicial to the public interest or public safety. Section 212(a)(28) excluded aliens who belonged to subversive organizations, or teach or advocate prohibited views. Section 212(a)(29) barred aliens deemed likely to engage in subversive activities once here.
[2]Calamia interview with author, 26 Jan 2006.
[3]Press Release, National Lawyers Guild <www.nlg.org>, May 1999, concerning the death of Margolis.
[4]*El Paso Herald Post*, 27 Jan 1953.
[5]Calamia interviews with author, 8 Sep 2004 and 29 Oct 2004.
[6]Thomason, 117. The convictions were reversed and remanded. The defendants pleaded guilty and Judge Thomason sentenced them to life imprisonment.
[7]*El Paso Herald Post*, 26 Feb 1953.
[8]El Paso County Historical Society, *Password*, Vol. XXXV, 130, "El Paso's Court of Appeals: Eighty Years of Judicial Service, 1911–1991," Schulte, Robert R., and Osborn, Max N. Williams (1894–2001) attended Southern Methodist University and obtained his law degree from the University of Texas law school. He served as an assistant U.S. attorney until his appointment in 1957 to the Eighth Court of Civil Appeals and later resumed private practice until he retired in 1984. Unlike the Texas system of electing state judges and district attorneys, a U.S. attorney is appointed by the president of the United States for a four-year term and may, in turn, appoint assistants. In the Western District of Texas headquartered in San Antonio, U.S. attorney Charles F. Herring, a Democrat, had been appointed by President Truman. Broaddus and Williams had served as assistant U.S. attorneys since about 1949.
[9]*El Paso Herald Post*, 5 Mar 1953.
[10]Lorence, James J., *The Suppression of Salt of the Earth*, 2003.
[11]Library of Congress, National Film Registry <www.loc.gov/film>.

FIRST JENCKS'S TRIAL: QUICK AND SIMPLE?

[1]*El Paso Herald Post*, 1–31 Dec 1953.
[2]*El Paso Herald Post*, 31 Dec 1953.

[3]Thomason, 117.

[4]*El Paso Herald Post*, 8 Jan 1954.

[5]*Jencks v. United States* 226 F.2d 540 (5th Cir. 1955); *El Paso Times*, 9–21 Jan; 1954; *El Paso Herald Post* 9–23 Jan 1954.

MATUSOW AND JENCKS: FALSE WITNESS, CONTEMPT AND DISCOVERY

[1]These plays included, *Waiting for Lefty* by Clifford Odets and *The Cradle Will Rock* by Mark Blizstein.

[2]U.S. Senate, Eighty-third Congress, 2nd Session, Resolution 301, 2 Dec 1954.

[3]*El Paso Herald Post*, 18 Mar 1955.

[4]226 F.2d 533 (5th Cir. 1955). The Fifth Circuit's opinion detailed the sub-rosa plot and quoted the chapter in part as follows: "Jencks was not alone. Others have been indicted for the same charge. Accused of being members of the Communist Party after they had signed the Non-Communist Affidavit of the Taft-Hartley (29 U.S.C.A Section 141 et. Seq.). "Jencks would have been a Communist Party member, yes. If he was I had no way of knowing it. And I didn't care," (*Id.* at 558).

[5]*El Paso Herald Post*, Dec 1954–21 Mar 1955; *El Paso Times* 7 Mar–21 Mar 1955; *Jencks v. United States* 226 F.2d 540 (5th Cir. 1955).

[6]*Matusow v. United States* 229 F.2d 335 (5th Cir. 1956); Calamia interview with author, 28 Jun 2006.

[7]*El Paso Herald Post*, 14 Mar 1955 and 17 Mar 1955.

[8]Calamia interviews with author, 28 Apr 2005, 14 Feb 2006 and 28 Jul 2006; *Matusow v. United States* 229 F.2d 335 (5th Cir. 1956).

[9]At the time, Rule 42(a) Federal Rules of Criminal Procedure provided that if the court could summarily punish a person who committed criminal contempt in its presence if the judge saw or heard the contemptuous conduct and certified the facts.

[10]At the time, Rule 42(b) provided that a person who committed criminal contempt could be punished after prosecution and notice, stating the time and place of trial and allowing the defendant a reasonable time to prepare a defense. All of the protections of the Bill of Rights applied, including the presumption of innocence and the requirement that the prosecution prove guilt beyond a reasonable doubt.

[11]Bass, 88. Cameron was appointed by President Eisenhower in 1955 and served as a Fifth Circuit judge until his death in 1964. Cameron did not share Rives, Tuttle and Brown's view on the *Brown* decision as evident in his dissent in *Denton v. City Carrollton* (235 F.2d 481 [5th Cir. 1956]), in

which he stood with the Tenth Amendment as one that gave the states a commission from the federal government observing that the states existed before the adoption of the U.S. Constitution.

[12]Jones was nominated by President Eisenhower to fill the seat vacated by Louis Willard Strum. Jones served from 1955 to 1966, when he assumed senior status. He along with judges Brown and Tuttle were reassigned to the Eleventh Circuit Court in 1981. He continued senior status until his death in 1993. Prior to his appointment, Jones had served as deputy district attorney in Denver, Colorado, and was in private practice in Jacksonville, Florida, from 1925 until 1955.

[13]Tuttle was one of the old Fifth Circuit Court of Appeals (later split into the Fifth and Eleventh Circuits) judges derisively called "The Fifth Circuit Four." Social and legal upheaval followed *Brown v. Board of Education* I [1954] and II [1955] and the Fifth Circuit was on the front line of following the *Brown* decision. Tuttle was born in California and grew up in Hawaii, returning to the United States to get his law degree from Cornell in 1923. In his Atlanta, Georgia, practice, Tuttle successfully defended one black man on charges of raping a white woman and another black man on charges of distributing communist literature. He was a Republican because of the segregation sentiment of the old Southern Democratic Party. Tuttle, along with Circuit Judges Brown, Rives and Wisdom, exhibited great courage in following the *Brown* decision as the courts faced integration delaying tactics, political pressures and threats. Tuttle's early decisions were in cases from his home state of Georgia declaring the Georgia legislative appointment system to be unconstitutional. (*Toombs v. Forston*, 205 F. Supp. 248 [D.C.Ga. 1962]). In a second appeal on congressional re-apportionment, his dissenting opinion was adopted by the U.S. Supreme Court. Other landmark cases involved the Jim Crow laws, voting rights, jury discrimination, employment discrimination and school desegregation. The latter included the order to admit James Meredith to the all-white University of Mississippi in 1962.

[14]*El Paso Herald Post*, 29 Jul 1955.

[15]Calamia interview with author, 14 Feb 2006; Mark Calamia interview with author, 29 Dec 2006.

AFTERMATH: JENCKS, MINE-MILL AND NO CALAMITY IN JOE

[1]Specifically, the opinion read: "The reliance of the Court of Appeals upon *Gordon v. United States*, 344 U.S. 414, is misplaced. It is true that

one fact mentioned in this Court's opinion was that the witness admitted that the documents involved contradicted his testimony. However, to say that Gordon held a preliminary showing of inconsistency a prerequisite to an accused's right to the production for inspection of documents in the Government's possession is to misinterpret the Court's opinion. The necessary essentials of a foundation, emphasized in that opinion, and present here, are that "[t]he demand was for production of [. . .] specific documents and did not propose any broad or blind fishing expedition among documents possessed by the Government on the chance that something impeaching might turn up. Nor was this a demand for statements taken from persons or informants not offered as witnesses." (Emphasis added.) We reaffirm and reemphasize these essentials. "For production purposes, it need only appear that the evidence is relevant, competent and outside of any exclusionary rule." Jencks, 353 U.S. at 666.

²Geraldine Calamia Michelbust interview with author, 5 Jan 2007.

³*El Paso Herald Post*, 11 Jun 1955; 29 Feb–21 Mar 195; 30 Aug 1956; 19 Sep 1956; 5–6 Jun 1959. Calamia interview with author, 3 May 2006.

TENACITY CALAMIA STYLE
THE 1960S: JUDGE THOMASON PASSES THE TORCH

¹*El Paso Times*, 8 Jun 1958.

²Kennedy, J. F. "A Special Address to Congress on the Importance of Space," 25 May 1961.

³*El Paso Herald Post*, 2 Jun, 1958, 13 Nov, 1961, 12 Feb, 1965 and 31 Jan, 1966. Federal Magistrates Act of 1968 (82 Stat. 1107). The act expanded the magistrates' authority to conduct misdemeanor trials with the consent of the defendants, to serve as special masters in civil actions and to assist district judges in pre-trial and discovery proceedings as well as appeals for post-trial relief. The act also authorized a majority of district judges on any court to assign to magistrates "additional duties as are not inconsistent with the Constitution and laws of the United States."

⁴Letter from Scott Segal, Unit Chief–Capital Crimes, to Texas Bar Foundation, 25 Jan 2006.

⁵Mark Calamia interview with author, 28 Dec 2006. El Paso Bar Association Resolution, presented by Frank Own III and Phillip Bargman on Mar 9, 1966: "It is the desire of the El Paso Bar Assn. to acknowledge,

applaud and publish the deeds of this man [. . .] who in the great tradition of his provision, well qualified and grounded, of character and courage, acted in the face of danger, placing his own life in jeopardy."
[6]*El Paso Times,* 17 Jun and 28 Jun 1969, *El Paso Herald Post,* 16 Jun 1969. Calamia received 105 votes out of a possible 144. Former U.S. attorney Holvey Williams received twenty-two and Corporation Court Judge Sam Callan received seventeen votes.

CLANAHAN: EVEN "LA MIGRA" DESERVES A FAIR TRIAL

[1]Craig, Richard B. *The Bracero Program,* U of Texas P, Austin and London, 127–132.
[2]8 U.S.C. § 1357 (a)(3). Any officer or employee of the Service authorized under regulations prescribed by the Attorney General shall have power without warrant—(3) within a reasonable distance from any external boundary of the United States, to board and search for aliens any vessel within the territorial waters of the United States and any railway car, aircraft, conveyance or vehicle, and within a distance of twenty-five miles from any such external boundary to have access to private lands, but not dwellings, for the purpose of patrolling the border to prevent the illegal entry of aliens into the United States.
[3]*El Paso Times,* 28 Apr 1963.
[4]*El Paso Herald Post,* 8 Jan 1963.
[5]Department of Justice letter to Mr. Joseph A. Calamia:
  "As an attorney and counselor at law, you are hereby specifically retained and appointed as Special Assistant to the U.S. attorney for the Western District of Texas to assist in the presentation of the case of *State of Texas v. Clanahan.* In that connection, you are specifically directed and authorized to conduct legal proceedings and perform other duties of an assistant U.S. Attorney."
  Please execute and forward the required oath of office at your earliest convenience.
  Sincerely,
  (signed) Nicholas B. Katzenbach, Deputy Attorney General."
[6]<www.tsha.utexas.edu/handbook/online/articles>.
[7]Calamia interview with author, 22 Jul 2005. *Washington Post,* 2 Mar 1954. The attackers had shot thirty rounds at the congressmen using automatic pistols from a House visitor's gallery. Congress was debating an immigration bill. Five lawmakers were wounded. The attackers, activists

for a free Puerto Rico, had unfurled a Puerto Rican flag before they began to shoot.
[8]*El Paso Herald Post*, 6 Jan 1964

NAGELL: DISCOVERY, INSANITY AND CONVINCING EVIDENCE

[1]U.S. House of Representatives, House Report No. 95-1828, Report of the Select Committee on Assassinations, 29 Mar 1979, 35.
[2]Review of events reported in the *El Paso Times* and *El Paso Herald Post*, Jan–Dec 1963.
[3]*El Paso Times* and *El Paso Herald Post*, 21 Sep 1963; Russell, Dick, *The Man Who Knew Too Much; Hired to Kill Oswald and Prevent the Assassination of JFK: Richard Case Nagell* (New York: Carroll & Graf Publishers/R. Gallen, 1992) 43–58.
[4]Jim Bundren conversation with author, 29 Aug 2006.
[5]*Ibid.*
[6]*Nagell v. United States*, 354 F.2d 441 (5th Cir. 1966) and selected transcripts *United States v. Nagell*, U.S. District Court for the Western District of Texas.
[7]U.S. Congress, House Report No. 95-1828, "Final Report of the Select Committee on Assassinations," U.S. House of Representatives, 2 Jan 1979.
[8]Jack Ruby Arrest Warrant for Murder of Lee Harvey Oswald," 24 Nov 1963 <www.history-matters.com>; "Admissions of Jack Leon Ruby in Capt. Fritz's office," 24 Nov 1963 <www.history-matters.com>.
[9]Office of the President, Executive Order No. 11130, 29 Nov 1963.
[10]*El Paso Herald Post*, 24 Oct 1963.
[11]*United States v. Nagell*, U.S. District Court for the Western District of Texas, 24 Jan 1964; *Nagell v. United States*, 354 F.2d 441 (5th Cir. 1966); *El Paso Times*, 27 Jan 1964.
[12]Judicial fiat governed the law on incompetency and insanity with the procedures being in 18 U.S.C. §§ 4241–4248 and Rule 12.2 of the Federal Rules of Criminal Procedure.
[13]*El Paso Times* 9–11 Jun 1964; *El Paso Herald Post*, 8–10 Jun 1964.
[14]*El Paso Herald Post*, 3 Jan 1963.
[15]*El Paso Times* and *El Paso Herald Post*, 8–19 Apr 1966.
[16]U.S. Bureau of Prisons, Report of Psychiatric Examination, Richard Case Nagell, 01029-H, 17 Jun 1966.
[17]Clinton served three consecutive six-year terms on the Texas Court of Criminal Appeals (1979–1996).

[18]William W. Turner, "The Garrison Commission on the Assassination of President Kennedy," *Ramparts*, Jan 1968.
[19]*El Paso Herald Post*, 5 Apr 1968; *Nagell v. United States*, 392 934 (5th Cir. 1968); Calamia interview with author, 29 Jul 2006.
[20]*Washington Post*, 25 Oct 1968.
[21]Russell, see note 2, Chapter 1.
[22]The Kennedy Assassination National Archives, <www.archives.gov/research/jfk>, has archived the following on Richard Case Nagell.

"In his book, *The Man Who Knew Too Much*, author Dick Russell wrote about Richard Case Nagell, a former Army Counterintelligence Officer who told Russell he: (1) had conducted surveillance on Lee Harvey Oswald for both the CIA and the KGB; (2) had been recruited by a KGB agent (masquerading as a CIA operative) to persuade Oswald not to participate in a plot against President Kennedy; (3) had been instructed by the KGB to kill Oswald if he could not dissuade him from participating in the plot; (4) was in possession of a Polaroid photograph that had been taken of himself with Lee Harvey Oswald in New Orleans; (5) had audio tape recordings of Oswald and others discussing a forthcoming assassination attempt on President Kennedy; and (6) had sent a letter, via registered mail, to FBI Director J. Edgar Hoover in September 1963, warning of a conspiracy to kill President Kennedy in late September 1963 in Washington, D.C. (and had documentary proof of the mailing of said letter).

"The Review Board sent a letter to Nagell dated October 31, 1995, requesting that Nagell contact the Review Board's Executive Director to discuss any assassination records he might have in his possession. Subsequently, the Review Board was informed that Nagell had been found dead in his Los Angeles apartment the day after the ARRB's letter was mailed. (The coroner ruled that he died as a result of natural causes.)

"A member of the Review Board staff traveled twice to California to inspect the effects of Nagell in an attempt to find assassination records. During the first trip, the Review Board staff member, along with Nagell's son and niece, inspected Nagell's apartment in Los Angeles. During the second trip, the Review Board staff member inspected, again with the assistance of the son and niece, material contained in some footlockers found in storage in Phoenix, Arizona. The Review Board staff did not locate any of the items that Dick Russell references above.

"A considerable amount of documentary material on Nagell from the U.S. Secret Service and the U.S. Army's Investigative Records

Repository (IRR) was placed in the JFK Collection as a result of the JFK Act and the efforts of the Review Board staff.

"The CIA processed as part of its sequestered collection a 201 and Domestic Contacts Division file on Nagell. The Review Board staff also reviewed a CIA Office of Security file on Nagell. The entire file was designated an assassination record."

[23]Calamia interviews with author, 1 Aug 2004 and 18 Aug 2006.

FEDERAL JUDGES: ATTITUDES AND THE LAW OF CONTEMPT

[1]*El Paso Herald Post*, 20 Mar 1969.

[2]The reference is to rules established by the Supreme Court in 1940 under 54 Stat. 688 (later 18 U.S.C. § 3771). Current authority since 1988 is in 28 U.S.C. § 2071.

[3]Burger was born in St. Paul, Minnesota. He received his law degree in 1931 from St. Paul (now William Mitchell) College of Law and was in private practice until his appointment as an assistant U.S. attorney general in 1953. He served in the U.S. Court of Appeals for the District of Columbia from 1955 through 1969. Burger's legacy was in improving the efficiency of the judiciary. Contrary to expectations, the Burger Supreme Court upheld *Miranda v. Arizona*, 384 U.S. 436, 86 S.Ct. 1602, 16 L.Ed.2d 694 (1966), allowed controversial busing as a means to end school desegregation, supported racial quotas in federal grants and contracts, and upheld a woman's right to an abortion in *Roe v. Wade*, 410 U.S. 113, 93 S.Ct. 705, 35 L.Ed.2d 147(1973). Burger retired in 1986.

[4]Black, Vincent, editor, *The Burger Court: The Counter-Revolution That Wasn't*, (Yale UP: New Haven, London, 1983,) 62–91 and 198–217.

[5]Calamia interview with author, 19 Sep 2006.

[6]Calamia interview with author, 30 Jun 2006.

[7]*Playboy*. "The Hard Hearts," 4 Jul 1974.

[8]Wood was born in Rockport, Texas, on Mar 31 1916. He obtained his law degree from the University of Texas in 1938 and was in private practice in San Antonio until his appointment by President Nixon to the federal bench in 1970. Wood, like Guinn and Suttle, was strict on courtroom decorum. He was tough on sentencing of drug traffickers and was quickly known in legal circles as "Maximum John." Wood was assassinated on May 29, 1979 outside his San Antonio home by contract gunman Charles Harrelson hired by El Pasoan Jamiel Chagra who was awaiting trial before Judge Wood in El Paso on drug trafficking charges. The assassination was the first of a federal judge in the twentieth century. *New York Times*, 24 Mar 1988. "Joe Chagra, a former lawyer who spent nearly six years in prison for plotting the assassination of a Fed-

eral judge, has been released on parole. Mr. Chagra, forty-one years old, pleaded guilty in 1982 to conspiring to kill Federal District Judge John H. Wood, Jr., who had been scheduled to preside over the drug trial of Mr. Chagra's older brother, Jimmy. He was released from a Federal prison in Stafford, Ariz., on Friday. Jimmy Chagra, who along with Joe Chagra was accused of hiring Charles Harrelson to kill the judge, was acquitted on a murder conspiracy charge and is imprisoned on a drug conviction. Mr. Harrelson was sentenced to two life terms."

[9]*El Paso Herald Post*, 9 Apr 1969.

[10]*El Paso Herald Post*, 3 Apr 1968.

[11]Speck's death sentence was vacated in 1972. He was re-sentenced to 400–1200 years. A year later, it was reduced to 300 years. Parole was continuously denied. Speck died in prison in 1991.

[12]Richard T. Marshall interview with author, 14 Sep 2006. Marshall recalled that it was by coincidence that Dr. Marvin Cyporyn was in New Mexico visiting friends, among them artist Peter Hurd, in the San Patricio area that facilitated his participation in El Paso.

[13]One possibility was in furtherance of 18 U.S.C. § 401(3) that empowers the court at its discretion to punish for contempt by fine, imprisonment or both, misbehavior of any person in the judge's presence or near the court so as to obstruct the administration of justice. Another was that of disobedience or resistance to its lawful writ, process, order, rule or command.

[14]*El Paso Herald Post*, 23 May 1969 and brief in support of appeal, In re Marshall, 423 F.2d 1130 (5th Cir. 1970).

[15]Hoffman's demeanor is described in Goulden, Joseph, *The Benchwarmers: The Private World of the Powerful Federal Judges* (New York: Weybright and Talley, 1974).

[16]Marshall interview with author, 14 Sep 2006.

FERNÁNDEZ AND THE FIFTH: NO SILVER PLATTER FOR THE FEDERAL TAXMAN

[1]Calamia interviews with author, 28 Jul 2006; 29 Sep 2006.

[2]"Mr. MADISON conceived this to be the most valuable amendment in the whole list. If there were any reason to restrain the government of the United States from infringing upon these essential rights, it was equally necessary that they should be secured against the State Governments. He thought that if they provided against the one, it was as necessary to provide against the other, and was satisfied that it would be equally grateful to the people." 1 Annals of Cong. 755 (1789).

[3]In summary, "Subpoenaed before a state grand jury which was conducting an inquiry regarding violations of state laws, petitioner refused to an-

swer certain questions on the ground of possible self-incrimination. After being granted under a state statute immunity from state prosecution and being ordered by a state court to answer, petitioner persisted in his refusal, on the ground that to answer the questions might expose him to federal prosecution for violation of a federal statute. For such refusal, he was convicted in the state court of contempt and sentenced to fine and imprisonment. Held: His conviction did not violate his rights under the Fifth Amendment, which limits only the powers of the Federal Government and not those of the States."

[4]"Criminal Justice in Times of Turbulence," Ramsey Clark, *Saturday Review*, 53 (19 Sep 1970) 21-48.

[5]26 U.S.C. § 7206.

[6]*United States v. Fernández*, Hearing before U.S. District Judge D. W. Suttle on Motion to Suppress, Nov 18 1968.

[7]Public Law 90-351, 42 U.S.C. Ch. 46, Justice System Improvement. The law authorized more than $100 million in block grants to communities to fight crime, half of which would assist law enforcement agencies. The law banned interstate commerce in handguns and established a national handgun license program.

Muñiz and Discrimination: No Mexican Americans in a Grand Jury

[1]The term is used in *Muñiz v. Beto*, 434 F.2d 697 (5th Cir. 1970). The term "Mexican descent" is used in *Sánchez v. State*, 181 S.W. 2d 87 (Tex.Cr.App. 1944), an unsuccessful appeal of murder conviction in nearby Hudspeth County, and in *Hernández v. Texas* 347 U.S. 475, 74 S.Ct. 667, 98 L.Ed. 866 (1954), a landmark case that established those of Mexican descent as an identifiable group for the purpose of the equal protection clause of the Fourteenth Amendment.

[2]Exchange of Notes, United States and Mexico concerning migratory workers, TIAS 1136 57 Stat. 1353.

[3]Establishment of a Joint U.S.-Mexico Defense Commission (Vol. 7, Federal Register, pg. 1607); Settlement of Mexican Claims Act, 1942 (56 Stat. Pt. 1058) and Exchange of Notes, United States and Mexico, 28–29 Sep 1943. Opened talks to arrive at the U.S.-Mexico Treaty relating to the utilization of waters of the Colorado and Tijuana Rivers and of the Rio Grande, and supplementary protocol, signed Nov 14, 1944. Signed at Washington, February 3, 1944. Effective November 8, 1945. (59 Stat. 1219; TS 994; 9 Bevans 1166; 3 UNTS 313).

[4]*El Paso Herald Post*, 13 Oct 1942.

[5]*El Paso Times,* 13 Oct 1942; *El Paso Herald Post,* 12–14 Oct 1942.

[6]Concerning the disputed evidence, the appeals court stated:

"It would serve no useful purpose to set forth the revolting facts showing the commission of the crime charged. It is sufficient to say that the prosecutrix, twenty years of age and weighing 103 pounds testified that she was, at night, by force, raped and ravished by the appellant. At the first opportunity after the commission of the crime, she reported such fact to her parents, with whom she lived, who in turn immediately notified the officers. The physical facts and other circumstances strongly corroborated the prosecutrix.

"Appellant, twenty-one years of age, testified as a witness in his own behalf, admitted having engaged in an act of intercourse with the prosecutrix, at the time and place charged, but asserted that it was with her consent and that she voluntarily entered into the act. He denied the use of any force or violence whatsoever upon prosecutrix." *Muñiz v. State,* 170 S.W.2d 565, 566-67 (Tex.Cr.App. 1943).

[7]Texas Forty-eighth Legislature, House Concurrent Resolution 105, 1943. Texas 49th Legislature, House Bill 804, 1945 establishing the Texas Good Neighbor Commission. The Department of State, Office of Inter-American Affairs, created in 1940, funded Texas's six-member Good Neighbor Commission in 1943 in large part to improve housing and health measures for migrant workers and deal with "human relations problems."

[8]Civil Rights Act of 1964, Public Law 88-352, 42 U.S.C. Ch. 21.

[9]18 U.S.C. § 3006A. Adequate representation of defendants. (a) Choice of Plan. Each U.S. district court, with the approval of the judicial council of the circuit, shall place in operation throughout the district a plan for furnishing representation for any person financially unable to obtain adequate representation in accordance with this section. Representation under each plan shall include counsel and investigative, expert and other services necessary for adequate representation. Each plan shall provide the following:

(1) Representation shall be provided for any financially eligible person who—

(A) is charged with a felony or a Class A misdemeanor;

(B) is a juvenile alleged to have committed an act of juvenile delinquency as defined in section 5031 of this title;

(C) is charged with a violation of probation;

(D) is under arrest, when such representation is required by law;

(E) is charged with a violation of supervised release or faces modification, reduction, or enlargement of a condition, or extension or revocation of a term of supervised release;

(F) is subject to a mental condition hearing under chapter 313 of this title;

(G) is in custody as a material witness;

(H) is entitled to appointment of counsel under the sixth amendment to the Constitution;

(I) faces loss of liberty in a case, and Federal law requires the appointment of counsel; or

(J) is entitled to the appointment of counsel under section 4109 of this title.

[10]Calamia interviews with author, 8 Sep 2004 and 6 Oct 2006.
[11]Calamia interview with author, 24 Aug 2006.

CHANGE AND REFLECTION
1970S AND BEYOND: TURMOIL AND CHANGE

[1]*El Paso Herald Post*, 21–25 Sep 1970. Five-Part Series on Project Bravo by Bob Ybarra.

[2]*El Paso Times*, 27 Dec 1978.

[3]Jerry Woodard was appointed Thirty-fourth District Court judge in 1969 when Judge Cunningham resigned to take a justice post with the Eighth Court of Civil Appeals in El Paso. Judge Mulcahy retired in 1966. Edward S. Márquez was appointed Sixty-fifth District Court judge in 1973. He received his bachelor and law degrees from the University of Texas. He served as assistant city attorney, a contract attorney with the International Boundary and Water Commission, assistant district attorney and assistant U.S. attorney. Hans Brockmoller was appointed 120th District Court judge in 1957 upon creation of the court. A graduate of the Texas College of Mines (UT El Paso), he received his law degree in 1938. Following his return from the Navy during World War II, Brockmoller served as an assistant city attorney. Edwin Berliner was appointed 171st District judge in 1965 when this court was created. He served as assistant county attorney and assistant district attorney with several years of private practice in between. He served as district attorney from 1961 until appointed to the district judgeship.

[4]Cross, Clinton, *El Paso Bar Bulletin*, "The Promise of Justice for All in our Community: The El Paso Public Defender's Office," Feb 2006, and

"The Promise of Justice for All in our Community: The Federal Public Defender's Office," Apr 2006.

[5]*El Paso Herald Post,* 4 Aug and 5 Aug 1977. There were 2,430 civil suits (1,396 divorces) in 1950 compared to 6,713 (3,327 divorce) in 1976. There were 257 felony indictments in 1950 compared to 795 in 1976.

[6]Western District of Texas, El Paso, *Woodard v. Federal Grand Jury Report* 72 CA 175, *White et al v. El Paso County* 72 319, *United States v. Bank Corporation* 72 CA 83, *Labor Relations Board v. Farah Manufacturing* 72 CA 128, 129, *Bencomo v. University of Texas at El Paso* 72 CA 166, *Karr v. Schmidt* 70 CA 229 and *Alvarado v. El Paso Independent School District* 72 CA 279.

[7]*El Paso Herald Post,* "Who Runs El Paso?" four-part series, 16-19 Aug 1986.

[8]The Supreme Court in *Baker v. Carr,* 369 U.S. 186, 82 S.Ct. 691, 7 L.Ed.2d 663 (1962) looked into the nature of political questions on which the courts have ruled and established that the high court has jurisdiction over questions of legislative apportionment. The Supreme Court in *Reynolds v. Sims,* 377 U.S. 533, 84 S.Ct. 1362, 12 L.Ed.2d 506 (1964) provided the reapportionment formula of one person, one vote.

[9]42 U.S.C. § 1973, signed Aug 6, 1965, with temporary provisions extended in 1970, 1975, 1982 and 2006. The last one extends through 2031.

[10]The Warren Court forced reapportionment on the states in *Baker v. Carr,* 369 U.S. 186, 82 S.Ct. 691, 7 L.Ed.2d 663 (1962) under the "equal protection" clause of the Fourteenth Amendment. The same court in *Reynolds v. Sims,* 377 U.S. 533, 84 S.Ct. 1362, 12 L.Ed.2d 506 (1964) required districts of equal population in both the houses of representatives and senates of state legislatures. Litigation in Texas began in 1965.

[11]*El Paso Herald Post,* 2 Apr 1968. Distribution by registered voters was as follows: Place 1–1,700 Place 2–33,000, Place 3–8,000 and Place 4–29,000.

[12]*El Paso Herald Post,* "Chicano Movement," a fifteen-part series by Bob Ybarra, 27 Dec 1971–11 Jan 1972.

[13]*El Paso Times,* 25 Aug 1973.

[14]Time Magazine, 3 Apr 1978.

[15]*State of Texas v. Michael Sullivan,* Thirty-fourth District Court.

[16]*El Paso Times* and *El Paso Herald Post,* 1978.

[17]Senior Judge Jerry Woodard letter to Texas Bar Foundation, 19 Apr 2005.

PATE AND FILING FEES: NOW CHUY DE LA O CAN RUN FOR MAYOR

[1]Fort Worth lawyer, William A. Blakely was appointed Senator in 1957 by Governor Daniel to fill the slot he left open when he was elected governor in 1956. He did not run in the special election to complete Daniel's term. One year later, he lost a bid for the same seat. Still later, Governor Daniel appointed Blakely to fill the seat vacated by Vice President Lyndon Johnson. Blakely lost the special election. In all, he served one month as senator in the two separate appointed terms.

[2]U.S. Constitution, Fourteenth Amendment, proposed August 25, 1962, and ratified January 23, 1964: "The right of citizens of the United States to vote in any primary or other election for President or Vice President, for electors for President or Vice President, or for Senator or Representative in Congress, shall not be denied or abridged by the United States or any State by reason of failure to pay poll-tax or other tax."

[3]Gettysburg Address by President Abraham Lincoln, 19 Nov 1863.

[4]*El Paso Herald Post*, 15 Jan 1970.

[5]*El Paso Herald Post*, 15 Sep 1969.

[6]*El Paso Herald Post*, 30 Sep 1969; *El Paso Times*, 3 Oct 1969.

[7]Oral history interview with Alicia Chacón, CMAS 2, Special Collections, University of Texas at Arlington Libraries, 22 Jun 1996.

[8]3 Apr 1970, preliminary injunction hearing before Circuit Judge Homer Thornberry, District Judge Hughes and District Judge William M. Taylor, Jr. in: Civil Action No. 3-3635, *Van Phillip Carter v. Martin Dies Jr. and Dr. Elmer C. Baum*; Civil Action No. 3-3733, Theodore H. Wischkaemper, on Behalf of Himself of others Similarly Situated; and Civil Action No. 3,3739, *William Pate, on Behalf of Himself and all Others Similarly Situated v. George A. McAlmon, Jr. et al.*

[9]*El Paso Times*, 22 Dec and 25 Dec 1970.

[10]*El Paso Times*, 27 Jul 1971.

[11]Calamia interview with author, 3, 10, 17 and 26 Nov 2006.

[12]*El Paso Times*, 28 Jan 1972.

[13]*El Paso Times*, 25 Feb 1972.

JUDGE V. JUDGE: INVESTIGATIVE GRAND JURIES

[1]*El Paso Herald Post*, 21–22 Sep 1970, analysis of Operation Intercept. *El Paso Herald Post* and *El Paso Times* reported on the campaign and election of Mayor Bert Williams (1971–1973) and actions taken by the Williams' city council. The city council departed from the traditional local political alliances reflected in the appointment to the various city

advisory boards and in transactions involving out of town investors. In his term as a city councilman, Williams led council action to enact an anti-discrimination ordinance. It had the effect of opening the Plaza Theater and other facilities to blacks and of erasing that dreaded yellow line of segregation on city busses that relegated blacks to the back of the bus. *El Paso Herald Post*, 14–17 Jul 1975, report on drug enforcement issues.

[2]*El Paso Herald Post*, 1 Apr 1972, 2 May 1972, 14 Oct 1972, 20 May 1972, and 28 Feb 1973.

[3]*El Paso Herald Post*, 2–3 Nov 1970.

[4]U.S. Senate Committee on Government Operations, 16 Oct 1973.

[5]*El Paso Herald Post*, 14–17 Jul 1975; 1–3 Oct 1975.

[6]*El Paso Herald Post*, 10 Feb 1971.

[7]*El Paso Herald Post*, 3 Jun 1969.

[8]Thirty-fourth District Court of El Paso county, *State v. Apolinario Mabini*, No. 24,575, Apr 1971; indictment returned by El Paso County Grand Jury 16 Nov, 1971; motion and order to dismiss 18 Apr 1972.

[9]Letter from assistant U.S. attorney Ralph E. Harris to Thirty-fourth District Judge Jerry Woodard, May 1, 1972. U.S. District Court subpoenas to David Rosado, Tom Peterson, April 26, 1972 and Sharon Rasberry, April 20, 1972.

[10]U.S. District Court, Western District of Texas, El Paso Division, transcript of proceedings, 15 Jun, 1972.

[11]U.S. District Court, Western District of Texas, El Paso Division, *Report of Grand Jury Proceedings*, 15 Jun 1972.

[12]*El Paso Herald Post*, 16 Jun 1972.

[13]*El Paso Times*, 10 Jul 1972; Calamia interview with author, 24 Nov 2006.

[14]U.S. District Court, Western District of Texas, El Paso Division. In Re: *Report of Grand Jury Proceedings* Filed 15 Jun 1972, EP 72 CA 175, "Application to Expunge Grand Jury Report," 7 Jul 1972.

[15]U.S. District Court, Western District of Texas, El Paso Division. In Re: *Report of Grand Jury Proceedings* Filed 15 Jun 1972, EP 72 CA 175, Order Aug 14, 1972 to U.S. attorney to produce a brief as Amicus Curiae on or before Aug 24 1972.

[16]U.S. District Court, Western District of Texas, El Paso Division. In Re: *Report of Grand Jury Proceedings* Filed June 15, 1972, EP 72 CA 175, Brief of the U.S. attorney, 28 Aug 1972.

[17]U.S. District Court, Western District of Texas, El Paso Division. In Re: *Report of Grand Jury Proceedings* Filed June 15, 1972, EP 72 CA 175, Plaintiff's Reply to the Brief of the U.S. attorney, 5 Sep 1972.

[18]U.S. Court of Appeals, Fifth Circuit, 72-3014, Thirty-fourth Judicial Court of El Paso county, Texas and *Honorable Jerry Woodard v. Honorable Ernest Guinn*, Judge U.S. District Court for the Western District of Texas, El Paso Division, *Petition for Writ of Mandamus*, 22 Sep 1972.

[19]U.S. Court of Appeals, Fifth Circuit, 72-3014, Thirty-fourth Judicial Court of El Paso county, Texas and *Honorable Jerry Woodard v. Honorable Ernest Guinn*, Judge U.S. District Court for the Western District of Texas, El Paso Division, *Order*, 22 Sep 1972.

[20]U.S. District Court Western District of Texas, El Paso Division. In Re: *Report of Grand Jury Proceedings* Filed on 15 Jun 1972, 72-314, *Response*, 19 Oct 1972.

[21]U.S. District Court Western District of Texas, El Paso Division, In Re: *Report of Grand Jury Proceedings* Filed on 15 Jun 1972, RP 72-CA 175, *Petition for Rehearing and for Rehearing En Banc*, 14 Jun 1973.

JONES: CRIMES OF SUDDEN PASSION AND REFLECTION

[1]*El Paso Times*, 8 Jul 1977.

[2]*El Paso Herald Post*, 24 Aug 1985.

[3]Carlos Bombach, *El Paso Times* 27 Sep 1975; *State v. Hervey*, County Court at Law, 3 Nov 1970; *El Paso Times*, 7 Jun 1974; Sheriff Mike Sullivan, 168th District Court, Eighth Court of Civil Appeals, Sep 1978; *El Paso Times*, 24 Jan 1978, El Paso Police Chief Robert Minnie; *El Paso Times*, 2 Feb 1974, 2 Aug 1978.

[4]U.S. District Court. Entrapment defense that won acquittal in the case of a licensed gun dealer who faced federal charges of allowing non-Texas residents to buy guns from his business. (*El Paso Herald Post* 1975-Howard C. Phelps, Jr.). U.S. District Court. In Re: John Edward Joyce, 1974 Feb. Drug cases where government informers may have pushed a little too hard to make a case. (*El Paso Times*, 16 and 17 Mar 1976-Delgado and Tate). *Amalia Olivares v. United States*, an alien smuggling warrantless search case in which the appeals court ruled that a low ride in a car with out of state plates in a high incidence area was not probable cause. (*El Paso Herald Post*, 24 Jun 1974). María Corral García, conviction was reversed on appeal ruling because she was searched and detained without a Miranda warning. (*El Paso Herald Post*, 27 Jun 1974.)

[5]*El Paso Times*, 8 May 1982; *El Paso Herald Post*, 7 May 1982.

[6]*El Paso Times*, 12 May 1982; *El Paso Herald Post*, 11 May 1982.

[7]Calamia interview with author, 2 May 2006.

[8]Notice of appeal was given on 18 Jun 1982, but the record was filed with the Eighth Court on 7 Oct 1983.

[9]The Texas Court of Criminal Appeals denied the petition on April 30 1986. A motion for rehearing and the petition were granted on June 18, 1986. The appeals court filed its ruling on November 26, 1986.

[10]El Paso county's public defender's office was established in 1987 to provide legal representation to defendants who cannot afford it. The office was created as part of the settlement of a lawsuit filed by El Paso county jail inmates who complained of being incarcerated too long before obtaining counsel. Private attorneys also participate under the El Paso Plan under which licensed lawyers in private under fifty-five years-of-age either represent indigents by court appointment or pay a $600 a year fee. Those funds are paid by the El Paso Bar Association to El Paso county to assist with the funding of the public defender's office.

[11]District Attorney's Office Miranda warning card read: "You have the right to have a lawyer present to advise you, either prior to any questioning or during any questioning. If you are unable to employ a lawyer, you have the right to have a lawyer appointed to counsel with prior to and or during questioning. You have the right to remain silent and not make any statement at all. Any statement you make may and probably will be used as evidence."

[12]*El Paso Times*, 13 Jun 1986.

[13]*El Paso Times*, 17 Dec and 21 Dec 1983; 1 Mar 1984.

[14]Sec. 19.02. MURDER.

(a) In this section:

(1) "Adequate cause" means cause that would commonly produce a degree of anger, rage, resentment, or terror in a person of ordinary temper, sufficient to render the mind incapable of cool reflection.

(2) Sudden passion" means passion directly caused by and arising out of provocation by the individual killed or another acting with the person killed which passion arises at the time of the offense and is not solely the result of former provocation.

(b) A person commits an offense if he:

(1) intentionally or knowingly causes the death of an individual;

(2) intends to cause serious bodily injury and commits an act clearly dangerous to human life that causes the death of an individual; or

(3) commits or attempts to commit a felony, other than manslaughter, and in the course of and in furtherance of the commission or attempt, or in immediate flight from the commission or attempt, he commits or

attempts to commit an act clearly dangerous to human life that causes the death of an individual.

(c) Except as provided by Subsection (d), an offense under this section is a felony of the first degree.

(d) At the punishment stage of a trial, the defendant may raise the issue as to whether he caused the death under the immediate influence of sudden passion arising from an adequate cause. If the defendant proves the issue in the affirmative by a preponderance of the evidence, the offense is a felony of the second degree.

[15]Knox Fitzpatrick, Senate Criminal Justice Committee, SB 1067, 14 Apr 1993.

[16]Texas Legislature, Senate Bill No. 1067, relating to the sentencing policy of the state and to offenses and punishments under the penal code, to offenses and punishments involving certain prohibited or dangerous substances, to the effect of certain convictions and acquittals, and to the civil consequences of certain offenses involving intoxication, providing conforming amendments, approved June 19, 1993.

[17]David Briones, with a law degree from the University of Texas, was appointed by President Clinton in 1994. An Army veteran, he was in private practice (1971–1991) and served as judge of El Paso county court at law No. 1 (1991–1994). Phillip R. Martínez, with a law degree from Harvard University, was appointed by President George W. Bush in 2002. He served as judge of El Paso county court at law No. 1 and of the 327th District Court in El Paso. Kathleen Cardone, with a law degree from St. Mary's School of Law in San Antonio, was appointed by President Bush in 2003. She had served as 388th District judge and as 383rd District judge as well as a family law master in El Paso. Frank Montalvo, with a law degree from Wayne State University Law School, was appointed by President Bush in 2003. He had been the 288th District Court judge in Austin since 1995.

[18]Richard P. Mesa, Michael S. McDonald and Norbert J. Garney.

[19]<www.txwd.uscourts.gov>.

[20]Thirty-fourth District Court, Forty-first District Court, Sixty-fifth District Court, 120th District Court, 168th District Court, 171st District Court, 205th District Court, 210th District Court, 243rd District Court, 327th District Court, 346th District Court, 383rd District Court, 384th District Court, 388th District Court and 409th District Court, Impact Court and Tax Court. More have since been added. County courts at law hear civil and criminal cases. In civil cases, the court exercises concurrent jurisdiction with the district courts. In criminal cases, the court

may hear all Class "A" and Class "B" misdemeanors other than those involving official misconduct and cases in which the highest fine that may be imposed is $500 or less.

[21]El Paso Bar Association certificate of December 14, 2004. El Paso Bar Bulletin, Oct 2004. Video tape of Bar luncheon of 12 Oct 2004.

[22]Letter, Edward F. Sherman, Professor of Law, Tulane Law School, 6 Jun 2005.

[23]The 2002 Calamia Warhorse Award, presented, October 4, 2002 by the El Paso Criminal Law Group, Inc.

[24]Letter, Senior Judge Jerry Woodard, 19 Apr 2005.

[25]Letter, David Wellington Chew, Eighth District Court of Appeals, 5 Jan 2006.

[26]Letter, Thirty-fourth District Judge Bill Moody, 4 May 2005.

[27]Letter, Albert C. Cuetter, M.D., Texas Tech University Health Sciences Center at El Paso, Department of Neuropsychiatry and Behavioral Sciences, 5 Jul 2006.

Additional Hispanic Civil Rights Series Books

The History of Barrios Unidos
Healing Community Violence
Frank de Jesús Acosta
Foreword by Luis Rodríguez
2007, 240 pages, Trade Paperback,
ISBN: 978-1-55885-483-3, $16.95

"The story and example of Barrios Unidos is an inspiration to everyone." —Harry Belafonte

Message to Aztlán
Rodolfo "Corky" Gonzales
Foreword by Rodolfo F. Acuña,
Edited, with an Introduction,
by Antonio Esquibel
2001, 256 pages,
Trade Paperback,
ISBN: 978-1-55885-331-7, $14.95

"Gonzales' poetry and plays . . . are historically important and represent the struggles encountered by Chicanos up to the 1980s."
—*Library Journal*

La Causa: Civil Rights, Social Justice and the Struggle for Equality in the Midwest
Edited by Gilberto Cárdenas
2004, 176 pages, Trade Paperback,
ISBN: 978-1-55885-422-2, $16.95

"A fine collection of essays . . . This readable book details the often-neglected history of Latino and Mexican immigrant life in the Midwest, and would make a fine undergraduate course volume or reference work for student research projects."
—*CHOICE*

Black Cuban, Black American: A Memoir
Evelio Grillo
Introduction by
Kenya Dworkin y Méndez
2000, 224 pages,
Trade Paperback,
ISBN: 978-1-55885-293-8, $13.95
Contains an eight page photo insert

Hector P. García: In Relentless Pursuit of Justice
Ignacio M. García
2002, 416 pages
Clothbound,
ISBN: 978-1-55885-387-4, $26.95
Trade Paperback,
ISBN: 978-1-55885-386-7, $14.95

"The author . . . makes the case for his central role in the history of the struggle of Mexican Americans for a place in society." —*MultiCultural Review*

A Chicano Manual on How to Handle Gringos
José Angel Gutiérrez
2003, 240 pages,
Trade Paperback,
ISBN: 978-1-55885-396-6,
$12.95

A Gringo Manual on How to Handle Mexicans
José Angel Gutiérrez
2001, 160 pages,
Trade Paperback,
ISBN: 978-1-55885-326-3,
$12.95

"This is a classic in Chicano politics."
—*Pluma Fronteriza*

The Making of a Civil Rights Leader: José Angel Gutiérrez
José Angel Gutiérrez
2005, 160 pages,
Trade Paperback,
ISBN: 978-1-55885-451-2, $9.95,
Ages 11 and up

We Won't Back Down Severita Lara's Rise from Student Leader to Mayor
José Angel Gutiérrez
2005, 160 pages,
Trade Paperback,
SBN: 978-1-55885-459-8, $9.95,
Ages 11 and up

The Struggle for the Health and Legal Protection of Farm Workers: El Cortito
Maurice Jourdane
2005, 192 pages,
Trade Paperback,
ISBN: 978-1-55885-423-9, $16.95
Contains an eight page photo insert

"[Jourdane portrays] an accurate picture of the struggle César and I and thousands of farmworkers have dedicated our lives to."
—Dolores Huerta, United Farm Workers of America AFL-CIO

They Called Me "King Tiger": My Struggle for the Land and Our Rights
Reies López Tijerina
Translated from the Spanish and edited by José Ángel Gutiérrez
2000, 256 pages,
Trade Paperback,
ISBN: 978-1-55885-302-7, $14.95

"His compelling, often controversial, story brings to life a time of great turmoil and a major civil rights leader who has faded into obscurity."
—*MultiCultural Review*

"Colored Men" and "Hombres Aquí" Hernández v. Texas and the Emergence of Mexican-American Lawyering
Edited by Michael A. Olivas
2006, 352 pages, Clothbound,
ISBN: 978-1-55885-476-5, $49.95

Commended Title, 2007 Tejano Book Prize

Enriqueta Vasquez and the Chicano Movement: Writings from *El Grito del Norte*
Edited by Lorena Oropeza and Dionne Espinoza
Foreword by John Nichols,
Preface by Enriqueta Vasquez
2006, 320 pages, Trade Paperback,
ISBN: 978-1-55885-479-6, $16.95

Recipient, 2007 PEN-Oakland Josephine Miles Literary Award, and Winner, 2007 International Latino Book Award—Best History Book-English

Memoir of a Visionary: Antonia Pantoja
Antonia Pantoja
Foreword by Henry A. J. Ramos
2002, 218 pages,
Trade Paperback,
ISBN: 978-1-55885-385-0, $14.95

"A winner of the Presidential Medal of Freedom in 1996, Pantoja has crafted a sincere and politically illuminating autobiography that sticks to ways and means, and the complex encounters and emotions that accompany them."
—*Publishers Weekly*

Flight to Freedom The Story of Central American Refugees in California
Edited by Rossana Pérez
English translation by Carolina Villarroel, Introduction by Henry A. J. Ramos. 2007, 144 pages,
Trade Paperback, ISBN: 978-1-55885-329-4, $16.95

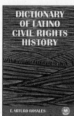